A Guide to Inner Healing:
16 Prayer Projects and Meditation Guides as Resources for Chaplains, Ministers, and Counselors

Yong Hui V. McDonald

A Guide to Inner Healing: 16 Prayer Projects and Meditation Guides
as Resources for Chaplains, Ministers, and Counselors
Yong Hui V. McDonald

Copyright © 2018 by Transformation Project Prison Ministry
All rights reserved.
Transformation Project Prison Ministry

P.O. Box 220, Brighton, CO 80601
www.tppmonline.org
Email: tppm.ministry@gmail.com

한국연락처: South Korean Contact Person:

이본 목사, 밝은빛교회,

Rev. Lee Born, Bright Light Church

인천시 남동구 구월동 1299-21, 청솔빌라 다동 301

Inchon-city, Namdong-gu, Guwal-dong, 1299-21, Chungsolbila, Da-dong 301

Cell: 010-2210-2504, 교회전화: 070-8278-2504

Published by Adora Productions.
Printed in the United States of America
First Printing: June 2018
ISBN: 978-1717130969

DEDICATION

I dedicate this book to my Heavenly Father, my Lord and Savior, Jesus Christ, and to the Holy Spirit and to all those who are longing to grow and experience healing through prayer, especially spiritual leaders.

ACKNOWLEDGMENTS

I am grateful for many people who worked hard and took the time to read and edit this story at different stages of my life. This book is the result of many amazing Christian friends who helped me write and edit: Mike Goins, Toni Gray, Lynette McClain, Carol Emery, and Laura Nokes Lang. I also thank Rev. Jeong Woon Yong who made a graphic of "A Room of Torment." God bless you all!

I pray that the Lord will use this book according to His will. I give glory to Jesus. Without him, this book couldn't have been written.

INTRODUCTION

How Did This Book Come About?

I have been working as a Chaplain at Adam's County Detention Facility (ACDF) since 2003 – 15 years now. This is one of the books that I wouldn't have written if the Lord hadn't asked me to. On March 16, 2018, I had a dream. In that dream, I saw two young women who were just hired on as prison chaplains. Somehow, I recognized one of them. She turned to me and asked, "Do you have a book on how to be a prison chaplain?" They were inexperienced, and had no idea how to help prisoners, and were looking for a resource book.

My answer was "no." It seemed it would be good if I wrote a book to help new chaplains. I occasionally have a nightmare about needing to do something and not being able to do it. I had many distractions in my dream so I wasn't able to do what I was supposed to do. This dream was like that: two young women already hired as chaplains, and me with no resource books to help them be more effective at what they do.

After I awoke from the dream, I asked the Lord why I had it. He replied, "My daughter, work on a book to help spiritual leaders. I have given you many resources." As I thought about it, the Lord was right: I had already developed many resources, I just needed to gather the information and put it together. If I had not worked at a jail, I couldn't and wouldn't have developed resources to help hurting people. The Lord blessed me with ministries and many resources for His work in healing inmates.

The Holy Spirit's presence in our facility brought revival in many inmates' hearts. I also know that the Holy Spirit has used many resources I included in this book. Now, I am thankful that more people will benefit from these resources because of the Lord. Praise God!

This is a guide book for any spiritual leader, or even those who want to help themselves experience inner healing. I am so thankful for the ministry opportunities the Lord has given me through worship services, prayer meetings, individual and group counseling, and critical counseling at ACDF. I give all glory to Jesus. Without Him, this couldn't have been written. I also thank the Holy Spirit for guiding and leading the writing of this book.

CONTENTS

DEDICATION

ACKNOWLEDGMENTS

INTRODUCTION

How to Use This Book

- An individual prayer and meditation for spiritual growth and to learn how to pray.
- As a group study guide to help lead and learn how to pray different prayers.
- A prayer resource book for those who want to teach others how to pray.
- As a 30-day prayer project guide for an individual or a group.
- You can start at any part of this book as you need.

Note: This book contains materials that can be copied and distributed to prisoners/individuals by ministers, counselors and/or chaplains.

Part One

Chapter One

Inner Healing: Closing the Door of Torment & Finding Peace and Healing through Prayer

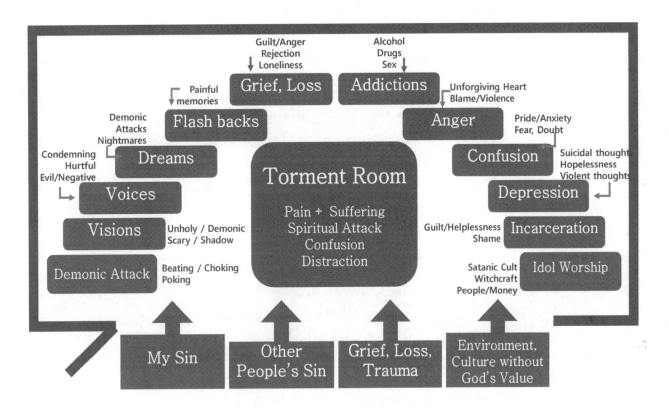

Many people are suffering from hurt and pain emotionally, mentally, spiritually and physically which is caused by torment, pain, suffering, confusion, and spiritual attack. Non-Christians can be in this room of torment, and Christians can be there, too.

You might question, "When people have faith in Jesus Christ, why do they suffer from spiritual attacks?" The reason for this is there are many ways we can be pushed into this room without realizing it. But the Lord can provide freedom from spiritual attacks and free people from spiritual pain. We need to process hurt and pain by doing what the Lord wants us to do. This healing and spiritual freedom comes from repenting of our sins, forgiving everyone, including ourselves, and asking the Lord to close the door of torment.

There are three steps to experience spiritual freedom and healing:
1) Recognize why you are stuck in the Room of Torment
2) Recognize that there are many doors inside the Torment Room and what they are.
3) Repent, and ask the Lord to close the doors one by one.

There are four things that cause us to enter this Room of Torment:
1) We fall into sin.
2) Others who are close to us or with whom we have contact with cause us to fall into sin.
3) We experience grief, loss, and trauma.
4) Our environment pushes us into a torment room where there are demonic attacks.

There are many doors inside this Room of Torment:
1) Physical attacks by demons – choking, poking, beating
2) Visions - unholy, scary, demonic visions
3) Voices – evil, negative, hurtful, condemning voices
4) Dreams – nightmares, demonic attacks
5) Flashbacks – living with painful memories every day
6) Grief and loss – loneliness, rejection, sadness, guilt, anger
7) Addictions – alcohol, drugs, sex, immoral thoughts and behaviors
8) Anger – unforgiving heart, blame, violence
9) Confusion – fear, anxiety, pride, doubt
10) Depression – hopelessness, suicidal thoughts, violent thoughts
11) Incarceration – shame, helplessness, despair, guilt
12) Idol worship - people, money, witchcraft, satanic cult

Repent, and ask the Lord to close the doors one by one:
1) Repenting of sins – Ask the Lord to forgive your sins one by one.
   Prayer: "Lord Jesus, forgive me for my sins. Holy Spirit, if there is any sin I haven't repented, please help me to repent. Please forgive me for my anger and unforgiving heart. Please take away my anger and fill my heart with your love and forgiveness."
2) Repenting of others – Ask the Lord to forgive others who sinned against you.

Prayer: "Lord, please forgive all people who have sinned against me. Help them to repent of their sins."

3) Forgiveness – forgive everyone, including yourself.
   Prayer: "Lord, I forgive everyone and I forgive myself. Thank you for dying on the cross for my sins."

4) Ask the Lord to close the doors of torment that were opened.
   Prayer: "Lord Jesus, please close all the doors of torment for me. Help me to live a pure life that will please you and help me experience healing from all the hurts and pain. Help me to spread your love and the gospel of peace to others."

If many doors are open, it takes a while to process all the pain and hurt, so keep focusing on the Lord to help you close the doors that need to be closed. When all the doors are closed, you will find God's peace and healing.

In order to keep this peace continuously, you need to live a life that will please God and avoid sin, so avoid people and environments that can put you in the room of torment again. Share your testimony of healing so others who are presently tormented can experience healing through God and be saved.

Why do we need to repent?

Repentance is related to the healing of our relationship with the Lord and to spiritual freedom from the devil's attack. Without repentance, we can't have a close, loving relationship with God because living in sin makes Him grieve and upset.

Having pain, torment, and spiritual attacks is a sign that we need repentance; and when you feel like you are far away so you don't feel the presence of God, there is a chance that you need to repent. God may have removed His presence from you so that you can recognize that something is missing in your life.

Without repenting and making changes in our thoughts and lifestyles according to God's holy word, we are continuously going farther away from Him. When you have a big empty heart, confusion, and lack of direction in life, this may be a sign that you need to turn to God's guidance on which areas you are not living in accordance with His will. Without leaving a sinful life, we can't have peace in our mind, and we can't create peace with people around us. The turmoil in our hearts shows that there is something we need to take care of, by doing something that the Lord wants us to do. We can sin by either commission or omission.

If you feel you don't know what to repent, ask the Holy Spirit to help you repent. This will invite the Lord to start the purifying process, and the Holy Spirit can help you.

Why we don't feel forgiven by God?

Why don't people feel forgiven after they have asked for forgiveness? There are two reasons for this: (1) When people ask for forgiveness but they do not truly want to leave sin; deep in their hearts they know that they have not truly repented. (2) Even if we have truly repented and are not going to repeat the sin we committed, the devil is condemning us for our sin.

We may not truly repent of our sins.

When we truly repent, we recognize that we need to make changes. Our thoughts, words, and actions will be transformed. If we are continuously sinning and living in sin, we know we are not truly repenting but constantly disobeying God. Therefore, we may be feeling guilty about our lack of sincerity. We know that this doesn't please God. We need to examine ourselves to see whether we truly intend to obey the word of God and change our sinful behavior.

"They promise them freedom, while they themselves are slaves of depravity--for a man is a slave to whatever has mastered him. If they have escaped the corruption of the world by knowing our Lord and Savior Jesus Christ and are again entangled in it and overcome, they are worse off at the end than they were at the beginning. It would have been better for them not to have known the way of righteousness, than to have known it and then to turn their backs on the sacred command that was passed on to them. Of them the proverbs are true: 'A dog returns to its vomit,' and, 'A sow that is washed goes back to her wallowing in the mud.'" (2 Peter 2:19-22)

To those who are in Christ who believe that Jesus died for their sins and when they fall into sin and repent, the Lord forgives: Be aware that if you continuously fall into sin and think that all you have to do is ask for God's forgiveness and have no intention of changing your lifestyle, you are opening the door to the devil's attack.

We need to leave sin and live a holy life to honor God and give Him glory with our lives. That's when we truly are free from the devil's attack and can have peace. We are in a spiritual warzone. Unless we are fully armored with the armor of God (Ephesians 6:10-18) and believe the word of God, we could open the door to the devil again. When we truly repent in both heart and behavior, we are closing the door of torment.

You may be attacked by a condemning demon.

God wants to save us, so He helps us to know what sin is so that we can repent and make changes. However, the devil will try to make us feel bad about our past sin and try to condemn us, even though we are not repeating the same sin anymore.

There is a difference between the Holy Spirit's conviction of our sins and the devil's condemning voice. The Holy Spirit's conviction of sins comes deep in our hearts, and we feel really bad about what we did. In this way, the Lord helps us to understand that we did something wrong and need to make changes, so we don't fall into the same sin again. The demonic condemning voice is deceptive. It is not coming from deep in our hearts with regrets of falling into sin, but it's a nagging voice behind us telling us how bad we are.

The demonic voice will tell people that God can't forgive them because their sin is so big. But the Scripture tells us that God will forgive those who confess their sin. We need to fight the devil's voice with the word of God.

"Therefore, there is now no condemnation for those who are in Christ Jesus, because through Christ Jesus the law of the Spirit of life set me free from the law of sin and death." (Romans 8:1-2)

Many Christians suffer from this condemning voice of the devil. When the voice troubles you after you repented for sins, you need to know that this voice is not coming from the Lord. The devil knows your weaknesses and knows how to attack you. The devil tries to disturb your peace and make you doubt God's love and forgiveness.

God forgives us when we repent of our sins. He doesn't even remember our sins. The devil will try to attack us if there is anything that could put us into the torment room. Recognizing the tactics of the devil and resisting them by having faith in God by resisting the devil in Jesus' name, obeying the word of God, and repenting when we sin will help us win the battle. Jesus has the power to help us and free us from spiritual oppression.

"The Spirit of the Lord is on me, because he has anointed me to preach good news to the poor. He has sent me to proclaim freedom for the prisoners and recovery of sight for the blind, to release the oppressed, to proclaim the year of the Lord's favor." (Luke 4:18-19)

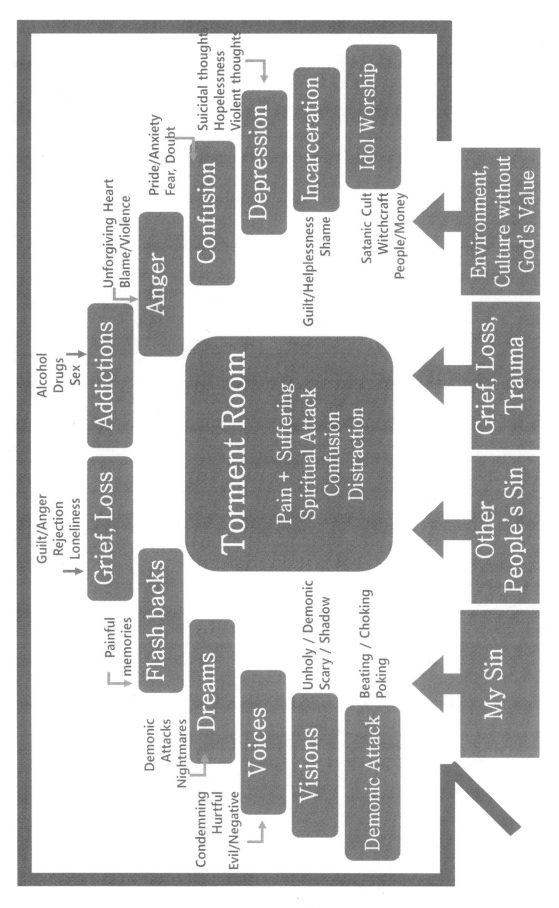

Chapter Two

Prayer Project: Daniel's Prayer of Repentance

Read Daniel 9:1-23 five times a day or once a day for the next 30 days. This prayer is Daniel's repentant prayer and it's a powerful prayer. It gives us guidelines on how to pray. Start asking God to forgive your sin, your family's sin, and our country's sin for purification.

Ask the Lord to help people to repent and find God. When we recognize our sin and ask for God's mercy, forgiveness, and a repentant heart, this will please the Lord. Here is God's promise which laid the foundation for Daniel's prayer.

"If my people, who are called by my name, will humble themselves and pray and seek my face and turn from their wicked ways, then will I hear from heaven and will forgive their sin and will heal their land. Now my eyes will be open and my ears attentive to the prayers offered in this place." (2 Chronicles 7:14-15)

Daniel's prayer for forgiveness: Daniel 9:1-23

In the first year of Darius, son of Xerxes (a Mede by descent), who was made ruler over the Babylonian kingdom--in the first year of his reign, I, Daniel, understood from the Scriptures, according to the word of the LORD given to Jeremiah the prophet, that the desolation of Jerusalem would last seventy years. So I turned to the Lord God and pleaded with him in prayer and petition, in fasting, and in sackcloth and ashes. I prayed to the LORD my God and confessed:

"O Lord, the great and awesome God, who keeps his covenant of love with all who love him and obey his commands, we have sinned and done wrong. We have been wicked and have rebelled; we have turned away from your commands and laws. We have not listened to your servants the prophets, who spoke in your name to our kings, our princes and our fathers, and to all the people of the land.

"Lord, you are righteous, but this day we are covered with shame -- the men of Judah and people of Jerusalem and all Israel, both near and far, in all the countries where you have scattered us because of our unfaithfulness to you.

O LORD, we and our kings, our princes and our fathers are covered with shame because we have sinned against you. The Lord our God is merciful and forgiving, even though we have rebelled against him; we have not obeyed the LORD our God or kept the laws he gave us through his servants the prophets.

All Israel has transgressed your law and turned away, refusing to obey you. Therefore the curses and sworn judgments written in the Law of Moses, the servant of God, have been poured out on us, because we have sinned against you. You have fulfilled the words spoken against us and against our rulers by bringing upon us great disaster.

Under the whole heaven nothing has ever been done like what has been done to Jerusalem. Just as it is written in the Law of Moses, all this disaster has come upon us, yet we have not sought the favor of the LORD our God by turning from our sins and giving attention to your truth.

The LORD did not hesitate to bring the disaster upon us, for the LORD our God is righteous in everything he does; yet we have not obeyed him. "Now, O Lord our God, who brought your people out of Egypt with a mighty hand and who made for yourself a name that endures to this day, we have sinned, we have done wrong.

O Lord, in keeping with all your righteous acts, turn away your anger and your wrath from Jerusalem, your city, your holy hill. Our sins and the iniquities of our fathers have made Jerusalem and your people an object of scorn to all those around us. "Now, our God, hear the prayers and petitions of your servant. For your sake, O Lord, look with favor on your desolate sanctuary. Give ear, O God, and hear; open your eyes and see the desolation of the city that bears your Name. We do not make requests of you because we are righteous, but because of your great mercy. O Lord, listen! O Lord, forgive! O Lord, hear and act! For your sake, O my God, do not delay, because your city and your people bear your Name."

While I was speaking and praying, confessing my sin and the sin of my people in Israel and making my request to the LORD my God for his holy hill- while I was still in prayer, Gabriel, the man I had seen in the earlier vision, came to me in swift flight about the time of the evening sacrifice.

He instructed me and said to me, **"**Daniel, I have now come to give you insight and understanding. As soon as you began to pray, an answer was given, which I have come to tell you, for you are highly esteemed. Therefore, consider the message and understand the vision."

Prayer: "Loving God, I pray for your favor, mercy, and forgiveness of my sin, my family, and my nation. Bless us with understanding and discernment to know what is right and wrong. Help us to understand your word and obey you. I pray this in Jesus' name. Amen."

Note: To learn more about how to repent, read the book, *Repentance Volume 2, The Way to Spiritual Freedom, Repentance Volume 3, Lost and Found & Repentance Volume 4, Finding Peace.*

Chapter Three

Prayer of Victory

After I had many car accidents on icy roads, I started having panic attacks on icy roads. So, I wrote a prayer of victory to be healed from anxiety attacks. This prayer has helped me immensely. I have not had an anxiety attack since I started proclaiming victory in Jesus Christ. Since then whenever I have anxious feelings, I read this victory prayer. This prayer helped me to find peace of mind.

I shared this victory prayer with many people who suffered from anxiety and panic attacks. Many people told me that this prayer helped them find peace and healing in their hearts.

Write your own prayer of victory and start proclaiming victory in your life. In everything, proclaim victory in Christ. John wrote, "You, dear children, are from God and have overcome them, because the one who is in you is greater than the one who is in the world." (1 John 4:4)

"For everyone born of God overcomes the world. This is the victory that has overcome the world, even our faith. Who is it that overcomes the world? Only he who believes that Jesus is the Son of God." (1 John 5:4-5)

Here is the victory prayer I wrote:

1) A victory prayer for myself
- I claim victory that I made a decision to love Jesus. He is the first priority in my life.
- I claim victory for God because He has the ultimate power over everything in my life, no one else does.
- I claim victory because I made a commitment to serve Christ.
- I claim victory over my guilt and shame because all my sins are washed away by the blood of Jesus Christ
- I claim victory that God is the source of my love, peace, wisdom, joy, and strength.
- I claim victory over my future belief that God is going to bless me beyond my imagination.
- I claim victory because I decided to love Jesus more than my sinful desires and passion.

- I claim victory over all my problems and concerns so that I am continuously surrendering everything to God.
- I claim victory that I made a decision to bless and forgive those who have hurt me.
- I claim victory over my fears because God is guiding my spiritual path.
- I claim victory over my life challenges knowing that God is going to give me wisdom to handle them.

2) A victory prayer for my family

- I claim victory that God will take care of my family for His glory.
- I claim victory that my family will be filled with the Holy Spirit and serve God to the fullest.
- I claim victory that God will give my children spiritual blessings beyond my imagination.
- I claim victory for my children that God will provide what they need, including godly mentors.
- I claim victory that my family will be blessed with spiritual gifts and use them for God's glory.
- I claim victory that God will take care of my family when I cannot take care of them.
- I claim victory that God will protect my family and help them grow in faith.
- I claim victory that other people will be blessed by my family's presence and ministry.

3) A victory prayer for my ministry

- I claim victory that God will provide an opportunity for me to spread the gospel of Jesus much more than I have ever imagined.
- I claim victory that with God's help, I will be able to help others use their spiritual gifts to the maximum for God's glory.
- I claim victory that the Holy Spirit will bring powerful Christian leaders to join me in building up the kingdom of God to win many lost souls and help them grow spiritually.
- I claim victory that God will help me use my time wisely to reach out to those who are in spiritual bondage, so they can find spiritual freedom in Christ.
- I claim victory because I am continuously surrendering all my plans and desires in order to love and serve Christ.

- I claim victory in managing financial resources with God's wisdom so that I will glorify God with my resources and help others to be saved and find hope and healing in Christ.
- I claim victory that the Holy Spirit will anoint me so much that others will experience the Holy Spirit's healing presence through my ministry and book projects.
- I claim victory that when God has different ministry plans for my life, I will obey Him because His plans are always better than mine.
- I claim victory over my selfishness that I will look after Jesus' interest, knowing that is the only way to build up Christ's kingdom.
- I claim victory because I will be focusing all my gifts, time, energy on loving Jesus and serving Him to the fullest.

Chapter Four

Forgiveness Meditation: Love Letter from God

When I was working as an intern chaplain at Denver Women's Correctional Facility in Denver in 2001, I taught a "Forgiveness" class. I learned that people can experience Jesus' love by writing a letter from Jesus. I wrote this letter for my forgiveness class. I tried to imagine how Jesus would write to me. You can also write a letter from Jesus.

My precious child, I watched you walking alone on the street. You looked so lonely, as if no one would understand how sad you were. I saw your gentle face with tears streaming down your cheeks, as if no one cared about you. The wind dried your tears. My pierced hands also dried your tears. Come to me and talk to me when you are sad and lonely. I will always listen and give you comfort. Remember, I care about you more than you can imagine or think. I created you and gave you life. You are my child. I can share my deepest love with anyone who comes to me. Come to me. I am Jesus, your friend. You deserve my love.

My wonderful child, I saw you lying in bed. The moonlight was the only light in your room. When no one else was looking, I saw your tears of grief and sorrow. You did not think anyone could understand you. I wanted you to turn to me so you could be comforted. You did turn to me as you went to sleep. I wiped your tears, and you did not even realize it. The pillow you had was my soft arm. You went to sleep in my arms. I understand you. There is no one who can give you peace and comfort as I can. Come to me. I am Jesus, your friend. You deserve my love.

My beloved child, I heard you asking for forgiveness. I checked your record, and I could not find the sins you were mentioning. In case you were talking about your old sins, the ones that you have already repented and thus erased from my record. I need to remind you that I cannot remember your sins anymore. I never condemn you for anything. My gift for you is my life. On the cross, I endured anguish, torture, pain and suffering so that you could be forgiven. I poured out my blood to forgive you and pardon you. I paid the price for your sins with my life. I clothe you with beautiful, spotless, and holy garments. You are so lovely, and there is no way I can forget about you, not even for a moment. You are forgiven, my child. I want to see your smiling face, knowing that you are free, because I have forgiven your sins of the past, present, and future. You are innocent. I can forgive anyone who comes to me. Come to me. I am Jesus, your friend. You deserve my love.

My gentle child, I saw you standing before the mirror reflecting on your past. I saw your tears of regret, remorse, shame, and guilt. You were sad that you could not share what happened to you with others. I saw your heart bleeding from the wounds. My heart ached with sorrow. Why? You did not commit any sins when you were not in control of situations that involved other people's words and behaviors. I am sorry about what happened to you. The Holy Spirit has the power to heal your wounds and painful memories. My child, I feel the pain of your suffering. I have compassion for anyone who comes to me. Come to me. I am Jesus, your friend. You deserve my love.

My beautiful child, I saw you carrying burdens of guilt and shame on your back. When you collapsed on the ground, the devil tried to put more burdens on your back by accusing you of past sins and reminding you of others' hurtful words and behaviors. I saw your tears of helplessness and hopelessness. Why? It was because you thought I had not forgiven your sins. You thought I had no power to help you. That brought tears to my eyes. I have suffered for you and carried your burdens, so you do not have to carry those burdens anymore. I want you to look at me and see my tears. I want you to touch my pierced hands and receive my forgiveness. Give all your burdens to me so I can heal your wounds. You can have my peace and joy. Remember everyone makes mistakes. It is time to forgive yourself and others because I have forgiven you. I died on the cross to free you from all your burdens. Hold my hands and get up and walk with me. Look up to me, and listen to my voice, then you will see my face. Listen to my words, and understand what I have done for you. Your sins were nailed to the cross. My blood has power to free anyone who comes to me. You are free and forgiven. Come to me. I am Jesus, your friend. You deserve my love.

My delightful child, I danced with you in my garden today. Your prayer brought joy to me. I was delighted that you remembered me and came to me. Your gentle voice touched my heart so much that I wanted to dance some more with you. It was your smile that brought a smile to my face. If you can dance with me by listening to me and talking to me, you will be able to handle the difficult situations with my power, the Holy Spirit. I want you to understand how much I love you and how sweet you are to me. You are like the light that shines in the early, fresh garden where the roses bloom. You are like the bright shining star that decorates my glorious sky. I can share my deepest thoughts with anyone who comes to me. Come to me. I am Jesus, your friend. You deserve my love.

My glorious child, I love you more than my life. You are my joy and my glory. Receive my love. Your love is all I ask for. I invite you to my table, that glorious, heavenly banquet that my Father has prepared for my children. I want you to see that your cup overflows because of the Holy Spirit's healing presence. I want you to walk with me so you can hear my voice and see my shining face filled with love for you. The Holy Spirit can fill you with visions, dreams, hopes, joy, peace, love, and power. I can give my gift of the Holy Spirit to anyone who comes to me. Receive spiritual blessings that I have prepared for you. Receive the Holy Spirit. Come to me. I am Jesus, your friend. You deserve my love.

My powerful child, I have called you to minister and to proclaim the message of forgiveness to those who are hurting, so others can experience the healing power of the Holy Spirit. Rely on the Holy Spirit's power to heal and transform you, then others can experience what you have experienced through your ministry. Most of all, you always have to remember that all the glory belongs to me, no one else. I am looking for people whom I can trust with the power to heal and transform others. If you can die to worldly desires, have my compassion, and obey the Holy Spirit, then you can experience the healing and transforming power in yourself and in others. Come and follow me. I am Jesus, your friend. You deserve my love.

My beloved child, it is time to go out and reach out to those who are suffering. Can you hear their cry? Can you feel their pain? Can you see their wounds? Can you understand what the Holy Spirit can do to help them? Many are living in emotional turmoil because they do not know me. Many innocent people are walking the roads of suffering because of injustices done to them. Many carry heavy burdens of guilt because they do not understand what I have done for them. Many are tormented by the devil's accusing voices because they do not know how to resist the devil by the power of the Holy Spirit. Many are lonely and sad. They need to be reminded of my love and power. Many do not have visions and dreams because they do not understand the plans that I have for them. Many feel helpless to help others because they do not understand the healing and transforming power of the Holy Spirit. Rely on my powerful words, pray constantly, and follow the Holy Spirit's guidance so you will be filled with the Holy Spirit. Then, others can experience healing and transformation through you. The Holy Spirit has unlimited power to transform and heal those who are suffering. I want you to experience that power because I live in you and you live in me. Come to my feast. I am Jesus, your friend. You deserve my love.

Chapter Five

A Love Letter to God

Learning to love God takes spiritual discipline and our determination to focus our hearts on God. Writing a love letter to God will help us in our spiritual disciple and reading it for Jesus will please Him. Here is my love letter I wrote for Jesus. If you want, you could write your own and read it to Jesus.

Lord Jesus, I love you,

It's you Lord Jesus. I've been looking for you for so long and I finally found you. Rather, I am found by you because of your grace and your great love for me. I love you Lord. I don't even have enough words to describe how much I love you. I can't even find a song that can describe my love for you.

As I look back to when I was unhappy, it was my love for you that was missing. All these years I did not even realize that I was created to love you. My big empty heart was created for you to fill with your love. I was looking elsewhere to fill this empty heart, but thank you for bringing me to the place where I could recognize your love, your grace, and my need to love you.

For a long time, I was wondering how I could love you more, but I just did not know how. Now, I understand what love is through the ministry you gave me. Love brings life, hope, passion, enthusiasm, excitement, fulfillment, joy, and peace. I love my ministry. It gives me so much joy, fulfillment, and excitement so much more than anything else! The Holy Spirit has blessed me beyond imagination through my prison ministry. The Holy Spirit reveals to me that my love for you brings life, passion, enthusiasm, joy, and excitement to you as well. Also, my love for you has to be the first priority in my life. I have this fulfilling life because you have given me many chances to make myself right with you. I learned that you want my love more than anything.

I made a decision to love you, my Creator, more than people, things, or even the ministry you created for your own glory. I declare to the world that no one and nothing is more important than you. Lord Jesus, I love you. I honor you. I cherish you. I praise you. You are my everything. I pray that my love for you will grow every day. You fill my heart with joy. I pray that you will be pleased with my love for you, like a rose in your garden. I pray that I will be able to give you my all, completely, as you did for me.

I made a decision to love you more than my sweet, fulfilling, joyful, life-giving ministry. I understand that when everyone and everything else is gone, you will be there with me always. You are the only one that matters because you will be with me till the end. No one else will be there like that. When I lose everything, even my breath, you will be with me, walking with me, holding me in your arms, carrying me to my permanent home which you prepared for me.

Let me love you, Jesus. Let my dedication to you and my service be pleasing to you. Let me be a blessing to everyone who comes in contact with me, like Abraham was. Let me be a passionate and effective servant like Peter and Paul were. Let me be a servant that you can use to the maximum for your glory. Let my service to you bring healing to so many people that there are too many to count. Let me see your smile today. Lord Jesus, I love you more than anyone and more than anything else.

Your beloved child

Chapter Six

Prayer Project: Silent Prayer

For the following 30 days, develop a habit of communicating with Jesus. Spend most of your time listening to Him. Many people listen to more than five different radio channels at a time in their mind. To hear God's voice, you need to learn to quiet your mind and listen in a state of silence. God doesn't speak to us all the time, so be patient. The more time you spend in the Bible and in prayer, the more you will recognize His voice. Try to understand His heart. Here are some guidelines on how you can practice silent prayer.

(1) If you can, talk less with other people and shut down any outside noises. Don't watch TV or listen to music. Instead, focus on listening to God in silence throughout the day as much as possible. It's hard to quiet your mind at first, but as time goes by it gets easier. You don't always have to sit down in order to quiet your mind. You can practice silence in your mind while you walk around.

(2) Scripture reading: Pick out any gospel and read it to understand Jesus' heart. There are two ways to practice this. One way is to read any gospel for 30 minutes each day. (The Gospels are: Matthew, Mark, Luke, and John). The second is to read from one gospel a day for the next 30 days: 1) Matthew has 28 chapters; 2) Mark has 16 chapters; 3) Luke has 24 chapters; 4) John has 21 chapters. Make a chart on how you progress with this reading every day.

Prayer: "Holy Spirit, bless me with wisdom, knowledge, and revelation to understand the Scripture, Jesus' heart, and His love for me."

(3) Write down your conversations with the Lord: After reading the gospel to learn about Jesus, write a letter from Jesus stating whatever he may be speaking to your heart.

Prayer: "Lord Jesus, please speak to me and teach me everything you want me to learn from the Scriptures I read. Holy Spirit, help me to understand God's love for me and help me to have love for Him."

(4) Pray for 30 minutes each day: Talk to God for 15 minutes and listen to His voice in silence for 15 minutes. Find a quiet time to do this, but try to practice

silence as much as possible throughout the day so that you can listen to God's heart.

(5) Worship God: We are created to love and worship Jesus. Paul wrote, "He is the image of the invisible God, the firstborn over all creation. For by him all things were created: things in heaven and on earth, visible and invisible, whether thrones or powers or rulers or authorities, all things were created by him and for him." (Colossians 1:15-19) Attend worship services and worship Jesus throughout each day. Loving God is recognizing His presence. You can offer your love through praise and worship as well by giving thanks to Him.

(6) Clean your spiritual house by repenting: We can't see ourselves clearly until the Holy Spirit convicts us of our sins. Ask Him to help you.
Prayer: "Holy Spirit, if there is any sin that I need to repent, please help me to see it and ask for forgiveness."

(7) Meditation: Try to memorize and meditate on the following Scripture to understand what Jesus can do for you and what you are supposed to be doing for the Lord: "The Spirit of the Lord is on me, because he has anointed me to preach good news to the poor. He has sent me to proclaim freedom for the prisoners and recovery of sight for the blind, to release the oppressed, to proclaim the year of the Lord's favor." (Luke 4:18-19)
This Scripture is not just for Jesus but for all those who believe in Him. Jesus was anointed by the Holy Spirit to do the work of God. We are anointed by the Spirit to live a victorious life and serve the Lord. The Holy Spirit is a gift to those who have accepted Jesus as their personal Lord and Savior. You receive this task when you become a Christian. This has to be your highest priority in life. We are made for the Lord. Our focus has to be to please Him.

(8) Practice silence and listen: If you have not experienced the Holy Spirit, try to listen to the Lord for one hour each day in silence. It's hard at first, but if you are persistent you will find this rewarding. It takes time to clear your mind and wait. You are telling God that what He has to say is important to you and that He is worthy of your time.
Prayer: "Lord Jesus, speak to me. I am listening." Then wait in silence, listen, and write a letter from Jesus. He will speak to you if you wait long enough. Solomon gave 1,000 offerings and God appeared in his dream. Be patient and wait. Eventually, you will hear from Him.

(9) Tell Jesus you love him: Make a habit of telling Jesus that you love him whenever you think about him. Love is a decision. You can show Jesus how important he is in your life by telling him that you care about him. You can think about him and tell him what's in your heart. He wants our deep, passionate love. He is not happy with us if we do our work without love for him. He sees your heart and knows if you are doing things out of love for him.

Prayer: "Lord Jesus, I love you more than anyone and anything. Let me love you and let love bring a smile to your face."

(10) Sing for Jesus: You can ask Jesus which song he wants you to sing for him. He may give you a song to sing. If you don't hear anything from him, sing a song that you think Jesus might like to hear from you. You can tell him, "Jesus, this song is for you," and sing silently or read it to Jesus if you are in a place where you can't sing. "Let the word of Christ dwell in you richly as you teach and admonish one another with all wisdom, and as you sing psalms, hymns, and spiritual songs, do so with gratitude in your hearts for God. And whatever you do, whether in word or deed, do it all in the name of the Lord Jesus, giving thanks to God the Father through him." (Colossians 3:16-17)

(11) Write a love letter to Jesus: Thank Him for what He has done for you. Also, you can write a love letter from Jesus to help you understand how much God loves you.

(12) Learn to let go of distractions in your life: If anyone or anything is consuming your thoughts all the time, to the point that you can't focus on loving God, you need to give them to the Lord. Loving people and things more than God can become a distraction. Confess your sins and ask the Lord to help you.

Prayer: "Lord, help me not to love people or things more than I love you. I give all my loved ones and things to you for your care. Please take away all my sinful desires and obsessions. Help me plant the seed of love for you in my heart. I give all my loved ones to you for your work and for your glory. Help me to have the wisdom, knowledge, understanding, and revelation to solve my problems according to your will so that I can let go of my concerns and worries. Help me to love you and worship you."

(13) If you are hurting from grief and loss, you have to make a conscious decision to let go of your loved ones.

Prayer: "Holy Spirit, please heal my broken heart so that I can focus on loving God. Help me to see the big picture that you see. Help me to let go of my loved ones."

(14) Learn to listen to God's voice: There are four voices we hear in our minds: 1) Your voice; 2) other people's voices; 3) the devil's voice; 4) the Holy Spirit's voice. When the devil speaks to you, it's impure, sinful, and tempting. When you obey his voice you fall into sin and lose peace. You have to repent in order to find peace. The devil's voice is hurtful and negative. You will fall into sin if you accept that voice. Resist any negative voices. Use them as a trigger to pray for other people's salvation. The voice of the Holy Spirit is gentle and soft. His voice will comfort you and direct you to do good things. You will have peace and joy when you obey the Holy Spirit's voice.
Prayer: "Lord Jesus, help me to recognize your voice and obey you."

(15) Be obedient: There are four ways we do things: 1) My way; 2) other people's way; 3) the devil's way; 4) the Holy Spirit's way. The best course is to listen and follow the Holy Spirit in order to do things that please the Lord.

(16) Meditate on the Holy Communion to understand Jesus' love for you. "While they were eating, Jesus took bread, gave thanks and broke it, and gave it to his disciples, saying, 'Take and eat; this is my body.' Then he took the cup, gave thanks and offered it to them, saying, 'Drink from it, all of you. This is my blood of the covenant, which is poured out for many for the forgiveness of sins.'" (Matthew 26:26-28)
Prayer: "Lord Jesus, help me to understand your love for me."

(17) Invite Jesus in: If you don't have a relationship with Jesus, invite Jesus into your life.
Prayer: "Lord Jesus, I give my life to you. Please come into my heart and my life. Forgive all my sins and cleanse my life so I can follow you. Bless me with the Holy Spirit. Jesus, guide and direct me to live a life that will please you. I pray this in Jesus' name. Amen."

Note: To learn more about Silent Prayer, read the book, *Journey With Jesus Two, Silent Prayer and Meditation.*

Chapter Seven

TLT Healing Model:

Tornadoes, Lessons, Teaching (TLT) Model for Healing of Souls

God asked me to write a book to help others who are grieving, traumatized and suffer from Post Traumatic Stress Disorder (PTSD), using the TLT (Tornadoes, Lessons, Teachings) model. The lessons that have helped myself and others who are lost in a "tornado" come from my own personal crisis plus from my counseling as a chaplain at Adams County Detention Facility (ACDF) and at the hospital where I help many who are dealing with "tornadoes" in their lives.

I saw a pattern after I counseled many people in crisis from grief, loss and trauma. Some were blown away by the tornado and were stuck in pain. Some, however, learned to process their pain, resolve the crisis, and then were able to move on. Those who moved on had similar patterns. They learned the lessons from their tornadoes of life. They became stronger and started helping others with what they had learned.

The TLT model was developed in my counseling to encourage people to focus beyond the tornadoes in their life. By focusing on the lessons learned through the tornadoes they experienced healing that helped them move on. Many who are stuck in pain and trauma, who have participated in this model, experienced an amazing recovery and are processing their pain allowing them to move on. In fact, I use the TLT model personally whenever I face any challenges. It's very simple and it works.

The Causes of Tornadoes

No one is exempt from tornadoes in life. Life is not free. We pay a price for living, and that price is facing tornadoes from time to time—some are small but some are very big (hurricane sized.) Some are easy to handle but some are overwhelming. How we handle and manage our tornadoes will determine whether we will grow and come out strong, or whether we will stumble, fall, and get stuck in pain and grief. If we don't know how to process tornadoes in life, they will immobilize us and we may continuously be stuck in the storms of life. This is a bad place to be. Let's look closely at what causes tornadoes in our lives.

There are seven areas that can cause tornadoes. Sometimes we experience several at once.

(1) **Ourselves:** Some troubles in life are caused by ourselves— failure –to make good judgments, immaturity, selfishness, bad temper, violence, low moral values and addictive lifestyles. Our poor choices can throw us into hardships and can cause debt, incarceration, or loss of everything which affects not only ourselves but our families and loved ones.

(2) **Our Family:** Our family members' low moral values, incarceration, addiction, selfishness, bad temper, violence, critical and judgmental attitudes, words and actions. Though we may not have done anything wrong, these actions of family members create turmoil and pain in our lives.

(3) **Others:** Painful events can be caused by other people's selfishness, critical attitudes, words and actions which affect us. If we come in contact with them at the wrong time in the wrong place, it can be devastating to us.

(4) **Environmental Hardships:** You can be affected by the environment in which you live, who you are, where you were born and what country you live in. Many other factors over which that you have no control are: cultural and moral values, religious backgrounds, economic conditions, education, job skills, inherited genetic weaknesses, war, plagues, gender, and the color of your skin, etc.

(5) **Natural Disasters:** Floods, earthquakes, famine, volcanic eruption, tornadoes, hurricanes, storms, etc. These are all beyond our control.

(6) **Spiritual Tornado:** Torment and pain caused by spiritual attacks from the devil or evil spirits. It brings spiritual confusion, oppression, pain, turmoil and bondage. When we are freed from demons, we will be healed from torment and pain. When Jesus cast out the demon from the man who lived in tombs and was hurting himself, he was healed from destructive behaviors. He came into his right mind and took care of himself instead of hurting himself further.

(7) **Divine Tornado:** Sometimes God will let people go through hardships to teach them lessons. When Jonah was disobedient and running away from the Lord, God sent the storm in the sea to get his attention. When Jonah was thrown in the sea, God prepared a fish to catch him. Jonah, in his suffering, repented inside the fish. Some people perceive incarceration as a wake-up call and God's

intervention because if they were outside, they may have been hurt badly or even ended up dead.

Tornadoes Lessons Teachings (TLT) Model

1. Tornado

We all face tornados in life is caused by crisis. Life is hard, and whether we want it or not, we all face our share of crisis either small or large in our lives. Sometimes one crisis can create many crises, like a ripple effect. Any life crisis can throw us into this unpleasant state. If you are in a tornado stage, you may experience turmoil, pain, fear, confusion, conflict, anger, devastation, disappointment or discouragement.

When you enter a tornado zone, you may be asking yourself the following:
(1) Why is this happening to me?
(2) What did I do to deserve this?
(3) Is this happening to me because I am bad?
(4) Why didn't I listen to the warnings of others?
(5) How can God let this happen to me? etc.

How do people react to a tornado?

Some may be upset, angry, and may blame someone or be confused. Many don't know how to land safely after they are thrown into the air. Some may fall onto a rock and be hurt. Sometimes they may have a safe landing if they learn to process their hurts and pain with new perception.

EXERCISE:
Reflect and answer the following:
(1) Who or what caused this tornado?
(2) What was my first reaction?
(3) What was my emotional response? Resentment, anger, disappointment, discouragement, betrayal, etc.
(4) How did I cope with the pain and emotional turmoil?
(5) Did I cause any other tornadoes after I was hit by this tornado?
(6) Is there anything God is trying to tell me through the tornado I am experiencing?

2. Lessons

Staying in a tornado is very painful. We need to process and learn why it has happened, what lessons we can learn from it, so we can come out a stronger person. Therefore, whenever I face any tornadoes in my life, I process them as soon as possible. I try to understand why it happened, who is responsible for it, and what the lesson is I need to learn, so that I can move on. Sometimes I can teach others what I have learned. You are invited to do the same. Understanding the causes of tornados will help you to learn what to avoid in the future. When people decide to learn the lessons, they begin the healing process.

EXERCISE:

Pick one incident where you experienced a tornado. If you can, share it with others whom you can trust or write it down and reflect to see what you can learn.

(1) What's the lesson I can learn from this?

(2) How can I experience healing from this?

(3) What do I need to do to find peace through this?

(4) Is there anything I need to adjust or change—attitudes, perception or behaviors—in order to process and heal?

(5) Do I need to forgive anyone and let go of my resentment or anger?

(6) What helped me the most in my difficult time?

(7) Have I had any regrets in dealing with this challenge?

(8) Is there anything I can do to prevent the same thing from happening to me in the future?

(9) What is God trying to teach me through this?

Each tornado has lessons to teach us. If we can learn the lessons, we can graduate from each tornado class and move on. We will learn what to do when we are hit by the same tornado the next time and how to process it.

3. Teachings

Those who have learned lessons from hardships have lessons to teach others. A little child usually does not have lessons to teach an adult about hard life lessons because they have not yet gone through the storms in life. Only those who have gone through life-changing experiences caused by tornadoes have learned lessons they can share with others.

Start focusing on what kind of lessons you may have for others who are going through the same problems. Our pain and suffering have lessons to teach us and others as well.

Reflect and try to answer the following:

(1) What can I teach myself and others with my tornado experience?

(2) Is there anything I can do to help others avoid the same pit falls?

(3) What do I need to do to help others? Is it sharing, writing my story or being involved with some kind of ministry?

This process gives direction to people as to what they can do with what they have learned to actively help others.

What is Your Tornado?

There are many tornadoes but the following list gives you some ideas where you are. Reflect and find out how many tornadoes you are dealing with now.

(1) Grief—You are grieving from the loss of your loved one from death, divorce or separation.

(2) Health problems—You are diagnosed with an illness.

(3) Trauma—You are traumatized by events such as physical, emotional, mental, or sexual abuse.

(4) Incarceration—Loss of freedom, loss of self-respect, separation from family, losing children to social services, divorce caused by incarceration, losing a car or house or other things that you value.

(5) Family incarceration—Your family is incarcerated.

(6) Mistreatment by others—You are hurting because of hurtful and destructive words or actions by others.

(7) Lack of resources—You feel you are running out of energy, resources and ideas as to how to handle problems in life.

(8) Lack of mentors—You feel you are desperately in need of help, but don't know whom to turn to for advice or solution.

(9) Emotional pain— Suffering from anxiety, panic attacks, anger, torment, resentment, etc.

(10) Unforgiveness—You are upset, angry or hateful, and cannot forgive those who have hurt you.

(11) Financial difficulties — You are having financial problems and you see no way out.

(12) Losing a job — You have lost jobs and cannot find employment.

(13) Depression — Lack of energy, helpless and hopeless feelings, suicidal thoughts.

(14) Lack of love —Your family or significant people in your life don't seem to value you or treat you with love and respect.

(15) Addiction—You are suffering from alcohol, drugs, or sex addiction.

(16) Your family's addiction problem—Your family is suffering from addiction and you feel helpless about it.

(17) Lack of direction and purpose in life—You don't know the purpose of your life.

(18) Lack of fulfillment in a job— Lack of education , work experience, etc. keeps you from getting a job that you would like to have.

(19) Cultural values—People around you don't value you because of the way you are shaped, your gender or skin color.

(20) Your own value system— You are having a difficult time valuing yourself.

All these things are tornadoes in life. The need is to learn to cope and value our life, learn lessons, and find peace in all situations.

I encourage you to start processing each area with the TLT model. Some areas will take time to process because you have to make changes and adjustments in your way of thinking, in habits, jobs or even education to find a job that you like. Whatever it is, change is something you have to make in order to process and learn the lessons from each storm in your life.

When you face problems in life, if you try to process all of them at once, it's overwhelming. Follow the process of the TLT model one by one and write down what you have learned and when you need to make changes—perception, lifestyle, your thinking process, etc. If you feel stuck and immobilized, I encourage you to find a professional counselor, pastor or a chaplain who could help you. The sooner you process the problem, the sooner you will experience healing from it and you will be able to function normally.

I encourage you to find people who have gone through a similar situation and have moved on. Ask them how they processed their trauma from tornadoes in their lives. People who are in a tornado cannot help you. But those who have learned from challenging problems in life and are able to move on can be your encouragement and your teacher. Find them if you can and learn from them.

In addition, there are many "tornado" stories in the Bible, and you can learn how others have dealt with them and how they overcame them. Read the different stories in the Bible to learn from them.

Note: To learn more about TLT Model, read the book, *Tornadoes, Grief, Loss, Trauma, and PTSD: Tornadoes, Lessons and Teachings—The TLT Model for Healing*.

Part Two

An Introduction to The Prayer Project

Since I started working as a chaplain at Adams County Detention Facility (ACDF) and the hospital on-call chaplain, I have ministered to many who are in need of spiritual guidance on how to pray. Many people I minister to are faced with critical conditions such as grief, loss, trauma, depression, and even suicidal thoughts. Many people have told me that they wanted to pray but didn't know where to start.

To meet these different prayer needs, I have created different prayer projects while leading a seven-week prayer project at ACDF. They were made into brochures and many of them were published in different books. I decided to gather them and make them into one book to help those who are in need of prayer.

What is emphasized in this prayer project?

I encourage people to read the Bible for 30 minutes and pray 30 minutes (15 talking to God and 15 minutes listening to Him) a day for the next 30 days with each prayer project. Every one emphasizes listening to God continuously. As you develop a habit of listening, you will be able to hear God's voice clearly. You can develop a close relationship with the Lord when you finally learn to listen.

Why do we need to pray?

The Bible teaches us to pray. Also, Jesus prayed and He told us to pray. He taught His disciples how to pray. If Jesus encourages us to pray and learn to communicate with God through prayer, we should do it. Prayer is a gift from God. I have received many blessings because of what I have asked God boldly through prayer. There is no relationship with God without prayer. Prayer is a direct communication line God created between us and Him.

I cannot imagine life without prayer; it would be like a fish trying to live without water. I constantly speak to the Lord and try to listen. I have experienced God's presence more than ever as I was praying and that changed my life. I have developed an intimate relationship with my Lord Jesus through prayer.

In addition, I have learned that spiritual healing is possible through prayer. God answers our prayers, miracles happen. I want to see others be healed through prayer. I pray this prayer project can guide them to experience growth and healing.

Which prayer project should I start first?

You can go through the prayer topics according to your needs. If you don't have any specific prayer need, or don't know which one to start with, I encourage you to start with "How to listen to God's Voice."

Many people who don't recognize God's voice are confused and don't know what to do when they face difficult situations. If they can learn to listen, they can follow the Lord's way and they can find peace and avoid lots of heartache and pain.

Learning to listen to God is a critical part of our spiritual growth and in our relationship with the Lord. When you learn to recognize and listen to God's voice, it will transform you and bless you.

May God bless you as you learn to walk with the Lord by talking and listening to His sweet voice.

Note: Each prayer project is treated as a separate prayer project so there will be some repetition in some parts. To read more about Prayer Project, read the book, *Prayer and Meditations, 12 Prayer Projects for Spiritual Growth and Healing*.

Chapter Eight

Prayer Project: Loving God

Many people think that loving God means attending church or being involved in ministry or missions. That is only a Chapter of loving Him. We need to do more than that if we truly want to love Him. Loving God requires our whole person: thoughts, words, and deeds. Always be mindful of what will please Him in every situation. We have the free will to love Him or reject Him. We need to make the decision to love Him more than anyone or anything else every day.

What are the benefits of loving the Lord? There are many, but I want to mention spiritual healing from lack of direction. There are many people who are spiritually and emotionally sick because they have not learned to love God. To overcome despair, hopelessness, loneliness, disappointment, and discouragement, and to find purpose and passion for life, you need to learn to love the Lord.

There is a spiritual war going on in our minds. The devil tries to plant the seeds of despair there by telling us no one loves us or God doesn't love us. The Holy Spirit, on the other hand, plants the seeds of love and hope, so we can understand God's love and learn to love Him.

The goal of this prayer project is to help your love for the Lord grow by working on three areas: loving God, loving yourself, and loving others. These are all connected. The most important thing is to love the Lord above all else, then to love ourselves and others.

Don't be discouraged if you don't feel any love for the Lord. As you learn about God, your love for Him will grow. Ask the Holy Spirit to help you for the next 30 days. That way you can develop a habit of thinking, talking, and doing things to please God. That will show Him how much you love Him.

Prayer: "Holy Spirit, pour out your love in my heart so I can understand God's love. I want to love Him with all my heart, mind, soul, and strength. Help me to love myself as God loves me and help me to love others as God loves them."

1. Love God

For the next 30 days, develop a spiritual habit of recognizing Jesus and communicating with him all the time.

(1) Scripture reading: Pick out any gospel and read it to understand Jesus' heart. There are two ways to practice this. One way is to read any gospel for 30

minutes every day. (Gospels are: Matthew, Mark, Luke, and John). Another way is to read one gospel a day for the next 30 days.

Prayer: "Holy Spirit, bless me with wisdom, knowledge, and revelation to be able to understand the Scripture. I want to understand Jesus' heart and his love for me."

(2) Write down your conversations with the Lord: After reading the Gospel to learn about Jesus, write a letter from Jesus detailing whatever he is speaking to you about.

Prayer: "Lord Jesus, please speak to me. Teach me from the Scripture I read. If you want to speak to me, I am listening. Holy Spirit, help me to understand God's love for me and help me to have love for Him."

(3) Pray for 30 minutes every day: Talk to God for 15 minutes and listen to His voice in silence for 15 minutes. We don't have any control over other people's voices or outside noises, but we can still practice silence in our thoughts. It's not easy but slowly, you will be able to tell that you are able to control your inner thoughts.

(4) Worship God: We are created to love and worship Jesus. Paul wrote, "He is the image of the invisible God, the firstborn over all creation. For by him all things were created: things in heaven and on earth, visible and invisible, whether thrones or powers or rulers or authorities, all things were created by him and for him." (Colossians 1:15-16)

Attend worship services and also worship Jesus throughout every day. Loving God is recognizing His presence. You can offer your love through praise, worship, and giving thanks to Him as you work throughout the day. What's important is learning to focus your heart on the Lord in every situation.

(5) Clean your spiritual house by repenting: We cannot see ourselves clearly until the Holy Spirit helps us to see what we have done wrong. He will convict us of our sins and teach us how to live a holy life to please God. Ask Him to help you.

Prayer: "Holy Spirit, if there is any sin that I need to repent, please help me to see it so I can ask for forgiveness and be cleansed."

(6) Meditation: Try to meditate on and memorize the following Scripture to understand what Jesus can do for you as well as what you are supposed to be doing for the Lord.

"The Spirit of the Lord is on me, because he has anointed me to preach good news to the poor. He has sent me to proclaim freedom for the prisoners and recovery of sight for the blind, to release the oppressed, to proclaim the year of the Lord's favor." (Luke 4:18-19)

This Scripture is not just for Jesus, but for all those who believe in Jesus. Jesus was anointed by the Holy Spirit to do the work of God. We are to be anointed by the Spirit to live a victorious life and serve the Lord. The Holy Spirit is a gift given to those who have accepted Jesus as their personal Savior and Lord.

(7) Pray for anointing: Put your hands on your head as if Jesus is putting hands on you then pray, "Lord Jesus, I love you. Please anoint me with the Holy Spirit and help me to think the way you want me to think. Help me to say the words that you want me to say. Help me to do things that you want me to do. Help me to minister to the people that you want me to minister to."

You have a task to do when you become a Christian. It is to love the Lord and serve Him, which pleases Him. That has to be your highest priority in life. We are made for the Lord. Our focus has to be to please Him.

(8) Practice silence to listen: If you have not experienced the Holy Spirit, try to listen to the Lord one hour every day in silence. I ask you to practice more silence here because in silence, you can be more sensitive to the Holy Spirit's guidance. It's hard at first, but if you are persistent, you will find this rewarding. It takes time to clear your mind and wait. You are telling God that what He says is important to you and He is worthy of your time.

Prayer: "Lord Jesus, speak to me, I am listening." Then wait in silence, listen, and write a letter from Jesus. He will speak to you if you wait long enough. Solomon gave 1,000 offerings and God appeared in his dreams. Be patient and wait. Eventually, you will hear from Him.

(9) Tell Jesus that you love him: Make a habit of telling Jesus that you love him whenever you think about him. Love is a decision. You can show Jesus how important he is in your life by telling him that you care about him. You can think about him. You can tell him what's in your heart. He wants our deep, passionate love for him. He is not happy with us if we live without love for him. He looks at your heart to determine if you are doing things out of love for him.

Prayer: "Lord Jesus, I love you more than anyone and more than anything. Let me love you and let my love bring a smile to your face."

(10) Sing for Jesus: You can ask Jesus, "Which song may I sing for you?" The Holy Spirit may give you a song to sing. If you don't hear anything from him, sing a song that you think Jesus might like to hear from you. You can tell him, "Jesus, this song is for you," and sing silently or read it to Jesus if it bothers others.

"Let the word of Christ dwell in you richly as you teach and admonish one another with all wisdom, and as you sing psalms, hymns and spiritual songs, do so with gratitude in your hearts for God. And whatever you do, whether in word or deed, do it all in the name of the Lord Jesus, giving thanks to God the Father through him." (Colossians 3:16-17)

(11) Write a love letter to Jesus: Write a love letter to Him. Thank Him for what He has done for you. You can also write a love letter from Jesus so you can understand how much God loves you.

(12) Learn to let go of distractions in life: If anyone or anything is consuming your thoughts all the time to the point that you are unable to focus on loving God, you need to give them to the Lord. Loving people and things more than God is a distraction. Confess your sins and ask the Lord to help you.

Prayer: "Lord, help me not to love people or things more than you. I give all my loved ones and things into your care. Take away all the sinful desires of obsession. Plant the seed of love for you. Help me to have the wisdom, knowledge, understanding, and revelation to solve my problems according to your will so that I can let go of my concerns and worries. That way I can love you and worship you."

(13) For those who are hurting from grief and loss, you have to make the decision to let go of your loved ones.

Prayer: "Holy Spirit, please help me and heal my broken heart so that I can focus on loving God. Help me to see the big picture that you see. Help me to let go of my loved ones."

(14) Learn to listen to God's voice: There are four voices we hear in our minds: 1) Your voice; 2) Other people's voices; 3) The devil's voice; 4) The Holy Spirit's voice. When the devil speaks to you, it's impure, sinful, and tempting. When you obey his voice, you will fall into sin and lose peace. You have to repent in order to find peace. The devil's voice is hurtful and negative. You will fall into sin if you accept that voice. Resist any negative voices and use them as a trigger to pray for other people's salvation. The voice of the Holy Spirit is gentle and soft. His voice may be comforting to you or directing you to do something good. When you obey, it will please Him. You will have peace and joy when you obey Him.

Prayer: "Lord Jesus, help me to recognize your voice so that I can obey you."

(15) Be obedient: There are four ways we do things: 1) My own way; 2) Other people's way; 3) The devil's way; 4) The Holy Spirit's way. The best course is to listen and follow the Holy Spirit in order to do things that please the Lord.

(16) Dance for Jesus: If you like to dance, you can show your love for the Lord by dancing for Him.

(17) Live as if you have only one year to live during this prayer project: Many people focus on loving people and things more than the Lord, as if they have eternity to live on earth. We need to be freed from distraction in order to love God. Prepare to meet Him and learn to spend time getting to know Him. Devote your time to prayer and let go of your selfish desires. Be generous with your time with the Lord and let go of distractions that don't help you grow spiritually. Don't get involved in conversations that do not honor the Lord. When we love the world and follow our own sinful desires, we get distracted and don't develop godly character.

Prayer: "Lord Jesus, help me to have the wisdom to spend my time wisely. Help me to know if there is anything or anyone that I love more than you. Please forgive me for not putting you above everyone and everything else. Help me to love you with all my heart, mind, soul, and strength."

(18) Meditate on Holy Communion to understand Jesus' love for you.
"While they were eating, Jesus took bread, gave thanks and broke it, and gave it to his disciples, saying, 'Take and eat; this is my body.' Then he took the cup, gave thanks and offered it to them, saying, 'Drink from it, all of you. This is my blood of the covenant, which is poured out for many for the forgiveness of sins.'" (Matthew 26:26-28)

Prayer: "Lord Jesus, help me to understand your love for me."

(19) Invite Jesus: If you don't have a relationship with Jesus, invite Jesus into your life.

Prayer: "Lord Jesus, I give my life to you. Please come into my heart and my life. Forgive all of my sins and help me to clean up my life so that I can follow you. Bless me with the Holy Spirit. Jesus, guide and direct me to live a life that will please you. I pray this in Jesus' name. Amen."

2. Love yourself

One of the things that that we can do to please the Lord is to love what He loves. He loves us. To please Him, we need to love ourselves. Loving ourselves doesn't mean being selfish. Selfishness means only focusing on our own needs and neglecting others. We need to value ourselves as God values us in Christ. We are created in the image of God. He wants our love to grow.

(1) Love yourself because God loves you: If you accepted Jesus in your heart and believe in Him, you are a child of God. He created you and saved you through Jesus, who died on the cross to save you from sin and eternal condemnation. Jesus did all that because he loves you. You have to love yourself. That is what God wants you to do. Love means taking care of yourself as His precious and beloved child.

(2) Love yourself by taking care of your soul through cleansing your heart: Read the following Bible passage as well as other parts of the Bible and reflect on if you have committed any sins. Repent of your sins one by one so that the Lord will purify your heart: "The acts of the sinful nature are obvious: sexual morality, impurity and debauchery; idolatry and witchcraft; hatred, discord, jealousy, fits of rage, selfish ambition, dissensions, factions and envy; drunkenness, orgies, and the like. I warn you, as I did before, that those who live like this will not inherit the kingdom of God." (Galatians 5:19-21)

(3) Forgive everyone, including yourself: 1) Make a list of all the bad things you have done and ask the Lord to forgive you. This list is not complete because your memory is selective, but it is useful and necessary; 2) Ask the Holy Spirit to help you remember if there is any sin you have committed that you still need to repent; 3) Go back to your childhood and all the people you got to meet: if there is anyone you have wronged, ask God for forgiveness; 4) Forgive everyone who has sinned against you. Bless them and pray for them whenever you think about them.

Prayer: "Lord Jesus, please forgive all my sins; I forgive myself and others who have sinned against me. I bless them in the name of Jesus. Thank you for your forgiveness."

(4) Work on your character: God created you. You have goodness in you. You need to continuously use that God-given character and resist your sinful nature. Find out which areas you are good at and which areas you need to work on more by asking for His wisdom. The Holy Spirit can help us develop those

godly character traits until they shine. Focus on positive character traits and resist your sinful nature.

Prayer: "Holy Spirit, help me to develop a godly, loving character that pleases you. Help me to understand which areas I need to work on so that I can think, say, and do things that please you."

(5) Pray for spiritual healing: We cannot freely love ourselves if we are living in a prison of despair or self-hate. Jesus frees us from the spiritual bondage of despair and disappointment. "He has sent me to proclaim freedom for the prisoners" (Luke 4:18b) Unless you are freed from spiritual bondage with the power of the Holy Spirit, you don't have true peace and freedom. Also, you need to learn to free yourself with the help of the Holy Spirit by living a godly life.

Prayer: "Lord Jesus, free me from all the destructive thoughts of despair, disappointment, hopelessness, and helplessness. Help me to find hope in you and help me to resist temptations and distractions in my life. Help me to love you and proclaim your love and power to others. Help me to love you and obey the Holy Spirit so I can have freedom, peace, and joy in my heart."

(6) Resist any impure thoughts: Paul tells us, "Finally, brothers, whatever is true, whatever is noble, whatever is right, whatever is pure, whatever is lovely, whatever is admirable—if anything is excellent or praiseworthy—think about such things." (Philippians 4:8) Godly behavior starts with your thoughts. Ask the Lord to help you think godly thoughts and make godly plans.

Prayer: "Holy Spirit, help me to think about Jesus today. Purify my heart so I can focus on loving God. Guide my thoughts so that I can make plans to love and serve God."

(7) Take care of your problems one by one: If you are grieving or hurting in any way, try to take care of the issues one by one so you don't feel overwhelmed. Many people who compile many problems in life have a difficult time loving anyone, including themselves. Ask the Lord if there are any areas where you need healing from a broken heart. Give him all your concerns one by one in prayer.

Prayer: "Lord Jesus, I am hurting. Help me to give everything to you so that you can help me find peace and joy. Please heal my broken heart. If there is anything that I need to give to you, speak to me now."

In order to be healed from grief, you have to let go of your loved ones. If you hold on to that person, your heart will be half frozen with grief. You won't be able to function or focus on loving God or others.

Prayer: "Lord Jesus, I give my loved one into your arms. Please take care of them. Help me to have confirmation that you are taking care of them. I give all my worries, concerns, and fears to you. Take away the desire to be with my loved one so that I can fully focus on loving you more than them. Thank you for blessing me with peace and healing."

3. Love Others

We are to love others as we love ourselves. People want to be treated with love and respect. We need to treat others with love and respect. Peter wrote, "Now that you have purified yourselves by obeying the truth so that you have sincere love for your brothers, love one another deeply, from the heart." (1 Peter 1:22) "Show proper respect to everyone: Love the brotherhood of believers, fear God, honor the king." (1 Peter 2:17)

(1) Seek peace with everyone if you can: "Whoever would love life and see good days must keep his tongue from evil and his lips from deceitful speech. He must turn from evil and do good; he must seek peace and pursue it. For the eyes of the Lord are on the righteous and his ears are attentive to their prayer, but the face of the Lord is against those who do evil. Who is going to harm you if you are eager to do good? But even if you should suffer for what is right, you are blessed. 'Do not fear what they fear; do not be frightened.'" (1 Peter 3:10-14)

(2) Love other people's souls and introduce Jesus to them: If we care about others, we will try to plant the seed of the gospel in their lives so they can be saved. The Great Commission we have received from the Lord gives us a guideline on how to love others by sharing our testimonies and leading them to Christ.

"Then Jesus came to them and said, 'All authority in heaven and on earth has been given to me. Therefore go and make disciples of all nations, baptizing them in the name of the Father and of the Son and of the Holy Spirit, and teaching them to obey everything I have commanded you. And surely I am with you always, to the very end of the age.'" (Matthew 28:18-20)

Prayer: "Lord Jesus, fill me with the Holy Spirit and help me to have a testimony so that I can spread the good news of Jesus to save people and help them grow in faith. Holy Spirit, bless me with courage and wisdom to be able to reach out to others as you want me to reach out. I pray that my gifts can be used for God's kingdom to glorify Him and to save the lost. Thank you for calling me to serve you, Lord Jesus. Please use me to the maximum for your glory. Amen."

(3) Take care of the poor: Besides saving souls and helping others to grow in faith, our Lord wants us to take care of the poor and needy. Volunteer to help others who are needy.

Prayer: "Lord Jesus, help me to help others as you would help them. Bless me with a generous heart."

(4) Pray for others: Love others by praying for them to learn how to love God.

Prayer: "Lord Jesus, I pray that my family and others learn about your love so that they can learn to love you too."

Conclusion

We are creatures of love. We want to be loved and we want to love. God created us in His image. Since God has a loving character, we also have a loving character. We are happy when we are loved by people, especially when we are loved by those whom we love. Many people are sad that no one loves them, sad when they have no one to love. Unfortunately, that's because people are focusing on human love.

Human love has limitations. Most of the time people's love is conditional, but God's love is deeper than we can think or imagine. God loves us even when we don't love Him. That's God. God is love. He also wants our love. He is happy when we love Him. He is not happy when we ignore Him. God made us so that He could love us. He also has the desire to teach us how much He loves us. That's why Jesus died on the cross for our sins. That's why the Bible was written: to teach us how much He loves us. Love starts with God. He wants us to know and understand how much He loves us so we can love Him and others.

Loving God

The lesson of loving God will never end until we die. We are all in a class about learning how to love God while we live on earth.

You don't just find love for the Lord in one day. Loving God is a process of developing an awareness of what is important in life. It is a way of developing a habit of thinking about God, as well as saying and doing things that will please Him more than anyone else. It is a way of recognizing the value of who He is and who we are in Christ.

We need to recognize that the most important thing in life is loving God. This awareness is only the first step. The next step is the desire to love God.

Ultimately, we need to continue to develop a habit of loving Him every moment.

In the process of learning how to love God, we learn how to love ourselves as He loves us and how to love others as He loves them. If you love God, you learn not to be selfish but to seek His plans and obey Him. Also, you will have a desire to teach others about God's love and how to love Him.

When we meet the Lord in heaven, we will complete this lesson on learning how to love Him. We will have perfect love and adoration for Him. Our eyes will be opened to see the glory and awesomeness of God. Deep in our hearts, we will have love for the Lord and He will be pleased with us. We are not there yet. We are still on earth learning how to love Him. This is not an easy course to pass due to our weaknesses, sinful nature, and distractions. It's easier to love the things we can see, rather than things we cannot.

The Lord knows the obstacles we face and He challenges us to continue to learn. Occasionally, we are tested as to whether we love the Lord or not. He wants us to pass this course because He loves us. It's a very difficult lesson, but if we rely on the Lord and develop the habit of loving Him daily, He will help us to do well in this course.

The Scriptures tell us what God wants from us. Pleasing Him moment by moment is loving Him. If we love someone, we try to make them happy. Loving God is like that. If we love Him, we will want to do things to make Him happy.

God gave us a choice. A person who makes a decision to love the Lord is a blessed person. God will be pleased when one makes the decision to love Him. Take this class of Loving God seriously. Learn to develop a habit of loving Him. This will please Him and bring a smile to His face.

There is nothing more important than learning how to love God. When you master it, you will find treasure - God's heart. He will have confidence in you. He trusts those who love Him.

May the Lord bless you as you read this book and learn how to love Him.

Note: To learn more about how to love God, read the book, *Loving God, 100 Daily Meditations and Prayers.*

Chapter Nine

Prayer Project: Jericho Prayer Walk

Prayer is sharing our hearts with God. It is essential to invite Him into our daily life whatever we do in order to build a close relationship with Him.

Prayer: "Lord Jesus, I invite you in my life today. Please walk with me, sit with me, listen to me and talk to me, so I can get to know you."

After I started working as a chaplain at ACDF, I felt the growing need to teach others how to pray, since many inmates told me they didn't know how. They were asking for a book on prayer but we were short of inspirational books, especially a book on prayer.

Then one day, I visited Rev. John Thompson after he was appointed as a senior pastor at Park Hill United Methodist Church in Denver, Colorado. Pastor John used to be my district superintendent, he is one of my spiritual mentors and I have lots of respect for him. He has become one of the most encouraging people in my ministry throughout the years.

There in his office, I learned something about his practice of prayer which I have never heard from anyone. When I asked him how he was preparing to minister to a new congregation, he said, "I start with prayer. Every time I am appointed to a new church, before I start ministering to my congregation, I go around the church seven times and pray for the church and my ministry. It's sort of like what Israelites did when they went around Jericho seven times and prayed. There are many walls that have to come down in order to work together and go forward with ministry."

What came out of this conversation?

I was in awe of what I heard. What a brilliant idea to pray and walk. Actually, I was practicing walking prayer but not intentionally like what pastor John did. His walk was intentional. The key word was "intentional" and that gave me an idea to create a prayer brochure called, "Jericho Prayer Walk," for inmates. It was the right timing because in our facility we hardly have any books on prayer. Many inmates started using this prayer brochure by walking around inside the pods (housing units) and praying.

I thank God for Pastor John's insight and sharing his story about how he prays as he did. It is not only inmates who used this prayer method, but I also started practicing it and it changed my prayer life. This prayer project suggests walking around seven times, but it helped me to develop a habit which extended my prayer to an all day prayer.

Jericho prayer became a blessing.

I used to pray about what I needed, but through Jericho Prayer Walk, I learned to focus on a relationship and sharing my love for the Lord and inviting Jesus to speak.

I started talking to God in my mind and sharing my heart with the Lord all the time. This spiritual practice has helped me be more aware of God's presence in my life. Whenever I am alone, and even when I speak to people, I can pray if I need to. As time went by, I started making less requests, but telling him how much I love Him. The focus of prayer became a relationship and not so much on my asking something from the Lord.

Inviting Jesus to walk and talk to me has blessed me. My relationship with the Lord doesn't have to be limited to when I am kneeling and praying, but I can have a relationship with him all the time. I learned that prayer is essential for our spiritual growth. It helps us to have a closer relationship with the Lord and with the Holy Spirit.

1. What is Jericho Prayer Walk?

God instructed Joshua what to do to win the battle with Jericho. "Now Jericho was tightly shut up because of the Israelites. No one went out and no one came in. Then the LORD said to Joshua, 'See, I have delivered Jericho into your hands, along with its king and its fighting men. March around the city once with all the armed men. Do this for six days. Have seven priests carry trumpets of rams' horns in front of the ark. On the seventh day, march around the city seven times, with the priests blowing the trumpets. When you hear them sound a long blast on the trumpets, have all the people give a loud shout; then the wall of the city will collapse and the people will go up, every man straight in." (Joshua 6:1-5)

The Israelites obeyed the Lord's instruction and the wall of Jericho fell. The spiritual wall we need to tear down is the wall between God and us. Also, between us and others. Our spiritual growth and peace comes when there is no wall between us and God or with others. We may not even realize what kind of wall we have been building to block God, and sometimes we try to hide behind this wall without even realizing it.

God is only visible in our lives as we start tearing down the walls by opening our hearts through prayer. The Scripture said, "If my people, who are called by my name, will humble themselves and pray and seek my face and turn from their wicked ways, then will I hear from heaven and will forgive their sin and will heal their land." (2 Chronicles 7:14)

The Jericho prayer is humbling ourselves, seeking God's face, opening our hearts to Him so He can help us to recognize our spiritual condition. Thus, we can change our ways to please God. So God can speak to us and deliver us from our own selfish, sinful or evil ways.

2. Where can I practice this prayer?

- **For those who are incarcerated:** Pray silently as you walk seven times around your pod. Each time you go around, try to pray the prayers listed below as well as your own prayers.
- **Praying in the sanctuary:** Arrive at the church before the worship service begins. Pray the seven prayers suggested ahead as you walk around the sanctuary seven times. Individual or groups can participate.
- **Praying at home:** Pray seven prayers as you walk around in your home seven times.
- **Pray whenever you walk:** Pray as you work at home, pray as you get to work and pray anytime you happen to be walking around.
- **Those who cannot walk:** Participate in this prayer even if you cannot walk. Close your eyes and visualize Jesus is sitting in front of you. You can share your heart and try to listen to His response.

3. How do I start?

As you start walking, invite Jesus to walk with you. Picture yourself walking with Jesus and start silent conversations with him.

Prayer: "Lord Jesus, I invited you to walk with me and listen to my heart and help me to hear from you."

(1) Relationship with the Lord:

Prayer: "Lord Jesus, I want to love you and serve you. Help me to understand your heart and your love for me and for others. Holy Spirit, teach me how to love Jesus and how to praise and worship Him. Help me to understand other people's pain so I can help others as I should. Help me to understand my gifts so I can share them with others. Help me to obey what I am called to do so I can be a blessing to others. I pray this in Jesus' name. Amen."

(2) **Family:**

Prayer: "Dear Jesus, help all my family and relatives to be saved and to learn how much you love them. Help them to love you. Surround them with godly Christians who could help them grow in faith. Provide Christian mentors for my family and my church family. Help them grow in faith and fill them with the Holy Spirit so they can love and serve Jesus to the fullest."

(3) **Forgiveness:**

Prayer: "Lord Jesus, if there is any sin I haven't repented, please help me to repent so I can be forgiven. Help me to have a clear conscience and throw away any habit of hurting myself or others with thoughts, attitudes, words and actions. Please cleanse me from all my sin and purify me so I can tear down all the walls that I have built around me. Help me to find peace with you, within myself, and with others. Help me to have wisdom on how to build other people up, instead of tearing them down. Lord Jesus, thank you for dying on the cross for my sins. I forgive others who have hurt me. I let go of my resentments, anger and bitterness. I pray for everyone who has hurt me and I ask you to bless them. Help others to forgive me if I have hurt them in anyway. I pray for my family and for others who are having a difficult time forgiving themselves and others. Help them, so that they can understand your love, forgive themselves and forgive others."

(4) **Salvation:**

Prayer: "Lord, Jesus, I give you my heart and life. I believe in you. Thank you for salvation and promise of eternal life. I pray for salvation for those who do not know Christ. Holy Spirit, open my heart so I can share Jesus' love with others. Bless me with the opportunities, courage and wisdom to help others grow in faith so they can be saved and find peace in Christ."

(5) **Addiction:**

Prayer: "Jesus, I pray for deliverance from any addictive, impure, obsessive, or ungodly thoughts and behaviors. Forgive me for following my sinful, selfish desires instead of loving you more than anyone or anything. Fill my heart with the love of Jesus and desire to know God. Help me to live a life that is holy, pleasing, and acceptable to God and to help me use my gifts to help others who are hurting. Help me to make a difference in my family and community so your will be done in my life. Holy Spirit, I ask you to deliver me from any ungodly thoughts and ungodly behaviors. Show me when I do wrong so I know what is right and wrong. I pray for others who are struggling with any kind of addiction. Give them the strength to change their lifestyle and serve Jesus."

(6) **Peace and thanksgiving:**

Prayer: "Come heavenly Father, come Lord Jesus, come Holy Spirit. Come and fill my heart with your peace and grateful spirit. I thank you for helping me in my walk with many blessings. I thank you for everything, even hard times, because your grace is sufficient for me. Jesus, I pray for peace in my heart, in my family, in my church and in the world. Help me to create peace. Bless the world leaders to have your wisdom to create peace instead of war and violence."

(7) **Holy Spirit's blessing:**

Prayer: "Lord Jesus, help me to understand how the Holy Spirit can guide, teach, and direct my life so I can obey. Holy Spirit, help me to give glory to Jesus whatever I do today: thoughts, words, and behaviors. Help me to share Jesus' love with others. Teach me Holy Spirit so that I can be a blessing to others. I pray for all the pastors, spiritual leaders, chaplains, and missionaries for the Holy Spirit's presence and blessing in their ministry. Comfort and bless the incarcerated, homeless, hungry, sick, abused, hurting, sick, and suffering."

(8) **Invite Jesus to speak:**

Prayer: "Lord Jesus, I have been talking to you and making requests but I want to hear from you. Is there anything you would like me to hear you say? If you do, please help me to listen. Help me to have a listening heart so I may hear from you. If there are any areas that I need to make changes, please help me to understand and help me to change. Speak to me, I am listening."

After inviting Jesus to talk to you, put aside your own thoughts and listen in silence for the answer. You may not hear anything, but silence. God has many languages and He may speak to you through Scriptures and words or understanding in your mind. God is not far away. The Holy Spirit lives in you and it's important to listen and obey the Holy Spirit. God can speak to our hearts with and without words.

4. Thought on persistent prayer.

You may not always get what you want or request, but He will answer your prayers according to His will in His time. Jesus told us to be persistent and to always pray if there is a need and ask God for favor. "Then Jesus told his disciples a parable to show them that they should always pray and not give up." (Luke 18:1) Jesus talked about a widow who constantly asked a judge for justice and her request was granted because of her persistence. Jesus said, "Be always on the watch, and pray that you may be able to escape all that is about to happen, and that you may be able to stand before the Son of Man." (Luke 21:36) Paul also reminds us to pray always, "And pray in the Spirit on all occasions with all kinds of prayers and requests. With this in mind, be alert and always keep on praying for all the saints." (Ephesians 6:18) "Pray continually; give thanks in all circumstances, for this is God's will for you in Christ Jesus." (1 Thessalonians 5:17-18)

Jericho Prayer Walk can lead you to pray constantly and persistently.

Chapter Ten

Prayer Project: How to Listen to God's Voice

If you have only been speaking and making requests to God, you have been missing out on a lot. God wants to speak to us and it's up to us to make the time to listen.

Prayer: "Lord Jesus, you said, 'My sheep listen to my voice.' I ask you to open my heart and mind to understand what you are trying to tell me. Help me to understand your heart and obey you with a willing heart."

In my ministry, one of the most frequent questions I am asked is, "How can I listen to God's voice?" That's the reason I created this prayer project.

Jesus told his disciples to wait for the Holy Spirit, and it took 50 days of waiting to experience the Holy Spirit. When the Holy Spirit came, the disciples' lives were transformed. Their ministry was not led by their timid, fearful hearts, but with boldness and the guidance of the Holy Spirit.

I have attended church all my life but no one encouraged me to wait and listen to God. I also thought when people told me to pray, I was asking God for something that I needed. I didn't realize that prayer is a conversation. I spoke and then instead of listening I ignored the Lord. That's all I had learned for a long time about prayer.

Think about what will happen when God speaks to you. You will be transformed. If you don't recognize God's leading and His clear voice, you are missing a lot. I cannot stress enough on listening, because listening prayer has changed my life. Relationship is the key to our spiritual growth. When God starts revealing things to you, your understanding will be clear and you will know many things that you could not have known and eventually understand what you are called to do.

After all, Jesus told us the Holy Spirit will guide, direct, teach, comfort, counsel and show God's children what is going to happen in the future. Prayer is a conversation that will help our relationship grow. God is willing to speak to us through the Bible. Also, the Holy Spirit speaks to us, and it's time for us to listen and obey God.

I believe listening to God's voice is what's missing in many of God's children who do not know what abundant life in Christ is about. Many of our problems will be solved if we can only listen to God's heart and see part of the big picture God sees.

How did God teach me to listen?

After God asked me to spend 10 percent of my time in prayer every day, I started praying more, mostly talking. Then one day, while I was praying, I heard a clear voice from God in my heart that He wants to talk to me and I should be quiet and listen in silence. I was surprised because up to that time I acted as if praying was leaving a request on an answering machine. I did all the talking and I didn't give God any chance to talk.

I started to practice listening to God, and He started revealing things to me. I had many misconceptions and one of them was that if I responded to a call to ministry, I had to do it on my own. All that was changed since God started revealing to me His heart and started changing my way of thinking. Prayer became a time to learn about God's heart and His passion.

My conversations with God through prayer have transformed my heart. I have received many spiritual blessings and learned a valuable lesson that prayer is a blessing in my spiritual journey. I learned to listen to God's heart.

Without growing in our relationship with the Lord, we will have an empty heart and we will feel that something is still missing. Yes, many of us are missing out big time because we ignore the Lord when we pray.

1. Who needs this prayer?

This prayer is for anyone who wants to learn how to listen to God's voice and to find God's plans for their lives. Jesus said, "My sheep listen to my voice; I know them, and they follow me." (John 10:27) Jesus seeks an intimate relationship with us and wants to speak to us; He wants to reveal His plans for our lives. People who do not hear or recognize God's voice are confused, lack vision, feel empty inside, and don't understand what God wants them to do with their lives. When we learn to listen and obey the plans that He reveals to us, we find purpose and fulfillment in life. Seeking Him with all our hearts is the key to listening: "You will seek me and find me when you seek me with all your heart." (Jeremiah 29:13)

Don't give up on this prayer because you don't hear immediately from God. Your persistent prayer of listening will help you find a new meaning of relationship with the Lord. Remember Solomon gave 1,000 offerings when God appeared to him in a dream and spoke to him. (1 Kings 3:1-15) You have to be persistent in prayer if you want to hear from God.

2. How does God speak to us?

God has spoken audibly to people, but most of the time, He speaks to us through the Holy Spirit. The Holy Spirit reveals to us what God wants us to know. Paul stated, "No eye has seen, no ear has heard, no mind has conceived what God has prepared for those who love Him – but God has revealed it to us by His Spirit." (1 Corinthians 2:9-10)

"But the Counselor, the Holy Spirit, whom the Father will send in my name, will teach you all things and will remind you of everything I have said to you." (John 14:26) "When the Counselor comes, whom I will send to you from the Father, the Spirit of truth who goes out from the Father, he will testify about me." (John 15:26)

"He will bring glory to me by taking from what is mine and making it known to you." (John 16:14) The Holy Spirit helps us to understand what Jesus is telling us. When we accept Jesus as our Lord and Savior, the Holy Spirit starts working in us and helps us to cultivate the gardens in our hearts, so we can understand what God wants us to do.

The Holy Spirit can speak to our spirits with or without words. The Holy Spirit may nudge us repeatedly in the same direction. When we try to go in a different direction, we may feel unsettled or ill at ease. The Holy Spirit also can give us spiritual understanding, wisdom, knowledge, and revelation, that we can understand God's heart. God's language is much broader than we can think or imagine. The Holy Spirit speaks to us in many ways.

(1) **God speaks to us through the words of the Bible:**

The Holy Spirit uses Scripture to guide, convict, direct, comfort, counsel, and teach us. We need to study the Bible if we want God to direct our paths. When we go through trials, God uses the Scriptures to console and comfort us; and when He does this it confirms for us that He is with us, and this helps us grow in faith. (John 14:15-17, 25-26, 15:26, 16:5-15) The Holy Spirit helps us understand when we are spiritually empty and need to be filled with the Holy Spirit.

The Word of God satisfies our spiritual hunger, and our spirit will know when He is near. Our spiritual hunger is something that Jesus understood when the devil tempted Him. Jesus said, "Man does not live on bread alone, but on every word that comes from the mouth of God." (Matthew 4:4)

Read Romans, John, Acts, Hosea, and other books of the Bible that have words that will help you listen.

Prayer: "Holy Spirit, bless me with wisdom, knowledge, understanding, and revelation, so I can understand the word of God and obey Him."

(2) God speaks to us as we spend time in prayer:

Many people think it is only important to talk to God, but it is more important to wait, to be still before Him, and to listen. Invite Jesus to speak to you.

Prayer: "Lord Jesus, please speak to me. I am listening. I love you." Then clear your mind and listen in silence. Let go of your scattered thoughts; write down whatever comes to your mind.

When God speaks to you, what you write will always agree with His written Word. Write down the questions you have for God and when you have an answer to a question, write it down.

It's not easy to clear your mind at first, but you will be able to do it if you keep practicing. I encourage you to count the days to see how many days it would take for you to recognize and hear the voice of God.

If you are persistent, God will eventually speak to you. He will also let us know that He will answer our prayers even before it happens. That happens when you recognize how to hear His voice so it's very important to learn to hear His voice.

When He says "no" to our prayer request, we need to change our prayers. When Paul's prayer was not answered the way he wanted, God gave him the reason. "But he said to me, 'My grace is sufficient for you, for my power is made perfect in weakness.' Therefore I will boast all the more gladly about my weaknesses, so that Christ's power may rest on me." (2 Corinthians 12:9)

Prayer: "Dear Jesus, I surrender my life and everything to you. Open my heart, so I can listen to your voice. I surrender all my plans because you have better plans for me. Break my hardened heart and work in me, so I can repent for all my sins. Forgive my sins and cleanse me, so that when you speak to me there will be no distractions."

(3) The Holy Spirit guides us:

Jesus told us the Holy Spirit will guide, direct, teach, comfort, counsel, and show God's children what is going to happen in the future. He speaks to our hearts. God has spoken audibly to people, but most of the time, He speaks to our spiritual senses in our hearts and minds through godly desires, feelings, understanding, conviction and understanding through the Holy Spirit.

The Holy Spirit reveals to us what God wants us to know: "No eye has seen, no ear has heard, no mind has conceived what God has prepared for those who love Him – but God has revealed it to us by His Spirit." (1 Corinthians 2:9-10a) "But the Counselor, the Holy Spirit, whom the Father will send in my name, will teach you all things and will remind you of everything I have said to you." (John 14:26) "When the Counselor comes, whom I will send to you from the Father, the

Spirit of truth who goes out from the Father, he will testify about me." (John 15:26) "He will bring glory to me by taking from what is mine and making it known to you." (John 16:14)

How can you prepare to listen to the Holy Spirit? Work on two important things: clean your heart by repenting and make peace with everyone. That will be a beginning of our growing relationship with the Lord who wants us to be pure and holy.

Many times we have a hard time listening to God because our mind is so cluttered with so many worldly things because we love the world more than God. We are created to love God more than things or people and living in sin blocks our spiritual ear to hear the voice of God. The sad thing is we may live in sin and don't even realize it.

Ask the Holy Spirit to reveal your spiritual condition to you so you can start cleaning and prepare your heart so your heart will have room to listen.

Prayer: "Holy Spirit, help me to see my spiritual condition. If there is any sin that I have not repented, please help me to repent."

Forgiving others is also essential to make room in our heart to listen. Many people are so overwhelmed with negative thoughts that they are filled with grief, resentment, anger, hate, and bitterness. They don't have room to listen.

Forgive yourself and others. Bless and pray for others who have hurt you. Let go of all the resentment, anger, hate and bitterness you have in your heart. Without repentance, there is no forgiveness and no spiritual blessing.

When Peter preached, he told others to repent, be baptized, and then they would be forgiven and receive the Holy Spirit. (Acts 2:37-41)

Try to live a life that will please God and create peace. Determine not to sin with your mouth: speak words that create peace, faith, and spiritual victory. Thank God for everything, even the hard times. Anything you have told God that you would do, follow through with it. (1 Peter 3:10-12)

If you want Jesus to answer your prayer, you need to have a relationship with Him. Invite Jesus into your heart and be saved.

Prayer: "Lord Jesus, I am a sinner. Forgive my sins. I give my heart to you. I surrender my life to you. Come into my heart and take control of my life. Fill me with the Holy Spirit and speak to me so I can obey you. In the name of Jesus, I pray. Amen"

(4) The Holy Spirit gives us assignments:

The devil will try to tempt you to fall into sin, but the Holy Spirit will give you assignments to guide you to grow in faith and to help others grow in faith. Also, the Holy Spirit tests you to see if you will obey Him from time to time. Obey the Holy

Spirit even the little things. When God can trust that you are a faithful and trustworthy servant, you will be anointed to do the work of God. Jesus said, "But you will receive power when the Holy Spirit comes on you; and you will be my witnesses in Jerusalem, and in all Judea and Samaria, and to the ends of the earth." (Acts 1:8)

Not everyone experiences the Holy Spirit even though they say that they are believers. Jesus spent more than three years with His disciples, and yet He told them to wait for the Holy Spirit. For you who have not experienced the Holy Spirit's power in your life, spend an hour clearing your mind, learn to wait before God in silence for the next one or two weeks, and ask the Holy Spirit to speak to you. Practice this until you experience the Holy Spirit.

(5) **God speaks to our spiritual senses:**

When we obey the Lord, the Holy Spirit will fill our hearts with joy and peace. Sometimes, the tears we often experience at such holy moments are the work of God. It's like God is watering our dried garden and helping us to grow in faith.

In the book of Hosea, God compares our hearts to a garden. "Judah must plow, and Jacob must break up the ground. Sow for yourselves righteousness, reap the fruit of unfailing love, and break up your unplowed ground; for it is time to seek the Lord, until he comes and showers righteousness on you. But you have planted wickedness, you have reaped evil, you have eaten the fruit of deception." (Hosea 10:11b-13a)

God speaks to us with comforting words, or convicts us of our sin. Our tears are the evidence of that. The Holy Spirit brings healing through our tears even though we might not know why we are crying.

(6) **God can speak to us through dreams:**

We need to ask God for interpretation of our dreams. The Holy Spirit gives us dreams to direct us and to help us understand our spiritual condition; they can also reveal something God wants us to know concerning our futures or the futures of our loved ones, so we will know what to pray. (Acts 2:17, John 16:13) For those who suffer from nightmares, read the Bible and pray more. The devil torments people by giving them nightmarish dreams, but prayer is powerful against him. Not all nightmares are from the devil, God can show us what is happening in our spiritual world, so we can pray.

Prayer: "Lord Jesus, help me to understand what you are trying to tell me with my dreams."

(7) God also speaks to us through visions:

He directs our spiritual path, or gives us understanding of what is happening in the spiritual world, or tells us what is going to happen in the future. (Acts 2:17, Acts 27:23-25) Write down your visions or images and ask for an interpretation. God may communicate with you through visions, and some spiritual visions come with images in your mind. The devil can also give you visions and images in your mind which will lead you to ungodly thoughts and destructive behaviors. Resist any ungodly thoughts and images and focus your heart and mind on Christ by meditating on the Scriptures. Pray for wisdom and discernment to know the difference. (James 1:1-18, 3:13-18)

(8) God can speak to us through other people:

Paul has helped many to grow in faith throughout many generations because of the letters that he wrote while in prison. God can use us regardless of our circumstances and will anoint us to do the work of Him if we are willing to obey Him.

(9) Reflection and a Journal can help us to listen to God's voice:

Write any questions you might have and ask the Lord to speak to you. Then, quiet your mind in silence, and write down what He may be speaking to you. As you start writing how God has helped you, the Holy Spirit can tell you the things that you need to know. God speaks to us through hardships and circumstances. Through reflection, God can reveal to us what He wants to teach us. Paul had hardships and he understood that through his suffering he learned to rely on God for comfort, no one else. He also learned that God can help him to comfort and encourage others even though he was going through suffering.

Prayer: "Lord Jesus, please speak to me. I am listening. I love you."

Clear your mind and listen in silence. Let go of your scattered thoughts and write down whatever comes to your mind. When God speaks to you, what you write will always agree with His written Word. Write down the questions you have for God and when you have an answer to a question, write it down. It's not easy to clear your mind at first, but you will be able to do it if you keep practicing.

During this prayer, add your personal prayer and count the days. If we are persistent, God will let us know that He will answer our prayers even before it happens. When He says "no" to our prayer request, we need to change our prayers. When Paul's prayer was not answered the way he wanted, God gave him the reason. "But he said to me, 'My grace is sufficient for you, for my power is made perfect in weakness.' Therefore I will boast all the more gladly about my weaknesses, so that Christ's power may rest on me." (2 Corinthians 12:9)

3. Discern the voices you hear.

(1) Our mind is a spiritual battlefield:
There are four voices we hear in our minds:
1) The voice of the Holy Spirit.
2) The voice of the devil.
3) The voice of other people.
4) Our own voices.

The voice of the Holy Spirit is positive, and listening to it helps us grow in faith. Until you obey Him, you will have a restless heart. However, as soon as you obey His voice, peace will fill your heart. On the other hand, the voice of the devil is negative, critical, ungodly, hurtful, and destructive. The devil always makes sin appealing so that people fall into sin and lose peace.

(2) What to do when you hear destructive voices and visions:
The devil can speak to us with an audible voice, but mostly speaks to us in our minds. Some people hear voices telling them to hurt themselves and others. Also, the devil can give us visions and images that will lead us to sin and destruction. Rebuke it: "In the name of Jesus, spirit of lies, destruction, and torment, leave me. I am covered by the blood of Jesus. I am a child of God and I am going to serve Jesus." Whenever you have destructive thoughts, hear voices, or see visions that are not from God, pray the Lord's Prayer again and again, especially the part: "Deliver us from evil."

(3) The Word of God has spiritual power:
We can be strong as we read the Bible and pray for healing of our minds. I believe many people who hurt themselves and others or who commit suicide are the victims of destructive voices and were tormented inside their minds and didn't know how to resist the devil. Many who hear voices have gone through traumatic events in their lives, and they need healing. If you hear destructive voices, forgive others and forgive yourself.

Prayer: "Lord Jesus, because you have forgiven me, died on the cross, and shed your blood for my sins, I forgive myself and forgive others who have hurt me. I bless others who have hurt me. Heal my wounds and my painful memories and fill my heart with your love, peace and joy. Help me to serve you."

Jesus was tempted by the devil to jump off a high building and kill himself, but he won the battle with the Word of God. So you can resist the devil's temptation with God's Word. Meditate whenever you can and be proactive on combating negative voices. Here is the Scripture that reminds us what Jesus has done for us and what we can do to help others by the power of the Holy Spirit.

"The Spirit of the Lord is on me, because he has anointed me to preach good news to the poor. He has sent me to proclaim freedom for the prisoners and recovery of sight for the blind, to release the oppressed, to proclaim the year of the Lord's favor." (Luke 4:18-19)

(4) **God has plans for all of us:**

Don't ignore what God is trying to tell you. You need to understand what His plan is in order for you to be productive in God's kingdom building business. So, ask the Lord what you need to do to serve Him because He knows what you need to do to be fruitful.

"'For I know the plans I have for you,' declares the Lord, 'Plans to prosper you and not to harm you, plans to give you hope and a future. Then you will call upon me and come and pray to me, and I will listen to you. You will seek me and find me when you seek me with all your heart. I will be found by you,' declares the Lord, 'and will bring you back from captivity.'" (Jeremiah 29:11-14a)

God gave you the gift of life so you can use it to help others. Volunteer to help others in the community, church or in a mission. "Then Jesus came to them and said, 'All authority in heaven and on earth has been given to me. Therefore go and make disciples of all nations, baptizing them in the name of the Father and of the Son and of the Holy Spirit, and teaching them to obey everything I have commanded you. And surely I am with you always, to the very end of the age.'" (Matthew 28:18-20)

Prayer: "God enlarge my vision and mission to serve you and others. Open the doors so that I will be able to make many disciples of Jesus and to help others who are hurting to bring healing with your help."

4. **Spiritual exercise for listening to God's voice through the Scripture:**

God can speak to you through the Scripture. Ask the Lord how He sees you then read the following Scriptures and see how God can use the Scriptures to speak to you.

Prayer: "Lord Jesus, please open my heart to understand how you see me. Please give me the wisdom to understand your heart. Speak to me, I am listening."

In the book of Revelation, we can learn how Jesus asked John to write letters to seven leaders in seven churches. We can learn from the letters how Jesus evaluates spiritual condition of people. Read the following seven letters and reflect on what Jesus may be telling you:

(1) "To the angel of the church in Ephesus write: These are the words of him who holds the seven stars in his right hand and walks among the seven golden lampstands: I know your deeds, your hard work and your perseverance. I know that you cannot tolerate wicked men, that you have tested those who claim to be apostles but are not, and have found them false. You have persevered and have endured hardships for my name, and have not grown weary. Yet I hold this against you: You have forsaken your first love. Remember the height from which you have fallen! Repent and do the things you did at first. If you do not repent, I will come to you and remove your lampstand from its place. But you have this in your favor: You hate the practices of the Nicolaitans, which I also hate. He who has an ear, let him hear what the Spirit says to the churches. To him who overcomes, I will give the right to eat from the tree of life, which is in the paradise of God." (Revelation 2:1-7)

(2) "To the angel of the church in Smyrna write: These are the words of him who is the First and the Last, who died and came to life again. I know your afflictions and your poverty-- yet you are rich! I know the slander of those who say they are Jews and are not, but are a synagogue of Satan. Do not be afraid of what you are about to suffer. I tell you, the devil will put some of you in prison to test you, and you will suffer persecution for ten days. Be faithful, even to the point of death, and I will give you the crown of life. He who has an ear, let him hear what the Spirit says to the churches. He who overcomes will not be hurt at all by the second death." (Revelation 2:8-11)

(3) "To the angel of the church in Pergamum write: These are the words of him who has the sharp, double-edged sword. I know where you live-- where Satan has his throne. Yet you remain true to my name. You did not renounce your faith in me, even in the days of Antipas, my faithful witness, who was put to death in your city-- where Satan lives. Nevertheless, I have a few things against you: You have people there who hold to the teaching of Balaam, who taught Balak to entice the Israelites to sin by eating food sacrificed to idols and by committing sexual immorality. Likewise you also have those who hold to the teaching of the Nicolaitans. Repent therefore! Otherwise, I will soon come to you and will fight against them with the sword of my mouth. He who has an ear, let him hear what the Spirit says to the churches. To him who overcomes, I will give some of the hidden manna. I will also give him a white stone with a new name written on it, known only to him who receives it." (Revelation 2:12-17)

(4) "To the angel of the church in Thyatira write: These are the words of the Son of God, whose eyes are like blazing fire and whose feet are like burnished bronze. I know your deeds, your love and faith, your service and perseverance, and that you are now doing more than you did at first. Nevertheless, I have this against you: You tolerate that woman Jezebel, who calls herself a prophetess. By her teaching she misleads my servants into sexual immorality and the eating of food sacrificed to idols. I have given her time to repent of her immorality, but she is unwilling. So I will cast her on a bed of suffering, and I will make those who commit adultery with her suffer intensely, unless they repent of her ways...Only hold on to what you have until I come. To him who overcomes and does my will to the end, I will give authority over the nations--'He will rule them with an iron scepter; he will dash them to pieces like pottery'--just as I have received authority from my Father. I will also give him the morning star. He who has an ear, let him hear what the Spirit says to the churches." (Revelation 2:18-22, 25-29)

(5) "To the angel of the church in Sardis write: These are the words of him who holds the seven spirits of God and the seven stars. I know your deeds; you have a reputation of being alive, but you are dead. Wake up! Strengthen what remains and is about to die, for I have not found your deeds complete in the sight of my God. Remember, therefore, what you have received and heard; obey it, and repent. But if you do not wake up, I will come like a thief, and you will not know at what time I will come to you. Yet you have a few people in Sardis who have not soiled their clothes. They will walk with me, dressed in white, for they are worthy. He who overcomes will, like them, be dressed in white. I will never blot out his name from the book of life, but will acknowledge his name before my Father and his angels. He who has an ear, let him hear what the Spirit says to the churches." (Revelation 3:1-6)

(6) "To the angel of the church in Philadelphia write: These are the words of him who is holy and true, who holds the key of David. What he opens no one can shut, and what he shuts no one can open. I know your deeds. See, I have placed before you an open door that no one can shut. I know that you have little strength, yet you have kept my word and have not denied my name. I will make those who are of the synagogue of Satan, who claim to be Jews though they are not, but are liars-- I will make them come and fall down at your feet and acknowledge that I have loved you. Since you have kept my command to endure patiently, I will also keep you from the hour of trial that is going to come upon the whole world to test those who live on the earth. I am coming soon. Hold on to what you have, so that no one will take your crown. Him who overcomes I will make a pillar in the

temple of my God. Never again will he leave it. I will write on him the name of my God and the name of the city of my God, the new Jerusalem, which is coming down out of heaven from my God; and I will also write on him my new name. He who has an ear, let him hear what the Spirit says to the churches." (Revelation 3:7-13)

(7) "To the angel of the church in Laodicea write: These are the words of the Amen, the faithful and true witness, the ruler of God's creation. I know your deeds, that you are neither cold nor hot. I wish you were either one or the other! So, because you are lukewarm-- neither hot nor cold-- I am about to spit you out of my mouth. You say, 'I am rich; I have acquired wealth and do not need a thing.' But you do not realize that you are wretched, pitiful, poor, blind and naked. I counsel you to buy from me gold refined in the fire, so you can become rich; and white clothes to wear, so you can cover your shameful nakedness; and salve to put on your eyes, so you can see. Those whom I love I rebuke and discipline. So be earnest, and repent. Here I am! I stand at the door and knock. If anyone hears my voice and opens the door, I will come in and eat with him, and he with me. To him who overcomes, I will give the right to sit with me on my throne, just as I overcame and sat down with my Father on his throne. He who has an ear, let him hear what the Spirit says to the churches." (Revelation 3:14-22)

Reflections:
- Which part of the Scripture touched you the most?
- What do you think God is telling you now?
- How does God see you now?
- Is He telling you something positive?
- Is He telling you to do something to make changes? What could that be?
- Write a letter from Jesus and see if God is telling you something that you need to hear.
- How has this exercise helped you?

Note: To learn more about how to listen to God's voice, read the book, *Four Voices, How They Affect Our Mind: How to Overcome Self-Destructive Voices and Hear the Nurturing Voice of God.*

Chapter Eleven

Prayer Project: Healing from Grief and Loss

God can bring healing from grief and loss from our loved ones. He understands our pain and broken hearts. He is opening His hands to ask us to give all our pain and grief to Him so He can take care of us.

Prayer: "Lord Jesus, you told your disciples, 'Do not let your hearts be troubled.' Help me experience healing from the loss of my loved one. I need you to show me how to walk this road of tears with your strength and comforting presence of the Holy Spirit. Help me to give my loved one to you completely so I can experience healing and find joy and peace in you."

I have experienced many deaths in my family. Each time the degree of pain was different and I suffered from it. But nothing can be compared to losing my husband, Keith, in a car accident in 2008.

I was immobilized with pain and couldn't work and I had to stop all my writing projects because I just couldn't continue to do it. The Lord guided me in my healing process and listening to God's voice was what helped me the most in my darkest times. God didn't want me to focus on my pain and live in the past.

God brought healing into my broken heart. Within three months I finally let my husband go. I was healed from grief, pain and triggers. He guided me to write a book, *Dancing in the Sky, A Story of Hope for Grieving Heart* which came from my journal to help others who are grieving and are in need of healing. By the time I finished this book, God asked me to write a prayer project and add it to the book to help others. This prayer project is what I included in this book.

I learned that we have work to do when we are grieving. As a chaplain I thought I knew how to process grief since I was helping many grieving people. But until I went through losing my husband, I didn't understand how to let him go.

I pray that you will find healing from grief and loss as you practice this prayer and let your loved ones go. As I have mentioned, listening to God's voice has helped me in my grieving process more than anything. So, if you don't know how to recognize God's voice, I encourage you to follow this project.

I. Who needs this prayer?
If you have lost a loved one, are grieving, and want to experience healing,

this project is for you. When you lose a person you love, it's like you are a leaf being blown away by a strong wind. In order to land safely from this disaster, you need healing from grief and pain. Healing is a process that involves many areas. You will be dealing with different emotions such as shock, denial, fear, frustration, anger, forgiveness, attachments, trust, faith, regrets, triggers, acceptance, idolizing the person, letting go of the person, and more. Your healing depends on how you process these areas. The time of grieving is the time to trust God more than ever. He has the power to heal your broken heart.

2. Understand the areas you need healing.
Reflect on four different areas so you will know where you need to focus.

(1) Do you have peace with God?
You need to know and believe that God is good, even during the loss of your loved one. Death and loss are a result of living in a fallen, imperfect world with frail bodies. Sometimes our loved one's tragic, sudden death may be caused by people's weaknesses and bad decisions. It's not God's doing. If you are angry with God because you think that He caused you pain by taking your loved one, you need to work on understanding God's love. When you can accept His love and healing power, this is the beginning of the path to restoration. God is for you and not against you. Jesus said, "I have come that they may have life, and have it to the full." (John 10:10b)

(2) Do you have peace with yourself?
If you had hurt the person in any way while they were alive, you need to forgive yourself. Also, you need to ask God to forgive you and accept that He does.

(3) Do you have peace with the person you have lost?
You may need to take care of the issues surrounding the death of the person. You need to forgive the person that you lost, in order to find peace.

(4) Do you have peace with everyone?
"If it is possible, as far as it depends on you, live at peace with everyone. Do not take revenge, my friends, but leave room for God's wrath, for it is written: 'It is mine to avenge; I will repay,' says the Lord." (Romans 12:18-19) Having peace does not mean that you have to reconcile with everyone face to face. It means you have accepted the reality of the loss, but you do not hold any resentment or anger toward anyone.

Prayer: "Holy Spirit, guide and direct me with your wisdom and strength. Help me to do what I need to do to find peace and healing so I can come out of this fire with strength and courage."

3. How to participate in this prayer project?

The following exercises will help you find peace as you work on different areas.

(1) Meditation:

Scripture reading and meditation bring healing. Read Job, Psalms, Proverbs, John, and other Scripture, to understand God's love and His healing power. You can learn from Job when you are grieving. He lost all of his seven sons, three daughters, and wealth all at once.

"At this, Job got up and tore his robe and shaved his head. Then he fell to the ground in worship and said: 'Naked I came from my mother's womb, and naked I will depart. The Lord gave and the Lord has taken away; may the name of the Lord be praised.' In all this, Job did not sin by charging God with wrongdoing." (Job 1:20-22)

Job praised the Lord in his loss. He didn't blame God for his losses. All our family, friends, material things, and our lives are temporary gifts from God. Job understood that and acted on it.

Read John 14:1-6, Psalm 23, Psalm 103, and Revelation 21 to understand God's plans for a better future for those who believe in Jesus.

The Scripture said, "He will wipe every tear from their eyes. There will be no more death or mourning or crying or pain, for the old order of things has passed away." (Revelation 21:4) Jesus said, "Come to me, all you who are weary and burdened, and I will give you rest." (Matthew 11:28)

(2) Prayer brings healing:

It is important to express your feelings and needs to God and ask Him to help you experience healing. Also, it is important to practice listening to God in silence. When you are grieving, there are many thoughts and attitudes that need to be adjusted and cleansed. Resist any disturbing thoughts so you can listen to God's voice without distraction.

Prayer: "I am listening to you. If there is any sin in my life for which I need to repent, please reveal it to me so I can experience healing."

(3) **Know that God cares:**

Our mind is a spiritual battlefield. The devil can speak to our minds and plant seeds of wrong attitudes, resentment, anger, and bitterness toward others and God. When we face difficult times through grief and loss, the devil will try to convince us that God doesn't care about us. Some people turn away from the Lord and this delays healing. (1 Peter 5:6-9) God cared enough to give His only Son, Jesus, to die for our sins. (John 3:16-17)

(4) **Write a prayer or letter to God:**

Write a letter of questions, wishes, pain, acceptance, releasing, and letting go of your loved one.

Prayer: "Lord Jesus, I give my fears, desires, plans, and unforgiving spirit to you. Take away the desire to hold on to my loved one. Please heal my heart."

(5) **Focus on God's blessings and grace:**

Read, meditate, and memorize Psalm 23:5-6 and make it your prayer whenever you are hurting: "You prepare a table before me in the presence of my enemies. You anoint my head with oil; my cup overflows. Surely goodness and love will follow me all the days of my life, and I will dwell in the house of the Lord forever."

(6) **Develop an attitude of gratefulness:**

Paul wrote, "Not only so, but we also rejoice in our sufferings, because we know that suffering produces perseverance; perseverance, character; and character, hope. And hope does not disappoint us, because God has poured out his love into our hearts by the Holy Spirit, whom he has given us. You see, at just the right time, when we were still powerless, Christ died for the ungodly." (Romans 5:3-6) We can praise God in any circumstances by focusing on God's grace.

(7) **Forgive everyone including yourself:**

You need to let go of all resentment, anger, and bitterness toward anyone associated with your loved one's death. One by one, tell God that you forgive your loved one or others who are involved. Jesus said, "But I tell you: Love your enemies and pray for those who persecute you." (Matthew 5:44)

Prayer: "God, I release all my anger, resentment, bitterness, and my unforgiving spirit. Please forgive me, if I have sinned against you and others. I forgive everyone responsible for my loved one's death. Bless them and forgive them, as you have blessed me and forgiven me."

(8) Have compassion for yourself and others who may be related to the death of your loved one.

(9) Start a journal to express your pain, feelings of hurt, restoration and how God is helping you.

(10) Write a letter to your loved one:
Write a love letter, forgiveness letter, releasing letter, or good-bye letter to your loved one.

(11) To help others, write a testimony or book about how God is helping you in your grieving process:
"Those who sow in tears will reap with songs of joy. He who goes out weeping, carrying seed to sow, will return with songs of joy, carrying sheaves with him." (Psalm 126:5-6)

(12) Let go of self-pity:
Don't expect others to understand your pain and meet your needs. Many people do not know how to help those who are grieving. By letting go of your expectations of how others should help you, you will be freed from a critical and judgmental spirit.

(13) Let go of your loved one:
You have to grieve and it is necessary. But, if you decide to grieve for the rest of your life, you will be immobilized by the pain and your relationship with God will also suffer. You have to let your loved one go, in order to experience healing from pain caused by grief.
Prayer: "God, I am giving you all of my desires, wishes, dreams, regrets, and unforgiving spirit associated with my loved one. Please take away any painful memories as well as my desire to be with my loved one. In Jesus' name I pray. Amen."

(14) Ask God to heal you from triggers of pain:
You will learn what makes you break down in pain when you lose someone. You may need to put away the items that trigger your grief and pain. However, you cannot put away everything since anything can be a trigger. The ultimate healing will come from the Lord when you put God first and not the person you have lost.

Prayer: "Lord Jesus, you are my joy and my love. I ask you to heal me so that I don't suffer from any triggers. I love you more than anyone and anything. Please help me focus my heart on you so grieving does not become a distraction between you and I. Amen."(Matthew 7:7, Colossians 3:1-4)

(15) Ask Jesus to anoint you for healing:

Prayer: "Lord Jesus, I am hurting. Please touch me and heal my troubled mind, heart, soul, and spirit. Holy Spirit, fill my heart with your peace and joy, and bring healing. Heavenly Father, I praise you for helping me in my troubled times. Lord Jesus, please heal my memories of the painful death of my loved one so I can forgive and have peace of mind."

(16) Sometimes do something to forget about your loss:

Take a break to enjoy small things in life – nature, drawing, exercise, dancing, or even humor. Don't turn to alcohol, drugs, violence, or follow destructive sinful paths to avoid the pain. When you do that, it will delay healing and the end result can be devastating.

(17) Find supportive friends:

Find friends who will listen and understand your situation, struggles, and feelings.

(18) Join a grief support group or start one if you can't find one:

Find people who will join this prayer project for 30 days. Discuss your loss, what you need to do to experience healing, how you are making progress, and how God is helping you. Pray for each other's healing.

James wrote, "Is any one of you in trouble? He should pray. Is anyone happy? Let him sing songs of praise. Is any one of you sick? He should call the elders of the church to pray over him and anoint him with oil in the name of the Lord. And the prayer offered in faith will make the sick person well; the Lord will raise him up. If he has sinned, he will be forgiven. Therefore confess your sins to each other and pray for each other so that you may be healed. The prayer of a righteous man is powerful and effective." (James 5:13-16)

(19) Help others who are hurting.

(20) If you do not have a relationship with Jesus, this is an opportunity to invite Him into your heart:

Prayer: "Lord Jesus, I invite you into my heart and my life. I give my heart to you. Forgive all my sins and wash me. Lord, I am hurting, but I believe that you can heal my broken heart. Fill my heart with your joy and peace. If there is any area that I need to work on, please teach me what I need to do."

(21) **Attend church:**
Get to know others who can encourage you to grow in faith.

4. What happens when you are healed from grief?
When you are healed, you are not immersed in grief and pain from your loss. Your heart is filled with gratitude, thankfulness, and compassion toward others who are hurting. Also, you will be free from triggers of grief and pain, and be able to function normally.

Note: To learn more about how to process grief and healing, read the book, *Dancing in the Sky, A Story of Hope for Grieving Hearts, Tornadoes, Grief, Loss, Trauma, and PTSD: Tornadoes, Lessons and Teachings—The TLT Model for Healing*, and The *Long Hard Road, U.S. Army Ranger Ricky's Story with Reflections*.

Chapter Twelve

Prayer Project: Healing from Nightmares

Nightmares can be a spiritual attack or sometimes God may be telling you what's going to happen in the future. To discern where these nightmares are coming from is important. Watch for reoccurring nightmares. If you are hurting because something is choking or troubling you, then you are under spiritual attack. God can release you from the nightmares.

Prayer: "Lord Jesus, you said you will give us peace that is not from the world. I ask you to help me to be strong so I will be able to win this spiritual battle and be freed from nightmares with your power."

1. Who needs this prayer?

This prayer project is for those who are suffering from nightmares and for those who want to find peace. Many people have no peace whether they are awake or asleep, and some are afraid to go to sleep because of nightmares. They feel helpless and wonder why they suffer so much.

Jesus said, "Peace I leave with you, my peace I give you. I do not give to you as the world gives. Do not let your hearts be troubled and do not be afraid." (John 14:27) Jesus is the Prince of Peace, and wants us to have peace all the time. The peace Jesus provides for us is a blessing in this troubled world. Many people, even those who proclaim that they are Christians, don't have peace.

This prayer project is to help you learn to have peace whether you are awake or asleep. Remember, there is no shortcut for this spiritual path of finding peace. Spiritual discipline takes time, and it is hard work. There are many areas you need to work on to keep this peace. Sometimes, you need to change your way of thinking, speaking, and behaving in order to have peace.

Ask the Holy Spirit to guide you and help you understand the Bible and understand yourself. If you cannot find peace and are not free from nightmares in the first 30 days, I suggest that you do another 30 days, or until you are healed from nightmares.

Jesus offers peace to all by inviting us to walk with him. Staying on that path is a lifelong process of learning through obedience. Many times we take the path of destruction and lose peace. The good news is that even if we lose peace, we can go back and find it because God's grace is greater than our weaknesses. We lose peace because there may be areas we need to change. We need God's wisdom and strength to make changes. Jesus said, "Everything is possible for Him who believes." (Mark 9:23)

Prayer: "God, help me to find peace in you, not only when I am awake, but in my sleep as well. Help others who are suffering from nightmares, so they will be delivered from the spirit of torment and fear and be filled with the Spirit of peace. In the name of Jesus I pray. Amen."

2. Spiritual exercises.

Sometimes we don't understand why we are having bad dreams. I know they make people feel helpless and hopeless. I am thankful that my mother was there to instruct me about my bad dreams. When you are having nightmares, there may be many reasons. Through dreams, we can see the spiritual condition of our souls. If we are not standing strong in our faith, the devil will try to torment us with destructive thoughts, attitudes and dreams.

Not all dreams are the work of the Holy Spirit. Even though God wants us to repent when we fall into sin, I don't believe God punishes people through their dreams. God does not terrorize anyone by giving them bad dreams, but we do encounter the spiritual realm. We need to put on the full armor of God to win the spiritual battle. Also, not all bad dreams are the work of the devil. The Holy Spirit may be warning us about what is going to happen in the future and that we need to pray.

Spiritual war is real. Those who have received the gift of spiritual discernment can see and feel the demonic attack. The devil can torment people. Therefore, not all spiritual encounters are the work of the Holy Spirit.

We can win the battle, however, if we follow the instruction of the Scriptures. Peter wrote, "Humble yourselves, therefore, under God's mighty hand, that he may lift you up in due time. Cast all your anxiety on him because he cares for you. Be self-controlled and alert. Your enemy the devil prowls around like a roaring lion looking for someone to devour. Resist him, standing firm, in the faith, because you know that your brothers throughout the world are undergoing the same kind of sufferings." (I Peter 5:6-9)

To win this battle I ask you to accept Jesus as your Lord and Savior if you have not already done so. Do not expect Jesus to help you if you don't have a relationship with Him. Here is a prayer so you can invite Jesus into your heart and be strong enough in the Lord to win even the spiritual battles in your dreams.

Prayer: "Lord Jesus, I am a sinner and I need your forgiveness. Please come into my heart and life and cleanse me from all my sin and help me to live a righteous life to glorify you. Bless me with your wisdom and discernment so I can understand you and love you. I pray this in Jesus' name."

(1) Learn about God's ways:
Start reading the Bible, either the gospel of John or Romans. While reading, see if there is anything you need to ask God to forgive. Ask Him to forgive you and ask Jesus to wash you with His blood to cleanse you of your sin. Ask God to give you the strength to live a holy life. We lose peace because of our sins, so try not to repeat your mistakes.

(2) Ask the Holy Spirit to help you cleanse your life:
The Holy Spirit is a gift to all Christians. When you accept Jesus, the Holy Spirit will be with you to teach, direct, guide, counsel, and comfort you. Ask Jesus to help you live a godly life.

(3) Forgive everyone including yourself:
Many of us are hurting because we have been wronged by others. We need to forgive them and learn to let go of anger and resentment. Start blessing people who hurt you and start asking God to help you forgive. God will give you peace when you forgive.

(4) Pray to God to help you experience healing:
If you have been abused or are a victim of violence, you need to experience healing from God. Ask Him to help you let go of your resentments and anger. Pray, so God can give you wisdom to let go of the painful memories. The devil will tell you that you don't have to forgive. Don't listen to him. If you don't forgive, you will open the door for the devil to hurt you more. If you see a demon in your dream, rebuke the devil to leave in Jesus' name. Keep reading the Bible and pray so you will be strong.

(5) Don't justify your sinful attitudes and behaviors:
The devil tries to tell our minds that it is all right to sin, but don't listen to his suggestions. Whatever suggestions come from the Holy Spirit to our minds are to help us grow. The devil's suggestions always sound good, but they invite us to fall into sin. This is not going to help us get closer to God, rather it will hinder our growth and in the process, we will lose peace only to end up in turmoil.

(6) Go to church and get to know other Christians:
If you feel weak like a newborn baby in Christ, you need to find others who can help you understand the Bible. They know what you are going through and have learned how to fight the spiritual battle. Don't be discouraged if you cannot find a mentor right away. The Holy Spirit is a divine person who lives in you and will help

you. Keep reading the Bible and ask the Holy Spirit to help you find a spiritual mentor who could help you.

(7) **Learn to clear your mind and listen to God:**

You can learn to control your destructive thoughts and start praying more, so the devil will not have room to attack you. You need to resist destructive thoughts and rebuke them in the name of Jesus. Quickly turn your mind to the powerful Word of God, He will help you in this process. It might take some time to win the battle of controlling your thoughts. In Jesus' name and in faith, you need to fill your mind with the powerful Word of God. The Holy Spirit within you is strong and will teach you, but you must learn to obey the Lord.

(8) **Dedicate your time to prayer and Scripture reading:**

I encourage you to do a 30-day prayer with a strong commitment to know Jesus. Read Luke or any gospel and pray that you will be set free from all nightmares. Bad dreams may not disappear right away, but as time passes you will be stronger and the devil will know that. Keep focusing your heart on Jesus if things don't improve. Try to follow Jesus so the devil has to flee, not only when you are awake, but also in your dreams. We need to learn to focus our hearts and minds on Christ to win the spiritual battle. Don't let the devil scare you because you are stronger than he is when you rely on Jesus.

(9) **Try to serve God by serving others:**

We will only grow if we obey the Lord. Jesus told us to make disciples of Christ and help others grow in faith. Taking care of the poor, underprivileged, undervalued in society and people who are hurting is our task. As we grow in faith and become a true servant of God, we will be strong spiritually and there is less of a chance that we will suffer from nightmares.

(10) **Try to read Ephesians 6:10-18 throughout the day and before you go to sleep. Try to memorize it if you can.**

"Finally, be strong in the Lord and in his mighty power. Put on the full armor of God so that you can take your stand against the devil's schemes. For our struggle is not against flesh and blood, but against the rulers, against the authorities, against the powers of this dark world and against the spiritual forces of evil in the heavenly realms. Therefore put on the full armor of God, so that when the day of evil comes, you may be able to stand your ground, and after you have done everything, to stand. Stand firm then, with the belt of truth buckled around your waist, with the breastplate of righteousness in place, and with your feet fitted with the readiness that comes from the gospel of peace. In addition to all this, take up the shield of faith, with which you can extinguish all the flaming arrows of the evil one. Take the helmet of salvation and the sword of the Spirit, which is the word of God. And pray in the Spirit on all occasions with all kinds of prayers and requests. With this in mind, be alert and always keep on praying for all the saints." (Ephesians 6:10-18)

2. Reasons for having nightmares.
(1) Critical events in your life:

You may have encountered traumatic events, like losing your loved ones, that you are still grieving about and don't know how to get over. Sometimes dreams about traumatic events or death are part of normal processing or grieving. When dreams reach the point they become nightmares, you are under spiritual attack. It is time to ask for God's help. When you are emotionally upset, you are vulnerable. Sometimes the devil takes advantage of these situations and torments people through their dreams. Ask God to bring healing in your heart so you can see the big picture and find peace. (Isaiah 43:1-5)

Prayer: "Lord Jesus, help me to let go of my painful memories. I forgive everyone. Please heal my memories and help me to have peaceful dreams."

(2) Spiritual attack:

Sometimes the spirit of torment comes after you with feelings of guilt, even after you repent of your sins. The devil will tell you that God will not forgive you or love you because you are no good. He will tell you that God will not answer your prayers. Rebuke the spirit of lies to leave you in Jesus' name. (John 10:10, 1 Peter 5:8-9, James 4:6-7)

Prayer: "Lord Jesus, surround me with angels to protect me from the tormenting spirits. Help me to repent if there are any sins in my life and please help me to change."

(3) Unforgiving spirit:

If you are filled with anger, bitterness and don't forgive, you invite the devil to put you into a state of hate and anger. Therefore, you cannot have peace. Sometimes other people's sinful actions have traumatized you and you may have nightmares. God understands the pain and suffering you have gone through. Let go of any expectations of others you might have, bless them and pray for them. Also, forgive yourself.

Prayer: "Lord Jesus, I forgive everyone including myself. Thank you for dying on the cross for my sins so I can be forgiven."

(4) **Sin in life:**

Your dreams may reflect your sinful condition. Every time we fall into sin, we invite the devil to have more space in our mind and we lose our peace. We need to repent every sin we have committed and ask God for wisdom to resist temptation. "When an evil spirit comes out of a man, it goes through arid places seeking rest and does not find it. Then it says, 'I will return to the house I left.' When it arrives, it finds the house swept clean and put in order. Then it goes and takes seven other spirits more wicked than itself, and they go in and live there. And the final condition of that man is worse than the first." (Luke 11:24-26)

Prayer: "Lord Jesus, help me to know in which areas I need to make changes if I live in sin. Please help me to change and live a life that will please you."

(5) **Lack of spiritual knowledge about the Bible:**

Even if you are a Christian, you may not know the Scriptures well enough to build up your relationship with the Lord or understand the spiritual battles in your life. Start reading the Bible to get to know Jesus and ask the Holy Spirit to teach you about Jesus. God will guide you. Pray to be filled with the Holy Spirit's peace.

Prayer: "Holy Spirit, help me to have wisdom and discernment to understand the Bible and help me to obey your Word so that I may be filled with your peace."

(6) **You don't have a relationship with Jesus:**

If you are not a Christian, Jesus cannot help you and you don't have the power to win the spiritual battle. You need to accept Jesus as your personal Savior and rely on His power to help you.

Prayer: "Lord come into my heart and forgive all my sins. Fill me with the Holy Spirit and bless me with your peace. Help me to have a new heart to obey you. In Jesus' name. Amen." Remember, you have to keep following Jesus to keep peace.

(7) **Disobedient heart:**

Many don't have peace because they don't obey God's call in their lives. Selfishness and disobedience are sin. Ignoring the Holy Spirit's direction in our life is sin. When we don't use our gifts for the glory of God, we sin. Misusing our gifts (even our lives are gifts from God) is sin. Hiding our gifts and not using them to build up the kingdom of God is sin.

The Holy Spirit comes after us to convict us when we try to run away from our call to serve the Lord. If we have sin in our lives, continuing to live in that sin may cause us to lose our peace. Jonah ran away from the Lord and was disobedient. Jonah and other people suffered greatly because he ignored God's plans. You need to surrender your life completely to serve the Lord. (Jonah 1:1-17, 2:1-2)

(8) God may be speaking to you through dreams to prepare your heart:
Sometimes we might have nightmares because the Holy Spirit is warning us what is going to happen in the future so we can pray for protection of ourselves and others. Also, God may be trying to prepare for the hard times ahead of us.

(9) You may not have learned to listen to God's voice:
Many people who don't know how to listen to God's voice get frustrated. They are confused when they have problems because they have not learned to listen to God's voice. When God starts speaking to us He will help us understand the big picture which will give us comfort.

(10) You may love people, material things, and sinful desires more than God:
When we do, we lose peace. Our physical life is temporary and all we have is a temporary gift from God. We are called to serve God not our temporary belongings. God has to be our first love. (Matthew 6:19-24, 10:37-39)

(11) You may not have experienced the Holy Spirit's power:
People who have not experienced the Holy Spirit are like people who have heard about God but never experienced being in the presence of God or felt Him in their hearts. The Holy Spirit has the power to release you from torment and fill your heart with peace. Ask the Holy Spirit to bless you with peace and other spiritual fruits.

3. Reflect on your spiritual condition.
When you are filled with fear, you are in a spiritual battle. You are losing ground for peace. When you have nightmares and lose peace, this shows that you need to work on trusting the Lord in any circumstances. Try to answer the following questions to find out which area you need to work on to experience healing.

(1) Understand yourself:
   1) When did I start having nightmares?
   2) Is there any sin in my life that I need to repent?

3) What was the event that contributed to this emotional turmoil?
4) Do I love myself and forgive myself when I fail?

(2) **Understand your relationship with others:**
   1) Is there anyone that you have not forgiven?
   2) Have you been disappointed because of others?
   3) Did you hurt others and disappoint them?
   4) Do you have anyone who is a mentor to you?

(3) **Understand your relationship with God:**
   1) How is your relationship with the Lord?
   2) Do you believe God forgives you and loves you no matter what?
   3) Do you believe God is on your side?
   4) What do you think God is telling you now?

4. Seven exercises to find peace.
(1) **Focus on your relationship with the Lord:**
Read the Bible for 30 minutes every day for the next 30 days to get to know Jesus. Read Daniel, John, Romans, Psalm 23, Psalm 103, 1 Peter, 2 Peter and other Scriptures for meditation. Ask the Holy Spirit to give you wisdom to understand the Scriptures.

Think about what Jesus has done for you and tell him you love him whenever you think about him. You can use your meal time so you can remember to talk to him. While eating you can pray: "Come Lord Jesus, I love you and thank you. I praise and adore you. Let me taste your beauty, love, power, wisdom, and peace today!"

(2) **Develop a close relationship with the Holy Spirit:**
Prayer: "Come Holy Spirit, come and speak to me. Fill my heart with peace day and night. Help me to live a holy life and help me to serve Jesus."

(3) **Forgive others:**
If you are obsessed with someone or some event in the past that is disturbing you, you need to forgive so God can heal you. When you don't forgive, you are opening the gate for bitterness, resentment, and anger. Bless others who have hurt you and pray for them so you can be released from the spirit of resentment. Write a forgiveness letter, but don't mail it unless it will help others.

Prayer: "Lord Jesus, I made a decision to forgive everyone who has hurt me. I bless them and pray for them. Heal my painful memories. I give my anger, bitterness, and resentment to you. Fill me with a spirit of peace and love."

You may have to say this prayer many times until your bitterness turns to compassion. Jesus said, "For in the same way you judge others, you will be judged, and with the measure you use, it will be measured to you. 'Why do you look at the speck of sawdust in your brother's eye and pay no attention to the plank in your own eye? How can you say to your brother, "Let me take the speck out of your eye," when all the time there is a plank in your own eye? You hypocrite, first take the plank out of your own eye, and then you will see clearly to remove the speck from your brother's eye.'" (Matthew 7:2-5)

(4) **Obey the Holy Spirit:**

Our mind is a spiritual battlefield. The devil plants destructive thoughts so we can fall into sin, and the Holy Spirit plants good thoughts for us to grow in faith, even if it is something small. If it is a good thing and will help you and others grow in faith, it is coming from the Holy Spirit. Obey the Spirit and know that until you obey Him, you cannot have peace.

Jesus gave us the power and authority to drive out demons. "When Jesus had called the Twelve together, he gave them power and authority to drive out all demons and to cure diseases, and he sent them out to preach the kingdom of God and to heal the sick." (Luke 9:1-2)

Watch what you think in your mind every moment. Recognize your weaknesses; then you will know which demon is after you. Rebuke any destructive thoughts and suggestions that can hurt you and others. It is not coming from the Lord. "In the name of Jesus, all the spirits that are not of God, spirits of lies, anger, resentment, bitterness, deception, fear, worry, destruction and violence, leave from me. I made a decision to forgive and bless everyone."

(5) **Write down your dreams and ask for interpretations:**

The devil can torment people through their dreams. But as we grow in faith and walk closely with Jesus, we can win the spiritual battle and be freed from nightmares. One of the signs of being filled with the Holy Spirit is having dreams, because God speaks to people through dreams.

They can teach us about our spiritual condition so we will know what to do to grow in faith; they can tell us about what is going to happen in the future. Write down your dreams and ask God to give you understanding. You might not get an answer right away, if you are not familiar with how God speaks to you. If you wait long enough, He will speak to you. God can speak to us with or without words.

Prayer: "As you have revealed dreams to Daniel, please give me wisdom, knowledge, understanding, and revelation to understand what you are telling me through dreams."(Daniel 2:1-49, James 1:5)

(6) **Speak the words that create peace, faith, victory:**

Think before you speak. Peter wrote, "Whoever would love life and see good days must keep his tongue from evil and his lips from deceitful speech. He must turn from evil and do good; he must seek peace and pursue it. For the eyes of the Lord are on the righteous and his ears are attentive to their prayer, but the face of the Lord is against those who do evil." (1 Peter 3:10-12)

Don't say defeating words or anything negative about yourself or others. Speak as though Jesus is standing right in front of you. Write a prayer of victory for yourself, your family, and your ministry.

Prayer: "Jesus teach me to say the words that will glorify you and help others to grow in faith. Anoint me with words of wisdom so that when I speak, I will build up God's kingdom and encourage others to grow in faith. Let me be a blessing to everyone who hears me."

(7) **Put God first in your life:**

Jesus said, "But seek first his kingdom and his righteousness, and all these things will be given to you as well." (Matthew 6:33) "Then Jesus came to them and said, 'All authority in heaven and on earth has been given to me. Therefore go and make disciples of all nations, baptizing them in the name of the Father and of the Son and of the Holy Spirit, and teaching them to obey everything I have commanded you. And surely I am with you always, to the very end of the age.'" (Matthew 28:18-20)

Prayer: "Lord, enlarge my vision and mission to serve you with my gifts and bring many people to Christ."

Note: To learn more about dreams and nightmares, read the book, *Dreams and Interpretations, Healing from Nightmares.*

Chapter Thirteen

Prayer Project: Forgiveness

Forgiveness is essential in order for us to have a close relationship with the Lord. The sooner you decided to forgive yourself and others, the sooner you will have peace and joy in your heart. If you have been hurt, don't ignore that nagging voice in the back of your mind. That is the voice of God. Until you obey, you cannot find peace. The Lord teaches us to pray: Forgive us as we forgive those who trespass against us.

Prayer: "Lord Jesus, reveal to me how you see me so that I can have spiritual understanding of myself. Help me to forgive myself and others. Fill my heart with your love, compassion and mercy so that there is no room for any resentment, bitterness, anguish, and anger. Wash me with the blood of Jesus and cleanse me from all my sin so I can love everyone."

1. Who needs this prayer?

This prayer project is for those who want to forgive, but have a difficult time doing so. One of the reasons why people have a difficult time forgiving is that they have developed a habit of hate, anger, bitterness and resentment in their hearts and they don't know how to clean it all up.

When we cannot forgive, we cannot have peace. The Lord clearly commands us to forgive, so when we disobey His command we remain troubled. To have peace with God, we have to obey and forgive; we must clean out all the garbage inside of us and start taking care of our relationship. Our relationships with others will affect our relationship with God.

To participate in this prayer, I encourage you to spend one hour with the Lord every day for the next 30 days through Bible reading and prayer.

Remember, you have to make the decision to forgive and forgiveness is a process and it might take time, so keep working at it. You will eventually be able to forgive with God's help.

2. Twenty-two ways to develop a forgiving spirit:
(1) Read the Bible:

Some suggested readings are: John, Romans, James, 1 John, Psalms 103 and Colossians. Every day meditate on the Scriptures that will help you develop a kind and gentle spirit so you can begin to forgive yourself and others.

(2) **Pray for 30 minutes every day (speak to God for 15 minutes and listen to God in silence for 15 minutes):**

Wait for God in silence and practice "listening prayer" by resisting any disturbing thoughts, then the devil will have less ground to influence you with destructive thoughts. It's going to be difficult at first to silence your thoughts, but as you practice more and more you will be able to completely shut them down.

Prayer: "God, release me from all my destructive, negative, critical thoughts and attitudes. Help me to develop a loving attitude even toward those who have hurt me. If there is any sin I have not repented, help me repent. Please speak to me, Lord Jesus, I am waiting."

(3) **Ask the Holy Spirit to fill your heart with the following characteristics:**

"But the fruit of the Spirit is love, joy, peace, patience, kindness, goodness, faithfulness, gentleness and self-control…Those who belong to Christ Jesus have crucified the sinful nature with its passions and desires." (Galatians 5:22-24)

For those who have not experienced the Holy Spirit's power in your life, spend an hour clearing your mind and asking the Holy Spirit to speak to you every day. Practice this for a week or two or until you have experienced the Holy Spirit. (Acts 1:4-5, Ephesians 5:15-21)

(4) **Resist the devil's accusing voice:**

The devil tries to tell us that God will not and cannot forgive us. Many people suffer from this negative voice. Don't accept this lie. Whenever you hear the voice in your mind that you cannot be forgiven, try to meditate on the Scriptures to overcome those condemning voices.

Jesus recited the Scriptures to fight the devil's temptation. Meditation on Scripture will help you when you have a difficult time with forgiveness. Here are some Scripture meditations for forgiveness.

"Therefore, there is now no condemnation for those who are in Christ Jesus, because through Christ Jesus the law of the Spirit of life has set me free from the law of sin and death." (Romans 8:1-2) "I, even I, am he who blots out your transgressions, for my own sake, and remembers your sins no more." (Isaiah 43:25)

"Do not judge, and you will not be judged. Do not condemn, and you will not be condemned. Forgive, and you will be forgiven." (Luke 6:37)

"Bear with each other and forgive whatever grievances you may have against one another. Forgive as the Lord forgave you. And over all these virtues put on love, which binds them all together in perfect unity." (Colossians: 3:13-14)

"For I will forgive their wickedness and will remember their sins no more." (Hebrews: 8:12)

"If we confess our sins, he is faithful and just and will forgive us our sins and purify us from all unrighteousness." (1 John 1:9)

We have no right to hold on to an unforgiving spirit for ourselves or others because Jesus already paid for our sins by dying on the cross for our sins.

Prayer: "Lord Jesus, help me understand your great love. Please forgive all my sins. Cleanse me with the blood of Jesus. You died for my sins, this I believe, so free me now from the guilt and shame I feel."

(5) **Recognize that the devil's destructive plan consists of watering the unforgiving spirit:**

The devil tries to remind us of our painful memories and tries to convince us that we are justified in not forgiving people. The devil's plan is a destructive one which will ultimately destroy us if we don't forgive others. When you are filled with anger, rebuke the devil saying, "I have made a decision to forgive and bless this person. Satan, leave me in Jesus' name."

Prayer: "Lord Jesus, it is my desire to forgive everyone who has hurt me. Fill me with your Spirit of love and compassion. I bless everyone, including those who have hurt me. Please restore to my heart a spirit of love and respect toward everyone." "But I tell you who hear me: Love your enemies and do good to those who hate you. Bless those who curse you, pray for those who mistreat you." (Luke 6:27-28)

(6) **If you can, ask others to forgive you:**

This will not only bring healing in your heart but also in others who are affected by your sinful attitudes and actions. "First go and be reconciled to your brother; then come and offer your gift." (Matthew 5:24b) In some cases, it causes more trouble when you try to reconcile. In this case, you should let God take care of the situation and pray for others.

(7) **Change your perception of others:**

There isn't anyone who is completely bad. Everyone has good in them, even those who have hurt us, because we are all created in the image of God. I believe everyone has 85% of the godly character that God has given us. We all have the capacity to do good as long as we resist sinful desires and follow our God-given character. (2 Peter 1:3-11) We also have 15% of the dark side and that is where our sinful desires, unforgiving spirits, and bad character come from. This dark side needs to be transformed in order for us to learn how to forgive.

The devil encourages us to fall into sin by appealing to our dark side. With no knowledge of God's Word we are victims of our own ignorance.

Therefore, in order for us to live godly lives we need to accept our Savior and be transformed by Him. We can follow the Holy Spirit's leading and the 85% of goodness, our God-given character, will come forth. If you don't have a relationship with Jesus, invite him into your heart and ask him to forgive you.

Prayer: "Lord Jesus, I give my life to you. Please come into my heart and my life and forgive all my sins. I believe you died on the cross for my sins and I am saved because of what you have done for me. Fill me with your Holy Spirit and teach me to forgive myself and others. Amen."

(8) **Avoid people who display bad character and porcupine personalities:**

Forgiveness does not mean that we have to keep putting ourselves in abusive situations and letting others hurt us. Instead, we need to spend time in prayer for discernment: look at the big picture, so that if someone might be continuously encouraging you to fall into sin, you need to stay away from that person.

In some cases you might need to cut off the relationship completely, for your own sake. Ask God's wisdom and protection before you make the final decision.

Paul warns, "Do not be misled: 'Bad company corrupts good character. Come back to your senses as you ought, and stop sinning; for there are some who are ignorant of God -- I say this to your shame.'" (I Corinthians 15:33-34) Most of the time abuse has to stop before we can start forgiving others. So, be kind to yourself.

(9) **Seek understanding of your own spiritual condition:** Many of us cannot forgive because we don't quite understand our own spiritual condition. Read Revelation chapters 1, 2, and 3. Try to understand how Jesus evaluates the seven church leaders. Do you think Jesus is evaluating your spiritual life now? Of course He is. We can ask Him how He sees us so we can change.

"He who has an ear, let him hear what the Spirit says to the churches. To him who overcomes, I will give the right to eat from the tree of life, which is in the paradise of God." (Revelation 2:7)

Prayer: "Jesus, open my spiritual eyes and help me to see my spiritual condition as you see me. Help me to understand what the Holy Spirit is trying to tell me."

(10) **Develop godly thoughts:**

Paul gives good advice about how we can control our thoughts. Philippians 4:8 says, "Finally, brothers, whatever is true, whatever is noble, whatever is right, whatever is pure, whatever is lovely, whatever is admirable — if anything is excellent or praiseworthy — think about such things. "Any kind of destructive division or prejudice is not from a loving God. If you have any disrespectful attitude toward anyone, it's time to ask for forgiveness.

(11) **Meditate to learn about others' spiritual condition:**

If you are upset with someone, sit still and imagine that the person you have a problem with is sitting right there in front of you. Close your eyes and ask the Lord to give you wisdom and understanding concerning that person's heart; and then start asking questions as if the person were sitting in front of you. Listen with your heart to what the person would say and, when God gives you understanding, you will be able to forgive that person. "If any of you lacks wisdom, he should ask God, who gives generously to all without finding fault, and it will be given to him." (James 1:5)

(12) **Practice waiting and listening to Jesus in silence:**

Invite Jesus to sit in front of you and ask the Lord to give you the wisdom to understand people or a situation that is bothering you. Take the time to understand what the Lord is saying, before you react, so you can resolve the conflict with peace and learn to forgive him/her.

"Everyone should be quick to listen, slow to speak and slow to become angry, for man's anger does not bring about the righteous life that God desires." (James 1:19)

Prayer: "Jesus, help me to see the big picture and help me to have your wisdom to solve this conflict peacefully and according to your word."

(13) **Meditate on the words of Holy Communion:**

Meditate or memorize the following words and imagine that Jesus himself is giving you Holy Communion, not a minister or a priest. Imagine that what Jesus is giving you is His body that was broken for your sins.

Communion meditation: "On the night in which Jesus gave himself up for us, he took the bread, gave thanks to God, broke the bread, and gave it to his disciples and said, 'Take and eat, this is my body which is given for you. Do this in remembrance of me.' When the supper was over, he took the cup, gave thanks to God and gave it to his disciples, and said, 'Drink from this, all of you. This is my blood of the new covenant, poured out for you and for many for the forgiveness of sins. Do this as often as you drink it, in remembrance of me.'" (This is written for communion for worship services but it came from Luke 22:19-20)

(14) **Learn to praise Jesus when you are upset or angry with your painful memories:**

The devil tries to remind you of your painful memories to keep you angry and bitter. When that happens, immediately start thanking Jesus and start praising Him.

Prayer: "Lord Jesus, I honor you. I love you. I praise you. I give you thanks. Thank you for forgiving my sins. Thank you for dying on the cross for my sins. I bless everyone even those who have hurt me. I forgive them."

(15) **Write your testimony of how God is helping you:**

List your pains and victories, write down how God has helped you and how He has forgiven you. This will bring healing in your heart. Our testimony is powerful and we need to share it to help others. (Revelation 12:11)

(16) **Write down the 70 x 7's of forgiveness:**

Every day for seven days, write 70 times: "I will forgive myself for _____. I will forgive _____ for _____." Each time you write this, try to let go of your resentments, and tear up the pages if you don't want others to read them.

(17) **Write letters of forgiveness:**
1) Write a letter of apology to God if you have held any resentment against Him, for He is innocent and holy.
2) Write a letter of forgiveness to yourself if you have had a difficult time forgiving yourself.
3) Write letters of forgiveness to others who have hurt you. Sometimes your letter might hurt you or others. In this case, just write your letters of forgiveness to get them off your heart, but don't send them.
4) Write a letter of forgiveness to yourself from Jesus.

(18) **Journal your reflections:**

Read Psalms 103, 139; John 3:16, Ephesians 1. When you feel you are ready, write short paragraphs starting with:
1) "To me, God is like…."
2) "God sees me as a person of…."

3) "God loves me because…."

Prayer: "Lord Jesus, help me to see myself as you see me: so loved and special in your sight that you even died for my sins, and not only mine, but for the sins of the world. Help me to love myself as you love me and help me love others as you love them."

(19) **Pray to understand God's vision for you:**

Lack of vision and commitment in serving God encourages our unfruitful thoughts, attitudes, and destructive lifestyles. If we are busy serving others, we don't have time for a bitter, negative, and critical spirit.

Prayer: "God fill me with visions and dreams of how I can serve you. Help me to have the passion to serve you and give me the opportunity to share your love with others."

(20) **Pray to God so He can heal your broken heart:**

When you are hurting, put your hands on your heart and ask God for help.

Prayer: "Come Lord Jesus, come Holy Spirit, come, heavenly Father, come and touch my heart and heal my wounds." Repeat this prayer until you can find peace in your heart. (James 5:13)

(21) **Pray the Lord's Prayer:**

When you are filled with anger or faced with situations and you need God's protection, pray the Lord's Prayer again and again, especially pray: "Deliver us from evil." Repeat it five times or until you can calm down. (Matthew 6:9-15, 1 Peter 5:5-11)

(22) **Pray for healing of memories:**

Prayer: "Lord, I have decided to forgive everyone who has hurt me, including myself. Holy Spirit, please heal my painful memories so that I can let go of my negative, critical, hateful and angry thoughts. Fill my heart with your love, peace and joy. I also want to pray for everyone I have hurt. Please heal their painful memories as well so they can forgive me."

Note: To learn more about how to forgive, read the book, *Maximum Saints Forgive.*

Chapter Fourteen

Prayer Project: Fasting Prayer

Fasting helps us to focus on God and take us to the throne of God. Spiritual understanding and lessons can come from intentional planning of our spiritual walk with the Lord through fasting and prayer.

Prayer: "Lord Jesus, you have blessed me in many ways and I want to get close to you. I want to know your heart and help me to prepare my heart to know you better."

To grow in faith and have a deeper relationship with Jesus, I believe spiritual discipline is a must. "'Come, follow me,' Jesus said, 'and I will make you fishers of men.' At once they left their nets and followed him." (Matthew 4:19-20)

Jesus is still calling His disciples. In order to follow Jesus, it takes discipline, persistence and determination to live a holy life. God's grace calls us to follow Jesus. Yet, our spiritual growth is dependent on how we plan and follow through on those plans.

When we love God and love our neighbors, we grow. When we read the Scriptures, pray and worship God, we grow. We grow if we obey the Holy Spirit by serving others. If we choose to live a holy life instead of following our sinful desires, we grow.

Fasting is a sacrifice for almost everyone but it's not for everyone. If we do it for the right reason, fasting will help us grow spiritually. Fasting itself is not spiritual discipline unless we are praying and focusing our hearts on God. Fasting while we are praying is our attempt to get God's attention, and it's an act showing God that we are serious about our spiritual growth.

In the past, God asked me to fast and pray from time to time. At times I resisted fasting because I thought I couldn't skip a meal but, when I obeyed, I was blessed.

Sometimes, God gave me reasons why I should fast, and there were spiritual lessons I had to learn. Most of the time God confronted me with my sins, and I had to repent. While fasting and praying, God helped me to see things that I wasn't able to see before. Other times, I fasted simply because God asked me to fast, and I learned some spiritual lessons that I didn't expect to learn.

We can fast and pray for the Holy Spirit to have a spiritual revival and renewal for our families and for our nation. We need to be serious about God's business of saving the lost and the purification of our souls for spiritual renewal. As we get closer to God and obey the Holy Spirit through prayer and fasting, God can empower us to serve Jesus instead of serving our selfish sinful desires.

1. Who needs this prayer?

If you feel you are in need of prayer and fasting, I invite you to skip a meal a week for the next four weeks. The goal is to have many Christians involved in fasting and prayer for the following four weeks so people can experience the Holy Spirit's blessing and to be transformed as a group.

For those of you who want to participate in this prayer who have medical problems, I suggest that you not skip the meal, and just join the prayer.

This prayer idea comes from the book of Joel. When the Israelites fell into sin and abandoned the Lord, God was ready to punish them. At the same time, God was merciful and asking them to repent and turn their hearts to the Lord through prayer, fasting and purification, so God could forgive them.

Joel wrote, "Even now, declares the Lord, 'Return to me with all your heart, with fasting and weeping and mourning.' Rend your heart and not your garments. Return to the Lord your God, for he is gracious and compassionate, slow to anger and abounding in love, and he relents from sending calamity….Blow the trumpet in Zion, declare a holy fast, call a sacred assembly. Gather the people, consecrate the assembly….Let the priests, who minister before the Lord, weep between the temple porch and the altar. Let them say, 'Spare your people, O Lord.'" (Joel 2:12-17)

This Scripture teaches us that we also need to repent, turn our hearts to the Lord, and change our ways. I am making a call to "Holy Fasting and Prayer" because I believe our prayers can make a difference.

We need to plant the seed if we want to see the fruits. If we plant the seed of spiritual revival and cleanse our hearts and lives, we will see the fruits of the Holy Spirit in our lives. Let's ask God for favor of a mighty outpouring of the Holy Spirit in our families and in this nation.

How do we pray and fast? You can kneel and pray but we don't always have to close our eyes and kneel. What's important is what is in our hearts. You can pray in your heart while you are walking around or standing or sitting.

2. How do you participate in this prayer?
(1) Read the Bible:
Read the Bible for 30 minutes every day for the next 30 days. Read the book of Acts once a day as the basis for your meditations for the following four weeks or pick out some Scriptures for purification of your heart and your life. Concentrate on reading materials that only have to do with God or spiritual growth. You might want to read Romans and other Old Testaments like Isaiah, Jeremiah, Daniel, Ezekiel, Hosea, Joel and other Scriptures and pay attention to the teaching of the Holy Spirit.

(2) Pray for 30 minutes for the following four weeks:
Try to speak to the Lord for 15 minutes and try to listen for 15 minutes. Ask Jesus a question if you have any questions, clear your mind, and try to listen to Him. Or you can ask Jesus to speak to you. Say, "Jesus speak to me, I am listening."

(3) Fast one meal a week on Saturday dinner:
This fasting and prayer starts at noon on Saturday. Read the Scriptures and pray to ask the Lord how you can purify your heart and be filled with the Holy Spirit.

(4) Pay attention to the Holy Spirit's voice:
Your desire to fast and pray could come from the Holy Spirit. He is planting the seed in your heart so you can learn to grow and seek the Lord. Also, the Holy Spirit helps you to clean your heart. If there is anything that has been bothering you for a long time, it's time to ask the Holy Spirit to help you sort out and let them go.

Prayer: "Holy Spirit, help me purify my heart by helping me to repent if there is any sin I have committed. Help me to take care of all the things that are holding me captive in spiritual prison. Please release me from any wrong perception and help me to see the big picture God sees. Help me to find peace and joy in my heart."

(5) Learn to wait for the Holy Spirit:
To those who have not experienced the Holy Spirit, clear your mind and wait for one hour every day. Ask the Holy Spirit to speak to you until you experience Him. Try one week of waiting then if you have not experienced the Holy Spirit, try another week or until you know that God has spoken to you.

Prayer: "Holy Spirit, come and speak to me I am listening."

(6) Conversations with others:

Your conversations with others should be focused on growing in faith at all times. Try not to get into arguments. Walk away from situations before you lose your temper. Avoid any conflict or violent situations so you can practice focusing on the Lord and not problems during prayer and fasting. If you get into a situation where you become very agitated, stop and think about what is happening to you. You are in spiritual battle so focus on God to win the battle instead of reacting to the situation.

(7) Watch TV programs if that will help your faith:

Many TV programs are written by people who don't understand what holiness is about. Listen to the voice of the Holy Spirit, and obey him but resist any destructive attitudes and behaviors.

(8) Drink as much water or other liquids as you can:

Your body is a temple of the Holy Spirit. While fasting, drink water or other liquids so you don't get dehydrated. Refrain from too much exercise while fasting or you will feel drained. If we get too tired, we cannot pray and focus our hearts and minds on God.

(9) Understand that the devil might try to attack you to stop your fasting:

All Christians are in a spiritual war regardless of whether we realize it or not. When we pray and fast, we are not just defending ourselves spiritually but we are being offensive to the realm of evil. We will be gaining spiritual ground, and the devil will try to fight back to gain control of our minds and lives. Be prepared for Satan's attack so you can win the spiritual battle.

(10) What do we need to ask in prayer?

The following prayers are for you to get started and then you can write your own prayers.
1) "Holy Spirit, purify my heart, mind, relationships and help me to live a godly life that will please you."
2) "Jesus, please forgive my sins. I forgive others who have sinned against me. I ask you to help others to forgive me if I have hurt them in any way."

3) "I pray for the salvation of the lost in our families and in the world. I pray that I will be empowered by the Holy Spirit so I can be a disciple of Jesus and be able to help others to find God and help them grow in faith."

4) "I pray for myself and others who may struggle with destructive thoughts and addiction. Free us from any negative and destructive thoughts and release us from the spirit of violence and destruction. Help me so I can create peace and not turmoil."

5) "I pray for all the church leaders and Christians so they can be filled with the Holy Spirit and have the passion to share Christ with others. I pray for a revival of this nation and the Holy Spirit's visit to convict their sins and start it from me so I can experience healing."

3. Scripture teaching about fasting.

God will pay attention to our fasting and answer our prayers when we are right with God. If your prayer is not answered, try to listen to God to see if there are any areas that you need to work on.

"Why have we fasted, they say, 'and you have not seen it? Why have we humbled ourselves, and you have not noticed?' 'Yet on the day of your fasting, you do as you please and exploit all your workers. Your fasting ends in quarreling and strife, and in striking each other with wicked fists. You cannot fast as you do today and expect your voice to be heard on high. Is this the kind of fast I have chosen, only a day for a man to humble himself? Is it only for bowing one's head like a reed and for lying on sackcloth and ashes? Is that what you call a fast, a day acceptable to the Lord? Is not this the kind of fasting I have chosen: to loose the chains of injustice and untie the cords of the yoke, to set the oppressed free and break every yoke? Is it not to share your food with the hungry and to provide the poor wanderer with shelter– when you see the naked, to cloth him, and not to turn away from your own flesh and blood? Then your light will break forth like the dawn, and your healing will quickly appear; then your righteousness will go before you, and the glory of the Lord will be your rear guard. Then you will call, and the Lord will answer; you will cry for help, and he will say: Here am I.'" (Isaiah 58:3-9)

God is saying that our true fast has to start from our own hearts and how we treat others will affect God's reaction to our prayers. We cannot please God if we only serve God with lips but not with sincere hearts and mistreat others.

Chapter Fifteen

Prayer Project: Overcoming Addiction

There are many forms of addiction and they are a distraction in our spiritual walk with the Lord. Addiction is misplaced priorities and destructive actions. The main cause is not loving the Lord with all our heart, mind, soul, and strength. Also, we lack dependency on the Lord's provision for our happiness and joy. We need to focus on loving the Lord more than anything or anyone in order to overcome addiction from our own selfish thoughts or actions.

Prayer: "Lord Jesus, help me to love you more than anything or anyone so I can live a life that will please you. Help me find joy and comfort in your presence. Help me to love you and serve you."

1. Who needs this prayer?

If you have been struggling with any kind of addiction, or destructive thoughts and behaviors, and want to change and overcome it, this prayer project is for you. If you don't suffer from any addiction, I ask you to join this prayer to pray for your family or others who suffer from addiction.

2. Different forms of addiction:

1) Addiction to alcohol, drugs, sex, TV, computer games, and many other ungodly behaviors.
2) Addiction to immoral, impure thoughts.
3) Addiction to anger, hate and violent thoughts and urges to hurt themselves or others.
4) Addiction to people and things.
5) Addiction to constant fears and worries.

Many people suffer from addiction, disturbing thoughts and behaviors, and live destructive lifestyles. Consequently, they cannot live a fulfilling, abundant, fruitful, joyful and peaceful life the Lord provides.

Even though there are many degrees and levels of destructiveness, addicted people have one thing in common: they love the world or are obsessed with things or people more than the Lord. If we love the worldly things and people more than God, we become addicted to the world and the result is a disaster, because whatever we have are temporary gifts.

John wrote, "Do not love the world or anything in the world. If anyone loves the world, the love of the Father is not in him. For everything in the world-- the cravings of sinful man, the lust of his eyes and the boasting of what he has and does-- comes not from the Father but from the world." (1 John 2:15-16)

The goal of this prayer is to help you to focus on loving the Lord, yourself, and others in a godly manner, so you can be freed from addiction.

3. You can overcome addiction.

Know that living in an addictive lifestyle is sin and cannot please God. You have to resist sin instead of living in it. No one can change your addictive thoughts and behaviors, not even God. You have to make that decision.

Healing from addiction is replacing your love for the world with love for the Lord. You will be putting God above your own desires and plans. When you suffer from addictive thoughts and behaviors, you are in a spiritual battle. You have to resist the devil and reject your own sinful desires.

You need to believe and know that you can overcome sin, sinful desires, the devil's temptation, and addiction with the help of the Holy Spirit. Freedom from addiction requires making a daily decision. It requires determination to follow the Lord not the world or your plans. Jesus has given you the authority and power to drive out all demons in his name. You need to exercise your power and authority to drive out the demon of addiction and many more demons that come along with it. (Luke 9:1-2)

4. How to participate in this prayer project?

The goal is to let go of your attachment to worldly desires. After 30 days, if you still feel that you have not developed love for the Lord, yourself, and others, start this prayer project again and continue until you learn to gain control over addictive thoughts and behaviors.

(1) Read the Bible:

To love a person, you need to know a person. Get to know Jesus by reading the gospels. There are two ways to do this: 1) Read John or any gospel for 30 minutes every day for the next 30 days; or 2) Read one gospel every day for the next 30 days. Make a chart to see your progress every day.

Learn from Paul's example. "But whatever was to my profit I now consider loss for the sake of Christ. What is more, I consider everything a loss compared to the surpassing greatness of knowing Christ Jesus my Lord, for whose sake I have lost all things. I consider them rubbish, that I may gain Christ." (Philippians 3:7-8) If you have a desire to know Christ like Paul and serve Jesus like him, you will be able to overcome addiction.

(2) **Pray 30 minutes every day:**

Talk to God for 15 minutes and listen to God in silence for 15 minutes. For those who want to spend more time with the Lord, try to spend 10% of your time in prayer everyday for the next 30 days, spending half of your time listening to God in silence to win spiritual battles. "For though we live in the world, we do not wage war as the world does. The weapons we fight with are not the weapons of the world. On the contrary, they have divine power to demolish strongholds. We demolish arguments and every pretension that sets itself up against the knowledge of God, and we take captive every thought to make it obedient to Christ." (2 Corinthians 10:3-5)

Prayer: "Holy Spirit, I am struggling with destructive thoughts and behaviors. Please help me to let go of my addiction so I can love you. Lord Jesus, help me to love you more than anyone or anything. I made a decision to change my life and work on loving you more than anyone or anything. Help me to repent from all my sins. Holy Spirit, remind me if there is sin that I need to repent. Lord Jesus, bless me with a clear conscience so I can see things as you see them. Lord Jesus, I have decided to love you and serve you. Help me to focus on you and take away any desire for an addictive lifestyle so I can live a pure, holy, and blameless life. Help me to help others who are in need of your healing. I pray this in Jesus name. Amen."

(3) **Repent:**

Destroying your body through alcohol, drugs, and violence is sin. "The acts of the sinful nature are obvious: sexual immorality, impurity and debauchery; idolatry and witchcraft; hatred, discord, jealousy, fits of rage, selfish ambition, dissensions, factions and envy; drunkenness, orgies, and the like. I warn you, as I did before, that those who live like this will not inherit the kingdom of God." (Galatians 5:19-21)

Write a confession letter going back to your childhood as far as you can remember. Write your sins down and ask God to forgive you, one by one. Also, if you haven't forgiven yourself or others, ask God to help you. Let go of the blame and bitterness.

Prayer: "Lord Jesus, I ask for your forgiveness for the sins I have committed. Please forgive me for all the things I put into my body to hurt myself and for neglecting my family's needs. Help me to recognize impure desires, thoughts, attitudes, words and actions that displease you and hurt others. I made a decision to love you more than the world or my sinful desires. Forgive me for hurting my family and other people in anyway. Help them to forgive me. I forgive everyone who has sinned against me. Come Holy Spirit, come and bless me with conviction of sins and a clear conscience, so that I will be able to see what is right and wrong, be transformed, and be freed from addiction."

(4) **Learn to love yourself as God loves you:**

Treat your soul and body with dignity, love, and respect. "Do you not know that your body is a temple of the Holy Spirit, who is in you, whom you have received from God? You are not your own; you were bought at a price. Therefore honor God with your body." (1 Corinthians 6:19-20) Your self love and respect comes as you understand how much God loves you. Read Scriptures that tell about God's love for you like John 3:16, Psalm 103.

Prayer: "Lord Jesus, I thank you for the life you have given me. Help me to glorify you with my thoughts and my body. Help me to love myself as you love me. I let go of all my anger, hate, guilt, and shame. Help me to stop all the destructive thoughts and behaviors that will hurt me and others."

(5) **In place of addictive thoughts and behaviors, develop a habit of worshipping Jesus daily.**

1) Worship Jesus. Paul wrote, "He (Jesus) is the image of the invisible God, the firstborn over all creation. For by him all things were created: things in heaven and on earth, visible and invisible, whether thrones or powers or rulers or authorities, all things were created by him and for him." (Colossians 1:15-19)
2) Attend church worship services, Bible studies, prayer meetings and learn from others who love God. Also, keep reading the Bible and pray so you can grow in your relationship with the Lord.
3) Tell Jesus you love Him whenever you think about him.
4) Sing a song for Jesus every day.

(6) **Develop a godly character so you will be a blessing to others and not a burden:**

From the following list from Paul, find out which area you need to work on and ask the Lord to help you change. "But the fruit of the spirit is love, joy, peace, patience, kindness, goodness, faithfulness, gentleness and self-control. Against such things there is no law. Those who belong to Christ Jesus have crucified the sinful nature with its passions and desires. Since we live by the Spirit, let us keep in step with the Spirit. Let us not become conceited, provoking and envying each other." (Galatians 5:22-26)

Prayer: "Holy Spirit, help me to develop a godly character that will please you. Help me to be a blessing to others."

(7) Work on your relationship with your family if you can:

If you hurt your family with addiction, immoral and violent behaviors, don't expect them to accept you or forgive you with just words, but show them you are truly changed and you are not going to hurt them anymore. Think about what your responsibility is, make plans about how you can bless your family.

Prayer: "Lord Jesus, please help my family to forgive me. Help me to overcome my addiction so they can see that I am changed, and I am a new person."

(8) Use your gifts to serve the Lord:

God gave you the gifts of life so you can use it to help others. Volunteer to help others in the community, church, or in a mission.

Prayer: "Holy Spirit, open the doors so I can spread the good news of Jesus Christ to bring healing to others who are hurting."

(9) Find a Christian godly mentor who can help you focus on loving the Lord.

Prayer: "Jesus, help me to find a mature spiritual mentor who could guide me. Help me to surround myself with people who love you more than the world."

(10) Avoid people who will tempt you to fall into sin of addiction:

Paul wrote, "Do not be misled: 'Bad company corrupts good character.' Come back to your senses as you ought, and stop sinning; for there are some who are ignorant of God-- I say this to your shame.'" (1 Corinthians 15:33-34)

Prayer: "Lord, help me to have spiritual discernment to avoid ungodly people so I don't fall into sin and grieve you and others that I love."

(11) Your mind is a spiritual battle field:

There are four voices we hear in our minds: our own voice, the devil's voice, the Holy Sprit's voice, and other people's voices. The devil can speak to our minds and he can lead us to make wrong choices. Resist the devil's suggestions and destructive voices.

The devil tried to deceive Jesus into committing suicide by falling down from a high place and Jesus fought back with the Scriptures. The devil is still working to destroy God's people with thoughts of suicide, murder, and violent behaviors. We need to resist the devil in the name of Jesus and with the Word of God.

(12) **Pray for anointing and healing:**
You can memorize and meditate Luke 4:18-19, and whenever you are troubled or have a craving for addiction and you are struggling, put your hands on your head and then pray, "Lord Jesus, anoint me with the Holy Spirit. Fill my heart with your peace and joy."

(13) **When you are tempted to sin, pray for others:**
When you start thinking about going back to the old addictive lifestyle, immediately start praying for other's salvation. You can develop a habit of praying for others whenever you tempted.
Prayer: "Father God, please open the hearts of my family, relatives, and friends who don't know Jesus so they can be saved. Bless me with wisdom and courage to share with others about your love."

(14) **Ask the Holy Spirit to help you focus:**
Prayer: "Holy Spirit, when I am tempted, stressed out, bored, hurting, please help me to focus on Jesus."

(15) **Obey the Holy Spirit:**
"Jesus replied, 'If anyone loves me, he will obey my teaching. My Father will love him, and we will come to him and make our home with him. He who does not love me will not obey my teaching. These words you hear are not my own; they belong to the Father who sent me." (John 14:23-24)
Prayer: "Lord Jesus, help me to obey you and love you with all my heart, soul, mind and strength."

(16) **Take care of distractions in your mind:**
Anything or anyone who is consuming your thoughts and overwhelms you so you cannot focus on the Lord is a distraction. Take care of things that you need to take care of with God's help.
Prayer: "Lord, I give you all my worries, fear, and anything that is not holy. Help me to create peace and find peace in my heart. Give me a new heart that is filled with love for you."

(17) A Writing project can help your healing process:

    1) Write a love letter to Jesus.

    2) Write a love letter from Jesus to you.

    3) Write a forgiveness letter from God.

    4) Write a letter to God asking for forgiveness.

    5) Write a victory prayer from addiction.

    6) Write a daily journal and reflect on your journey.

Chapter Sixteen

Prayer Project: Praying for Children

Children are gifts from God but at the same time they come with a responsibility. We, parents, have the responsibility to help them to be prepared to live a life that will please the Lord. What God wants us to do is to help our children to know Him so they can rely on Him and live a godly life. But we have no control over them when they start making decisions for themselves. However, we can pray for God's intervention and pray for miracles so that they can find God, and understand the purpose of their lives. Remember, prayer doesn't always guarantee the smooth sailing of your children's life but it helps us to learn how to trust God when we face tornadoes of life.

Prayer: "Lord Jesus, you have blessed me with my children and I love them. I thank you for the gifts you have given me. I am learning that unless I can rely on you, I cannot have peace about what's going to happen to my children. I ask you to give me wisdom and faith to help my children. Help me to show your love to my children so that they know I love them and I care for them. Bless them in every area of their lives and protect them from all harm. Surround them with godly people who can help them."

1. Who needs this prayer?

This prayer project is for all parents who are anxious and overwhelmed with concern for their child or children. For those who don't have a child, I encourage you to join to pray for the children of the incarcerated and any children who are hurting. Jesus knew what we parents need to do. On the way to the cross, "Jesus turned and said to them, 'Daughters of Jerusalem, do not weep for me; weep for yourselves and for your children.'" (Luke 23:28)

It's time to weep for our children and ask God for mercy and to bring healing in our children's hearts and lives. If you have already been weeping and praying for a long time, it's time to ask God for instructions on how to help your children and find peace.

2. How do I start it?

For the next 30 days, try to follow the guidelines for meditation, prayer, reflections, and practices as they suit you.

(1) **Fasting:**

If you feel God is leading you to fast for your children, read "Fasting Prayer" and pray the following the prayer.

Prayer: "Lord Jesus, I pray for my children, all the children of the incarcerated, and the children of the world to open their hearts to receive Jesus to be saved and find peace. Help those who feel abandoned and hungry for their parents' love, attention and care, especially the children of the incarcerated. Jesus, please bring comfort and healing to the homeless, neglected, and abused children. Please raise the workers to help children who are hurting."

(2) **Read the Bible 30 minutes every day:**

Read 1 Samuel Chapters 1-3. Learn how Hannah dedicated her son, Samuel, to the Lord even before he was conceived. God blessed Samuel and he became one of the faithful spiritual leaders who learned to hear God's voice when he was a young boy.

Prayer: "Lord Jesus, I give my children into your big hands. Please take care of them. I dedicate them for your work for the rest of their lives. Surround them with good Christian mentors and bless them with pure hearts, clear consciences, and faith that could move mountains. Save them from all harm and temptation and help them to know what is right and wrong according to your will. Bless them with obedient hearts and fill them with the Holy Spirit. Bless them with many spiritual gifts and help them to serve you and to help many people."

Remember, dedicating your child to the Lord doesn't always mean that your child will grow up to be a pastor or a priest. Not everyone receives the call to be a pastor or priest or spiritual leader. If they have God in their hearts and help others, whatever they do will become their service for the Lord. Their light will shine because of their faith, and that will be serving the Lord.

(3) **Pray for children:**

Pray for 30 minutes every day (15 minutes talking to God and 15 minutes in silence listening to God.) The Holy Spirit speaks to our minds and hearts and can help us to pray for our children. Read John Chapters 14 - 16 to learn how the Holy Spirit can help you.

Prayer: "Holy Spirit, bless me with wisdom, knowledge, understanding and revelation; so you can guide, teach, and counsel me in my relationship with my children. Help me to obey you so I will be a blessing to my children and my children's children."

(4) Work on loving God and neighbors:
Prayer: "God, help me to focus on you even when I am hurting for my children. I love you; help me to love you more. Help me to help others who are hurting. Help others to help my children when they are hurting."

(5) Rebuke the spirit of fear and worries:

Many parents live in a spiritual prison of fear and worries. Jesus comes to free the spiritual prisoners. Read Luke 4:18-19 and try to memorize it to understand that Jesus can help you. Read Proverbs one Chapter a day for the next 30 days and meditate on it. Learn to be free from fear except fear of the Lord.
Prayer: "God, I am confident that you will help me in any circumstances. I let go of my spirit of fear and worries. Fill my heart with your peace, joy, and confidence that you will take care of my children."

(6) Praise the Lord in any circumstances:
When you pray, things may not change the way you want right away. In fact, sometimes things seem to get worse because we expect things will change or improve right away. The devil will try to discourage you from continuing to pray by telling you God is not doing anything to help your children. When you are discouraged, that's the time you need to thank and praise God for His mercy and compassion. When Job lost seven sons, three daughters, and everything else he owned, he still praised the Lord. (Job 1:21)
Prayer: "Lord, thank you for helping my children."

(7) Find a spiritual mentor for yourself:
Prayer: "Lord, help me to find a spiritual mentor who will guide, counsel, direct and pray for me to be a nurturing, godly, kind, compassionate parent."

3. Help your children to develop faith.
(1) Teach them about God's love and the Bible stories:
If they are little, read them the Bible stories and take them to church whenever you can. There are many Bibles with pictures that can capture young minds. It's important for them to know how much God loves them, so they can be saved and learn to love the Lord. "Train a child in the way he should go, and when he is old he will not turn from it." (Proverbs 22:6)
Children who believe in God have higher moral standards, and they tend to follow the higher law and have concern for others and are less selfish. Also, they are happier because they know life is hard but they also learn to pray to God so they can get help.

Prayer: "God, please help my children to understand your love, so they can love you. Help them understand the Bible to know you better and have the Holy Spirit's conviction of sin so they can obey you." If you cannot read the Bible for your children, ask others to do it for you.

(2) **Teach them how to pray:**

Teach your children the Lord's Prayer and also read Psalms to them so they can learn how to pray. Remind them to learn to communicate with Jesus when they are hurting and when they are happy. Also, tell them to wait and listen, so God can speak to them, and they learn prayer is not a one way communication.

Prayer: "Lord, help my children to communicate with you through prayer. Help them hear your voice clearly, like Samuel. Bless them with the gift of faith and help them to have the heart and desire to obey you."

(3) **Believe in your kids and be their cheerleader:**

Work on having close relationships with your children, even when their behavior is not acceptable. They are in the process of growing, and no one is perfect. Let them know your standards and values, but also communicate that you love them, so they can come to you when they are in trouble and need help. Tell them how much you are proud of them so they know you value them.

Prayer: "God, thank you for the gift of my children. Help me to raise them with love and respect, so they can learn about God's love through me."

(4) **Teach them how to forgive:**

Never call your children bad names or curse or hurt them emotionally, mentally or physically, even when they make a mistake. If you have hurt your children, ask them to forgive you. When you discipline them, talk to them firmly, but forgive them immediately. Children are frail, and they desperately need your affirmation, even when they make a mistake. When they see how you forgive them with compassion and kindness, they will follow your example. "Fathers, do not embitter your children, or they will become discouraged." (Colossians 3:21)

Prayer: "Lord Jesus, help me not to be harsh with my children when they make mistakes. Help me to forgive them as you have forgiven me, so they can learn to forgive."

(5) **Treat your children with love and respect:**

Everyone is special in God's eyes, and you need to communicate that to your children with words and actions. You need to believe there is goodness in everyone, including children, because everyone has inherited God's good characteristics. If you have seen only badness in your children, you need to ask God for help.

Prayer: "Lord, help me so I can see goodness in my children as you see them, so I can help them to use their God given good character and gifts to glorify you. Help my children understand how much I love them so they can learn to love you, love themselves and love others."

(6) **Listen to them when they talk to you:**

This will help them to know that you care about them and they are valued. When you don't listen and ignore them, they will stop talking to you. They will look for others with whom to share their feelings, and you will miss being involved in many things where you might make an impact on their life journey.

Prayer: "God, help me to be a good listener so my children can realize that I care about them and I can help them with your wisdom."

(7) **Teach your children how to help others:**

Encourage your children to be involved with helping the poor, homeless, sick, or hurting. Mission trips are one way to help them to develop nurturing spirits. When they understand other's pain and try to help others, they will grow and become productive citizens. People who help others are healthier and happier than those who are selfish and only think about their own needs.

Prayer: "Lord Jesus, help our children to understand other's pain and do something to help them. Help them so they can spread love, healing and justice."

(8) **Be a good role model for your children:**

If you have grieved, hurt, and/or brought shame to your children with alcoholism, drugs, violence, any harsh words, or immorality, repent and change your lifestyle. Ask the Lord and your children to forgive you.

Prayer: "God please forgive me for not being a good example for my children. Help my children to forgive me. Help me to be free from alcoholism, drugs, violent and immoral behaviors. Help me to guide my children to live a godly life."

(9) **Ask the Lord to help you find a mentor for your children:**
Prayer: "Lord Jesus, help my children to have Christian mentors who could help them with your love."

Note: To learn more about how to pray for your children, read the book, *The Ultimate Parenting Guide, How to Enjoy Peaceful Parenting and Joyful Children.*

Chapter Seventeen

Prayer Project: Overcoming Depression

Life is a gift from the Lord. Don't let the devil lie to you that pain is what life is about. Yes, life is difficult and painful at times, but God can bring healing and give us hope and encouragement so we can heal from pain and hurts and gives us peace and joy in the midst of turmoil.

Prayer: "Lord Jesus, I am in pain and I ask you to help me get out of this mess. Help me to find healing in you. I ask for your forgiveness for all my sins including devaluing my life and what you have given me. Please forgive all my sins and help me change my perception so I can see myself as you see me. Help me to understand your Words so I can have a clear direction on how to love and serve you. Help me to understand your love and help me to love myself. Help me to reach out to others who are hurting with your love and power."

1. Who needs this prayer?

This prayer is for those who suffer from depression and also suicidal and destructive thoughts. Some people suffer from hearing voices that life is not worthwhile and no one cares about them. They hear voices that they are worthless. When they accept these voices, they open the door for the spirit of torment. The spirit of torment literally torments people with much pain. People can feel pain without any physical reasons. Some depressed people hear that their pain will end when they end their lives. If they continuously accept the lies and don't resist the voices, they can be suicidal and can commit suicide.

2. How to participate in this prayer?
(1) Read the Bible:

Read the Bible 30 minutes a day for the next 30 days to develop a habit of listening to the Lord and not destructive voices. Read John or any gospel everyday for 30 minutes a day or read one gospel a day. Loving God has to be our first priority and not to be obsessed with hurting ourselves. To love a person, you need to know a person.

Make a chart to see your progress every day. Also, read and memorize Luke 4: 18-19 "The Spirit of the Lord is on me, because he has anointed me to preach good news to the poor. He has sent me to proclaim freedom for the prisoners and recovery of sight for the blind, to release the oppressed, to proclaim the year of the Lord's favor."

You are in a spiritual battle. Reading the Bible will give you spiritual strength to fight and win because God gives you reasons to live and directions on how to help others. You need to rely on the Word of God for healing. God values us.

Jesus came and died for our sins. He opened the door for salvation and allowed us to build a relationship with God. God values us so we should value ourselves. Read Psalms and find prayers that help you express your feelings. Ask God for help.

Try to find a Bible verse that touches you, meditate and memorize it throughout the day. "Trust in the Lord with all your heart and lean not on your own understanding; in all your ways acknowledge him, and he will make your paths straight. Do not be wise in your own eyes; fear the Lord and shun evil. This will bring health to your body and nourishment to your bones." (Proverbs 3:5-8)

(2) **Pray for 30 minutes every day (speak to God for 15 minutes and listen to God in silence for 15 minutes):**

Wait before God in silence and practice "listening prayer" by resisting any disturbing thoughts, then the devil will have less ground to influence you with destructive thoughts. It's going to be difficult at first to silence your thoughts, but as you practice, more and more you will be able to completely shut them down. Don't get frustrated when you have distractions and thoughts you don't want to focus. They are normal. Just let your thoughts go without focusing on them.

Prayer: "Lord, Jesus, I ask you to deliver me from the spirit of torment, hopelessness, despair, suicide and murder. I give you all my pain, my problems, and my loved ones. Please fill me with the fruits of the Holy Spirit: love, joy, peace, patience, kindness, goodness, faithfulness, gentleness and self-control. Lord, in your mercy, hear my prayer. In Jesus name, I pray. Amen."

(3) **Pray the Lord's Prayer:**

Whenever you are tempted by depressed or suicidal thoughts, repeat, "Deliver me from evil." Jesus asked us to pray: "And lead us not into temptation, but deliver us from the evil one.'" (Matthew 6:13)

(4) **Repent:**

Repent for all your sins so God can hear your prayer and forgive you if you love someone or something more than the Lord. "Do not love the world or anything in the world. If anyone loves the world, the love of the Father is not in him. For everything in the world-- the cravings of sinful man, the lust of his eyes and the boasting of what he has and does--comes not from the Father but from the world. The world and its desires pass away, but the man who does the will of God lives forever." (I John 2:15-17)

(5) **Develop a Relationship with God:**

If you don't have any relationship with God, this is the time to invite Him and ask Him for help.

Prayer: "Lord Jesus, I accept you as my Lord and Savior. Please forgive my sins. Help me overcome these destructive thoughts. Fill my heart with your peace. In Jesus' name I pray."

(6) **Know God's Plans for You:**

God has good plans for you. "For I know the plans I have for you," declares the Lord, "plans to prosper you and not to harm you, plans to give you hope and a future. Then you will call upon me and come and pray to me, and I will listen to you. You will seek me and find me when you seek me with all your heart. I will be found by you." (Jeremiah 29:11-14)

Prayer: "God, help me to understand your plans for my life. Lord Jesus, help me understand your love and guide me with your wisdom, so I can love and serve you."

(7) **Recognize the origin of the voices:**

Any voice that is telling you to do something to hurt yourself or others is not coming from the Lord but from the devil. Rebuke the devil: "In the name of Jesus, the demon of suicide and murder, leave from me."

(8) **Resist self-hatred spirit:**

Love yourself because God loves you. Believe that and meditate on the Word of God which talks about God's love. You are born to be loved by God. You are to love God and to love your family and others. God can give you peace, joy, and healing, but you have to seek it. Work on your relationship with the Lord so you can experience God's power in your life.

(9) **See the bright side:**

Resist any negative thoughts. God loves you. Recite John 3:16: "For God so loved the world that he gave his one and only Son, that whoever believes in him shall not perish but have eternal life." (John 3:16)

(10) **Write Journals:**
It will help you process your pain.

    1) Write a letter to God asking for help so you can learn to process the pain caused by grief and loss.
    2) Write a letter to God asking for forgiveness.
    3) Write a forgiveness letter from God.
    4) Write a victory prayer for yourself and your family.

(11) **Prayer for healing of emotional pain:**
Some people suffer from constant emotional and spiritual pain. If you don't have any physical problems, you might be suffering from the spirit of torment who goes around hurting people with unbearable pain in spirit and body.
Prayer: "Lord Jesus come and deliver me from pain and anguish. I ask for healing of my mind, soul and body."

(12) **Process Grief:**
If you have lost anyone, give them to God. Also find a professional grief counselor or minister or grief support group to give you support and pray with you. Also, follow through "Healing from Grief and Loss Prayer."
Prayer: "Lord Jesus, please heal my broken heart. Help me to experience healing. I give my loved ones into your arms so you can take care of them. I give you my pain, hurts, and all these problems. Heal my grieving heart."

(13) **Praise God for your blessings:**
Write down all the good things that Praising God does for you. It is important for you to see changes while going through your healing process. If you rely on God, you may not see it right away, but you will eventually see the fruit if you are persistent.
Prayer: "Thank you Lord for all my blessings. Help me to be a blessing to everyone I meet, including my family and friends. Lord Jesus, I love you more than anyone or anything in the whole world. Lord Jesus, help me to obey you and love you with all my heart, soul, mind and strength."

(14) **Work on fruit of the Spirit:**
From following the Scripture, find out which area you need to work on and ask the Lord to help you change. "But the fruit of the spirit is love, joy, peace, patience, kindness, goodness, faithfulness, gentleness and self-control. Against such things there is no law. Those who belong to Christ Jesus have crucified the sinful

nature with its passions and desires. Since we live by the Spirit, let us keep in step with the Spirit. Let us not become conceited, provoking and envying each other." (Galatians 5:22-26)

Prayer: "Holy Spirit, help me to develop a godly character that will please you. Help me to be a blessing to others."

(15) **Use your gifts to help others:**

Your life is a gift to be shared. God gave you the gifts of life, talents and resources so you can use them to help others. Volunteer to help others in the community, church, or in missions. When you focus only on your pain, the pain will grow, and you will be miserable. When you help others to relieve pain, your pain will also be relieved. "'When did we see you sick or in prison and go to visit you?' The King will reply, 'I tell you the truth, whatever you did for one of the least of these brothers of mine, you did for me.'" (Matthew 25:39-40)

There are times we need to receive other's help but if you are always focusing on what you want to receive from others, you will be miserable. The reason for that is you are forgetting your blessings in life. There are many others who are less fortunate than you. Usually other people cannot meet your expectations, so why keep being disappointed?

God can only fill our empty hearts with peace and joy when we have Him as our first love and first priority. As soon as we lose our focus on God, we lose peace and joy. We also lose joy when we only focus on our needs but when we try to meet others' needs, overflowing joy comes.

Prayer: "Lord, Jesus, free me from all the destructive thoughts of despair, disappointment and hopeless and helpless feelings. Help me to find hope in you and help me to resist temptation and distractions in my life, so I can love you and proclaim your love and power to others. Help me to love you and obey the Holy Spirit so I can have freedom, peace, and joy in my heart."

Unless you are freed from spiritual prison with the power of the Holy Spirit, you don't have the true freedom. Also, you need to learn to free yourself with the help of the Holy Spirit by living a godly life.

(16) **Affirm yourself:**

Many people don't have confidence in themselves and they don't love themselves. We need to see ourselves as God sees us and learn to accept ourselves as a valuable human being and love ourselves as God loves us. The following statement is an example of a personal affirmation to boost your confidence and yourself how God sees you.

Personal Affirmation:
- I am beautifully and wonderfully made and created by God.
- I am special because I am loved by God.
- I am created for the divine purpose of giving God glory.
- I am a reflection of God's glory.
- I am valuable to God and His kingdom business.
- God created me in His image.
- I am precious in God's sight.
- I am created to be a partner in God's kingdom building business.
- I am a conqueror of the dark world and the devil cannot stand against me.
- I am a child of God because I believe in Jesus.
- I am clothed with Christ so the Holy Spirit is working with me.
- I am blessed beyond measure, and I will be a blessing to others.
- God didn't make a mistake creating me.
- God has visions, dreams, and plans for my life.
- I am worthy of God's love because Jesus died for my sins.
- I am filled with the Holy Spirit who can bring healing.
- I am forgiven. God has forgotten my mistakes and failures.
- I am hopeful because I know Jesus is preparing a place for me.
- I am encouraged that my trials and difficulties are a purifying fire.
- I am joyful because the Holy Spirit is leading my path.
- I value myself and others because God values us.
- I am hopeful because God is going to help me overcome depression.
- I am blessed that God is training me to be a disciple of Jesus.

Prayer: "Lord Jesus, help me to understand your love so I can learn to love myself and others. Help me to value myself and others so I can love you, love myself and love others as well. Thank you Lord Jesus for loving me and dying on the cross to forgive me. Please fill my heart with love for you, myself and others. Help me to love as you love me. Please forgive me for not loving myself. Cleanse me from all my guilt and shame. Free me from the unforgiving spirits and fill my heart with loving spirits. Help me to love what you have given me – my life, all my family and other people you created in your image."

3. God has the power to heal you.

I suffered from depression and nightmares after I lost my sister in a car accident. I was immersed with grief and I suffered from pain. After I started reading the Bible and praying more, God eventually healed me from depression, nightmares and pain caused by grief. I experienced the power of God. I believe the ultimate healing from emotional and spiritual pain comes from God, who gives you peace, not pain. Take the initiative to get closer to God by reading the Bible and praying for healing.

You also have to be determined to fight the voices of destruction moment by moment. Recognizing the battle you are in is the first step of healing, but you have to walk the steps to go forward by resisting the voices and changing your perception. You have the power to change your life through faith.

Note: To learn more about how to overcome depression, read the book, *Twisted Logic, The Window of Depression*. If you are struggling with suicidal thoughts, or affected by suicide, read the book, *Twisted Logic, The Shadow of Suicide*.

Chapter Eighteen

Prayer Project: Overcoming Fear

Fear can immobilize us. Those who conquer fear are free in the spirit and can be productive in what they do. How can we be freed from fear? We cannot predict the future and we cannot see what's ahead. That's our short sighted statement. God knows what's ahead and He already knows what we will be facing. He understands what we are afraid of. He has a big plan—an eternal plan to comfort and encourage us to focus on Him, and He is always with us.

We are passing through this life. By having faith, we know what's ahead because God is in control over everything in our life. We are here, we will go through fires of testing of our faith and also dark valleys where our faith will be again be tested. Our victory comes when we can rely on Him for strength in times of adversity. The key preparation: work on your relationship with the Lord more than anything else, then you can learn to conquer fear with His strength in times of peace or turmoil.

Prayer: "Lord Jesus, teach me how to let go of my fear. Fear of losing, fear of pain, fear that can distract my relationship with you. Teach me how to keep your peace in my heart. Let me have your peace. In the time of pain and facing death, let me see your gentle and kind face."

1. Who needs this prayer?

This prayer is for anyone who is afraid and fearful of any situation, faces uncertainty of the future, and for those who want to learn how to rely on the Lord for strength.

2. How to participate in this prayer?
(1) **Read the Bible:**

Read the Bible 30 minutes a day for the next 30 days to develop a habit of listening to the Lord and not destructive voices. Read John or any gospel everyday for 30 minutes a day or read one gospel a day.

(2) **Pray for 30 minutes everyday (speak to God for 15 minutes and listen to God in silence for 15 minutes):**

(3) **Pray for the best and prepare for the worst:**

One inmate told me that he was so filled with fear because he may receive a death sentence for his crime. I told him to pray for the best but prepare for the worst. I told him to prepare for his death by saying good-bye to his family and taking care of everything as if he had received a death sentence.

When people are facing a court date, many people are restless, worried, and filled with fear because they don't know what's going to happen. I tell people the same thing: Pray for the best but prepare for the worst. If they are prepared to receive a maximum sentence be prepared and pray that the Lord's will be done. They can rely on the Lord for the outcome. They have to learn to deal with the consequences. They don't have to be angry with God, or blame God because that doesn't solve anything.

(4) **To deal with fear, meditate and memorize the Scriptures:**

Ricky, a former Army Ranger who served in Afghanistan, met another Ranger who was called, "Preacher." This preacher's favorite Scripture was Romans 8:31-39; he died as a POW in Afghanistan. When they found him, his head was cut off and the body was unrecognizable and the only way they could identify him was a unique cross tattoo on his body.

When Ricky was captured as a POW, he found Romans 8:31-39 inscribed in a cave wall where he was. Ricky knew it was the Preacher's work because this was his favorite Scripture. That's the first Scripture the Preacher read to Ricky. Ricky was rescued eventually to share this amazing story.

What could bring more fear than being in a war and having a possibility of being captured and tortured? The preacher prepared his heart by focusing on God's love in any circumstances.

Paul faced lots of hardships, persecutions, and painful situations after he was converted and decided to preach the gospel. Because of his own hardships, pain and suffering, he was able to write his confession and statement of faith even though he faced death many times. It shows how he handled his own fear. You can meditate on what Paul wrote and have confidence knowing that God is for you even though the circumstance may be hard.

Paul wrote, "What, then, shall we say in response to this? If God is for us, who can be against us? He who did not spare his own Son, but gave him up for us all-- how will he not also, along with him, graciously give us all things? Who will bring any charge against those whom God has chosen? It is God who justifies. Who is he that condemns? Christ Jesus, who died-- more than that, who was raised to life-- is at the right hand of God and is also interceding for us. Who shall separate us from the love of Christ? Shall trouble or hardship or persecution or famine or nakedness or danger or sword? As it is written: 'For your sake we face death all day long; we are considered as sheep to be slaughtered.' No, in all these things we are more than conquerors through him who loved us. For I am convinced that neither death nor life, neither angels nor demons, neither the present nor the future, nor any powers, neither height nor depth, nor anything else in all creation, will be able to separate us from the love of God that is in Christ Jesus our Lord." (Romans 8:31-39)

(5) **Write down what God has done for you:**
When King Saul decided to kill David, David ran away and wandered around many years until King Saul died in the battle.

David knew what it felt like to be chased and fear death. He had the chance to kill Saul, but he didn't. He said God anointed Saul. David let God take care of his enemies. David focused on his relationship with the Lord like a shepherd and a sheep. His faith tells us we can proclaim victory in any circumstance even in the presence of enemies. Here is Psalm 23 and as you read it, think about how God is leading your path.

"The LORD is my shepherd, I shall not be in want. He makes me lie down in green pastures, he leads me beside quiet waters, he restores my soul. He guides me in paths of righteousness for his name's sake. Even though I walk through the valley of the shadow of death, I will fear no evil, for you are with me; your rod and your staff, they comfort me. You prepare a table before me in the presence of my enemies. You anoint my head with oil; my cup overflows. Surely goodness and love will follow me all the days of my life, and I will dwell in the house of the LORD forever."

(6) **Praise God for all hardships and use them for God's glory:**
Paul talked about how he felt like he was sentenced to death but instead of focusing on his fear, he learned to focus on God who gives him strength. In any situation, Paul learned to give God credit and praise for His strength. This is what he wrote:

"Praise be to the God and Father of our Lord Jesus Christ, the Father of compassion and the God of all comfort, who comforts us in all our troubles, so that we can comfort those in any trouble with the comfort we ourselves have received from God. For just as the sufferings of Christ flow over into our lives, so also through Christ our comfort overflows. If we are distressed, it is for your comfort and salvation; if we are comforted, it is for your comfort, which produces in you patient endurance of the same sufferings we suffer. And our hope for you is firm, because we know that just as you share in our sufferings, so also you share in our comfort. We do not want you to be uninformed, brothers, about the hardships we suffered in the province of Asia. We were under great pressure, far beyond our ability to endure, so that we despaired even of life. Indeed, in our hearts we felt the sentence of death. But this happened that we might not rely on ourselves but on God, who raises the dead. He has delivered us from such a deadly peril, and he will deliver us. On him we have set our hope that he will continue to deliver us." (2 Corinthians 1:3-10)

Share your stories of how God brought you out of fearful and painful situations so others can be encouraged by your testimony. Even if you are fearful, go back and review your life and how God brought you out of the fearful situation, and start believing that God will help you even in the midst of pain and hurts.

(7) Find the Scriptures that comfort you and meditate on them day and night. Read the Scriptures and find strength and peace.

"Do not let your hearts be troubled. Trust in God; trust also in me. In my Father's house are many rooms; if it were not so, I would have told you. I am going there to prepare a place for you. And if I go and prepare a place for you, I will come back and take you to be with me that you also may be where I am." (John 14:1-3)

"And I will ask the Father, and he will give you another Counselor to be with you forever--the Spirit of truth. The world cannot accept him, because it neither sees him nor knows him. But you know him, for he lives with you and will be in you. I will not leave you as orphans; I will come to you" (John 14:16-17).

"'For the eyes of the Lord are on the righteous and his ears are attentive to their prayer, but the face of the Lord is against those who do evil.' Who is going to harm you if you are eager to do good? But even if you should suffer for what is right, you are blessed. 'Do not fear what they fear; do not be frightened.'" (1 Peter 3:12-14)

"For God has not given us a spirit of fear, but of power and of love and of a sound mind." (2 Timothy 1:7, NKJV)

Chapter Nineteen

Prayer Project: Healing from Spiritual Attacks

Many people are hurting from grief, loss, trauma and PTSD (Post Traumatic Stress Disorder) and God can bring healing in their shattered minds. The tornadoes in life can create other tornadoes if we don't take care of them properly. With God's help, healing is possible.

Prayer: "Lord Jesus, give me a new heart and spirit so I can experience healing from hurts, pain and trauma. Help me to follow you and love you and obey you. Help me to focus on your love, your grace and your healing power. Open my heart to receive your blessing and healing because I cannot do it by myself."

1. Who needs this prayer?

If you are suffering from grief, loss, or trauma and PTSD, and suffer from triggers and flashbacks, spiritual attacks and are immobilized with pain, this prayer project is for you.

2. How to participate in this prayer?
(1) **Read the Bible:**
Find answers from the Word of God for healing of mind, soul and spirit. The lessons we can learn in life's crises are found in the Scriptures and God's Word will bring healing. God's Word is medicine for hurting souls. Our healing depends on how we walk with Jesus everyday as we rely on His Word and the Holy Spirit's leading. Try to develop a close relationship with Jesus who can bring you healing. Also, develop a habit of reading the Bible and ask God to guide you in your healing from grief, pain and trauma.

Prayer: "Lord Jesus, please give me the discernment to understand the Bible so I can get to know you and your love and power so I can experience healing."

(2) **Pray for 30 minutes everyday (speak to God for 15 minutes and listen to God in silence for 15 minutes):**
Spend time in prayer whenever you can. You can pray throughout the day and focus on what God can do for you.

Prayer: "Lord Jesus, all things are possible through you. Please heal my heart with the power of the Holy Spirit. Help me to forgive everyone who hurt me. I give you all my painful memories and thoughts. Please help me to be free from any negative voices. I will not grieve with sad feelings or ponder my past any more. Help me to look up to you every moment. I ask you to give me a new heart and make me into the person that you want me to be. I ask you for forgiveness for holding any resentment, hate or anger. I give up all my bad attitudes toward all who have hurt me. I forgive everyone including myself. Please heal my memory so I don't suffer from triggers and flashbacks any more. Fill my heart with your peace and joy. Please heal me so I can help others. Amen."

(3) Practice TLT (Tornadoes, Lessons, Teachings) model through writing your story:

We all experience tragic events that could immobilize us with pain and traumatize us. I call these events tornadoes of life. Write down your story of tornadoes in your life and focus on the lessons you have learned and the teaching that you may have for others. This writing practice will help you process your tornadoes.

When you don't take care of tornadoes of life, it can create other tornadoes and you feel stuck in pain and you can be traumatized more than before. By focusing on the lessons and what you can teach others, you can move forward. Ask the Lord to help you in this healing process.

Healing may take time because healing is a process but God can heal a wounded person. In order to be healed, we need to exercise our faith. We also need to process hurting and pain and letting go of them or painful memories that hurt us. Writing can facilitate this process.

Prayer: "Lord Jesus, please help me to understand the lessons you want to teach me through this. Help me to help others with what I have learned from tornadoes of life. Help me to let go of all the painful memories so I will be healed."

(4) Forgive everyone including yourself:

When we face tornadoes in life and are hurting, we may be resentful, angry, bitter and blame someone or sometimes God. We need to let go of all those negative emotions by forgiving and letting go of our blame. God forgives us and He asks us to forgive. God is not to blame when others have caused us harm. It's us and other people that are hurting each other. Or sometimes it is natural disasters or sickness which we don't have any control over. Whatever happens, we need to forgive and let go of them to find peace and be healed from trauma and hurtful memories. We can forgive with God's help.

Prayer: "Lord Jesus, you prayed for those who were crucifying you. You said, 'Father forgive them they don't know what they are doing.' Please Lord, help me to forgive everyone who has sinned against me. I made a decision to forgive and I need your help. Help me to see myself as you see me so I don't blame anyone anymore. I have made many mistakes and you have forgiven me. I forgive everyone including myself. Lord Jesus, let my heart be filled with your peace and forgiving heart. Let me share your love and grace with others who are in need of your healing presence. Open my heart and let me see if there is any sin that I have committed so I can repent. Help me to have a humble heart and learn to forgive others. Thank you, Lord Jesus, for dying on the cross for my sins. You have blessed me with forgiveness and let me bless others the same way. Let me be delivered from the spirit of blame and anger."

(5) **Practice silence:**

Jesus calmed the sea by saying, "Be still." We need to say to ourselves, "Be still" to calm our minds as much as we can especially in times of turmoil and pain. The Scripture says, "Be still before the LORD and wait patiently for him." (Psalm 37:7a) Silence brings healing when we are hurting. Many traumatized people suffer from negative and destructive voices. You can control your mind by learning to silence your thoughts with the Scripture meditation when disturbing thoughts come to you and by asking the Lord to speak to you.

Prayer: "Lord Jesus, I am hurting. Please heal my mind with your loving words. Speak to me. I am listening."

(6) **Meditate on the Scriptures:**

Find the Bible verses that touch you and meditate on them every day. The following Scriptures have helped me in my troubled times.

Jesus said, "Do not let your hearts be troubled. Trust in God; trust also in me. In my Father's house are many rooms; if it were not so, I would have told you. I am going there to prepare a place for you. And if I go and prepare a place for you, I will come back and take you to be with me that you also may be where I am." (John 14:1-3)

"When you pass through the waters, I will be with you; and when you pass through the rivers, they will not sweep over you. When you walk through the fire, you will not be burned; the flames will not set you ablaze." (Isaiah 43:2)

"Do you not know? Have you not heard? The Lord is the everlasting God, the Creator of the ends of the earth. He will not grow tired or weary, and his understanding no one can fathom. He gives strength to the weary and increases the power of the weak. Even youths grow tired and weary, and young men stumble and fall; but those who hope in the Lord will renew their strength. They will soar on wings like eagles; they will run and not grow weary, they will walk and not be faint." (Isaiah 40:28-31)

"So do not fear, for I am with you; do not be dismayed, for I am your God. I will strengthen you and help you; I will uphold you with my righteous right hand." (Isaiah 41:10) "Jesus replied, 'What is impossible with men is possible with God.'" (Luke 18:27) "If that is how God clothes the grass of the field, which is here today and tomorrow is thrown into the fire, will he not much more clothe you, O you of little faith? So do not worry, saying, 'What shall we eat?' or 'What shall we drink?' or 'What shall we wear?' For the pagans run after all these things, and your heavenly Father knows that you need them. But seek first his kingdom and his righteousness, and all these things will be given to you as well. Therefore do not worry about tomorrow, for tomorrow will worry about itself. Each day has enough trouble of its own." (Matthew 6:30-34)

"Be strong and courageous, because you will lead these people to inherit the land I swore to their forefathers to give them. Be strong and very courageous. Be careful to obey all the law my servant Moses gave you; do not turn from it to the right or to the left, that you may be successful wherever you go. Do not let this Book of the Law depart from your mouth; meditate on it day and night, so that you may be careful to do everything written in it. Then you will be prosperous and successful. Have I not commanded you? Be strong and courageous. Do not be terrified; do not be discouraged, for the LORD your God will be with you wherever you go." (Joshua 1:6-9)

(7) **Avoid alcohol or drugs or any addiction to numb your pain:**

This will only delay your healing. Try to find positive groups like church and attend worship services and Bible studies to find healing through God and others who have experienced healing. Try to surround yourself with positive people and avoid any negative people so you can experience healing instead of hurting.

(8) **Find pastors or counselors for continued healing:**

There are others who are trained to help you in your healing process like pastors, chaplains, and other mature Christians. Contact them and ask them to pray for you. Contact professional counselors if you need help.

(9) **Surround yourself with positive and godly people:**

Some people will drag you down, and hurt you more than help you. They create tornadoes in our lives. Ask the Lord for discernment so you are not in a place where you can be hurt by others. Find people who are loving and caring. Stay away from any people with low moral values who don't have any respect for themselves or others. This will prevent you from some tornados caused by other people. There are some tornadoes beyond your control, but try to prevent the ones you can control. Attend church and find people who have high moral values. Not all the people who attend church have high moral values either so be careful with whom you associate. Sometimes it will be best to find places where people are helping others. So, volunteer for church and community organizations where there are people who have the goal of helping others who are hurting. The more you focus on helping others instead of trying to get others to meet your needs, the more you will experience healing.

Prayer: "Lord Jesus, help me to have the wisdom to stay away from places and people who will cause tornadoes in my life. Help me to live a peaceful life by surrounding myself with people who love you and live a godly life."

(10) **Write a journal:**
Write a journal and your story about how God has helped you. This will help you process your deep wounds and will bring healing in your mind.

(11) **Find a song and sing in your mind whenever you can:**
Find some inspirational music which can help you focus on God and healing. Inspirational music brings healing. What you put it into your mind is very important in this healing process.

(12) **Share your story with others:**
God can use your painful tornado story to help others who are in a similar situation. Many are in need of guidance and healing. Start sharing your tornado story and the lessons you have learned and how you were able to move on. This will give others hope that they too can experience healing and can move on.

3. How to process and overcome nightmares, hurtful voices and spiritual confusion:
Anyone can have spiritual encounters because we are living in both a physical and a spiritual world. No one is exempt from stepping into the realm of the spiritual world. We can learn to find peace and healing from it with God's help. However, there are people who experience the spiritual world more than others and they are troubled by it. The following groups of people have a greater tendency to be bothered by spirits or spiritual world bringing confusion and fear:
- Those traumatized by abuse or have seen others being abused.
- Those who suffered from terrorizing events such as war or have seen the traumatic deaths of others.

- Those who have experienced traumatic or devastating death or loss such as suicide or brutality.
- Those who are involved in Satanic ritual or cult.
- People who use alcohol, drugs, or other addictive substances which can affect their mind.

(1) **Nightmares**

Some people, awake or asleep can hear, see and feel bad spirits not only in their minds, but also with their physical senses. This sounds scary but it happens to some people.

I believe nightmarish dreams are not natural but are caused by tormenting spirits. These spirits attack people and try to choke them not only in their sleep but while they are awake. With God's help, you can be freed from these bad spirits and nightmares. If you have problems like that, you don't have to be scared.

In my earlier years, I have seen scary looking spirits working in people and the spirits attacked me physically to the point of exhaustion. I also suffered from terrible nightmares after my sister died in a car accident. I was afraid to go to sleep because I felt spirits choking me and I had a difficult time breathing in my dream and had a difficult time waking up.

I didn't know what was happening. My mother told me that it was a spiritual attack and I need to pray more so I don't have nightmares any more. She was right. As I started reading the Bible and prayed more and relied on God for spiritual healing, He delivered me from nightmares and spiritual attacks. I am not afraid of these attacks anymore because I learned how the demons try to scare me. I can win and overcome them with God's help. If you are suffering from nightmares, start reading the Bible and praying "The Lord's Prayer." Keep praying until you can find peace. Many nightmares are spiritual encounters with bad spirits.

Prayer: "Lord Jesus, I believe that you have the power to help me and release me from nightmares. I ask you to help me to be strong so I can win this spiritual battle with your power. Please surround me with angels and protect me day and night from bad spirits. I ask for forgiveness if I have sinned against you and others. If there is any sin I need to repent, please help me to repent. Thank you for your forgiveness. I forgive everyone who has sinned against me. Help me to love you and serve you as you want me to. I pray for the salvation of all my family and relatives and others who don't know you. I pray this in Jesus' name. Amen."

(2) **Hurtful voices**

Many people suffer from hearing negative and destructive voices and thoughts that come to their mind and some even hear it audibly. How do you deal with these destructive, negative, hurtful voices?

First, you need to realize from where these voices come. When people hear voices in their mind, many think these are their own voices or thoughts. That's not always true. There are four voices people hear in their minds: 1) Their own voice 2) The voices of other people 3) A bad voice (The devil's destructive voice) 4) A good voice (God's voice).

Other people's voices may be something that we remember from the past and it could be good or bad. Our own voice is our own thoughts, which can be good or bad. We have freedom to make choices about which voices we will accept and this will determine how we think and how we live. If we accept bad voices, we will be in turmoil and could fall into sin by following them. If we accept good voices, which are God's voice, we will find comfort and healing.

Where do you think the devil attacks first? It's our mind where we hear bad, wrong, negative, destructive, and sinful voices. They need to be resisted by rebuking them in the name of Jesus, and replacing them with the life-giving, positive Word of God. People who have suffered from depression and suicidal thoughts have shared with me that they have heard many bad voices telling them how bad and worthless they are and sometimes give directions on how to hurt themselves and others.

Peter warns us about spiritual attack. He wrote, "Be self-controlled and alert. Your enemy the devil prowls around like a roaring lion looking for someone to devour. Resist him, standing firm in the faith, because you know that your brothers throughout the world are undergoing the same kind of sufferings. And the God of all grace, who called you to his eternal glory in Christ, after you have suffered a little while, will himself restore you and make you strong firm and steadfast. To him be the power for ever and ever. Amen." (1 Peter 5:8-11)

Prayer: "Lord Jesus, please help me to have discernment; to know what is a good voice or a bad voice, so I can follow the Holy Spirit's voice. I ask for your guidance and wisdom to follow you and learn to resist destructive voices. I let go of all the blame and hurtful thoughts. I bless everyone."

If you have been involved in Satanic cult rituals and have turned to God, but you suffer from a destructive voice saying that God cannot forgive you, know that God has forgiven you. Don't believe any voices undermining God's love for you. I encourage you to memorize the following Scripture: and recite it whenever you feel you need God's comfort: "The Spirit of the Lord is on me, because he has anointed me to preach good news to the poor. He has sent me to proclaim freedom for the prisoners and recovery of sight for the blind, to release the oppressed, to proclaim the year of the Lord's favor." (Luke 4:18-19)

Here is a prayer for those who want to turn to God.

Prayer: "Jesus, I invite you to be the Lord and Savior of my life. I ask for your forgiveness and protection from spirits which are hurting me and tormenting me. Please forgive all my sins and cleanse me. I believe in the power of your blood which was shed on the cross for my sins. Bless me with the Holy Spirit and clothe me with the armor of God. Surround me with angels to protect me from the devil's lies and attacks. I believe you died on the cross and shed your blood to forgive me. Thank you for your forgiveness. Help me so I can win this spiritual battle with your power. Bless me with wisdom and discernment so I can understand the Bible. I pray this in Jesus' name. Amen."

(3) **Spiritual confusion**

Not all spiritual encounters are bad; some are from the Lord. God can give us spiritual visions about our loved ones who passed away, to give us comfort and healing. What God gives us is always good and helps us to grow in faith. He would not scare us by showing dead people walking in daylight or through nightmares.

However, there are some people who see dead people in physical forms and this encounter brings turmoil to the point that they may wonder if they are going crazy. They are not crazy. They are seeing the spiritual world which is hidden to many, but they are seeing, feeling and hearing it. This spiritual encounter is caused by demons who are trying to confuse people. Bad spirits can disguise themselves as the deceased person and appear to people.

When people die, their spirits are no longer here. Jesus tells a story of where dead peoples' spirits are. Luke 16:19-31 tells us the story of Lazarus and the rich man. The rich man who was tormented in hell, asked Abraham to send Lazarus to warn people so they don't have to be in the place of torment, but his request was not granted.

Avoid talking to a dead person's spirit because the Lord tells us not to communicate with them. "Do not turn to mediums or seek out spiritists, for you will be defiled by them. I am the Lord your God." (Leviticus 19:31)

Mediums in this context are people who seek to talk to the spirits of dead people. Demons can disguise themselves to look like a dead person to deceive us. If that happens and you are scared, then rebuke that spirit. James wrote, "Submit yourselves, then, to God. Resist the devil, and he will flee from you." (James 4:7) So, resist them by saying, "In the name of Jesus, leave from me. I am a child of God."

Prayer: "Lord Jesus, I believe in you. I ask you to surround me with angels and protect me from confusing spirits. Bless me with your peace and joy. Amen."

Note: To learn more about spiritual battle, read the book, *Tornadoes of Spiritual Warfare, How to Recognize & Defend Yourself From Negative Forces.*

Chapter Twenty

Prayer Project: Praying for Revival

I wanted to see a revival in America and God helped me to experience this at the least expected place –jail. God's grace is sufficient. He shows up where people are hurting and seeking God. I thank God for calling me to the prison ministry to show me that He is alive and He cares. A lot of my mountain top experiences come from the transformation stories of Maximum Saints books and testimonies of inmates at Adams County Detention Facility. That's God's grace. Many of my books could not have been written without the inmates' help. Praise God. Now, I know seeing a revival is possible when the Holy Spirit shows up and when people humble themselves and pray. He has been teaching me about God's grace and I believe that many miracles I have seen are all due to God's grace.

Prayer: "Lord Jesus, please help us to experience a revival in our hearts. Help us to love you and love ourselves and others. Help us to hear, feel, and understand the suffering of others and help us to equip and to help them with your wisdom and strength. Teach us so we can seek you with all our heart and mind so that we can find you and feel your presence. Bless everyone who is seeking you with the Holy Spirit's presence and bring healing to those who are hurting. Help us to help others to whom you want us to reach out, too. Guide us so we can be a part of a revival that will bring transformation of the people around me and around the world."

1. Who needs this prayer?

If you feel you are in desperate need of prayer and don't know how to start, or feel something is missing in your spiritual walk, and have a deep spiritual hunger but don't know how to fill that empty heart, or if you want to have a deeper relationship with the Lord, I encourage you to start this prayer project.

Spend one hour each day with the Lord. Read the Bible for 30 minutes. Then spend 30 minutes in prayer, talk to God for 15 minutes and listen for God's voice in silence for 15 minutes.

If you spend one hour with Jesus every day for the next 30 days, you will be transformed. I assure you that you will learn something new from the Lord, and your walk with Him will not be the same.

2. What is the prayer focus for this project?

God gave me the desire to pray more for incarcerated people and their families, especially children. I come with a heavy heart, and I believe it is time to start praying for not only ourselves, but our families, and this nation. In recent years, America has been hit by many natural disasters. Katrina in New Orleans is an example of this. We have seen the devastation of many people who lost the homes and everything for which they had worked for.

I see disaster slowly taking over America. This is not a natural disaster but a disaster caused by sin resulting in incarceration. This disaster I call "The Flood of Incarceration." Some lose everything when they become incarcerated. The incarcerated can be like people in New Orleans or more because of separation from their loved ones, their families, and even losing self-respect.

In America, 2.3 million people are incarcerated. There are many reasons for incarceration. Many are incarcerated because of alcohol and drug abuse. Addiction to ungodly living is the cause of incarceration and in some cases, the cause is the lack of economic resources and mental problems. Also, spiritual poverty leads many to the same situation; lack of direction, and lack of purpose in life. Because of "The Flood of Incarceration," many homes, families, and communities have been devastated. Churches are not exempt. Many Christian homes have been hit hard by "The Flood of Incarceration." As Adam and Eve's sin affected everyone, sin resulting in incarceration is affecting everyone everywhere, especially in Colorado.

3. What is happening in Colorado?

The following statistics come from the Colorado Prison Crisis Report:

1) The Colorado prison population has increased 604% since 1980. During the same time, the population of the state has grown 59%.

2) Colorado's average annual prison population growth rate of 7% far exceeds the national average of 4.3%.

3) In Colorado, the incarceration rate of women has grown faster than the rate for men. Between 1993 and 2003, the women's prison population grew at more than double the rate of the male prison population.

4) Children with an incarcerated mother are 5 to 6 times more likely to become incarcerated than other children who live in poverty and whose mothers have never been to prison.

5) The Colorado state General Fund appropriation to the Department of Corrections for fiscal year 1985 - 1986 was $57 million. Twenty years later, the appropriation for 2006-2007 is in excess of $644 million.

4. What is the reason for this disaster?

We need to understand that ungodly lifestyles invite the devil's attack. We are in a spiritual war and many are losing when so many families are broken down because of our sin. The incarcerated families are going through so much suffering and the devil can plant the seed of despair, helplessness, hopelessness, resentment, bitterness, and anger.

The enemy has attacked and without a prayer the children are an easy target since they don't understand what is going on. All they know is that their mom or dad or sometimes both parents are taken away from them. We are raising many innocent children soaked with a flood of shame and anger and many are heading toward "The Flood of Incarceration." Many are beginning to recognize the ripple effects of incarceration.

The reason for this disaster is because we have disobeyed the Lord. Paul said, "The wrath of God is being revealed from heaven against all the godlessness and wickedness of men who suppress the truth by their wickedness." (Romans 2:18)

"There is no one righteous, not even one; there is no one who understands, no one who seeks God. All have turned away; they have together become worthless; there is no one who does good, not even one. Their throats are open graves; their tongues practice deceit. The poison of vipers is on their lips. Their mouths are full of cursing and bitterness. Their feet are swift to shed blood; ruin and misery mark their ways, and the way of peace they do not know. There is no fear of God before their eyes….for all have sinned and fall short of the glory of God." (Romans 3:10-23)

Our sin invites disaster and the first sign of disobedience is that we lose peace. The devil has a part in this and we need to recognize the spiritual battle. Paul said, "For our struggle is not against flesh and blood, but against the rulers, against the authorities, against the powers of this dark world and against the spiritual forces of evil in the heavenly realms." (Ephesians 6:12)

Paul stated, "Therefore put on the full armor of God, so that when the day of evil comes, you may be able to stand your ground, and after you have done everything, to stand. Stand firm then, with the belt of truth buckled around your waist, with the breastplate of righteousness in place." (Ephesians 6:13-14)

Our determination to live godly lives and to obey the Lord will help us to put on the armor of God. When we turn to God and leave the life of sin, God will help us win the spiritual battle.

5. What do we need to do?

James said, "Is anyone of you in trouble? He should pray." (James 5:13a) We can ask God to help us change this pattern of "The Flood of Incarceration." This is the main reason for this prayer project.

It's time to ask God to forgive us and pray for protection for ourselves, our families, so God can help us to overcome our addiction to sinful desires and passion. Peter wrote, "God opposes the proud but gives grace to the humble. Humble yourselves, therefore, under God's mighty hand, that he may lift you up in due time. Cast all your anxiety on him because he cares for you. Be self-controlled and alert. Your enemy the devil prowls around like a roaring lion looking for someone to devour. Resist him, standing firm in the faith, because you know that your brothers throughout the world are undergoing the same kind of sufferings." (1 Peter 5:5-9a)

Self-control comes from our spiritual discipline and this prayer is a part of learning how to discipline ourselves to pray and to learn to focus our heart on Christ so we can learn to obey.

6. How to participate in this prayer?

God said, "My people are destroyed from lack of knowledge." (Hosea 4:6) It's important to learn about God through the Scriptures to understand Jesus' heart. Read the Bible ask the Lord for wisdom, understanding, knowledge and revelation so the Holy Spirit will help you and remind you of the Scriptures when you need it.

Many of our problems are caused by not paying attention to the small voice of the Holy Spirit who lives in us. When we pray, we tend to talk all the time. We shout in our minds most of the time, and our minds are so cluttered that we cannot have peace. We talk way too much to God. If we talk less and reflect more, there will be more healing in our relationship with God and in our relationship with others.

Waiting in silence is difficult at first but if you practice, you will be able to quiet your mind and listen. Learning to wait in silence can help us to listen to God's voice and to find peace in our minds. Prayer helps us to communicate with God only if we try to listen to Him.

Ask God to help you understand His plans for you. God has visions, dreams, and plans for you. Our problem is that we make our own plans and follow through without asking God if that's what He wants us to do. We have received a Great Commission, that we are to make disciples for Jesus and to teach others to obey the Lord. Try to understand God's plans for you and obey the Lord.

7. Here are eight prayer suggestions:
(1) Pray to raise the workers:
Prayer: "Jesus forgive me and others who have sinned against you. Raise godly workers for your kingdom inside and outside prison walls. I pray for all the incarcerated and their children. Please help me break the cycle of incarceration with your power and love. Provide godly Christian mentors for the children of the incarcerated."

(2) Repentance:
Prayer: "Jesus, bless me and this nation with the spirit of repentance so we can be saved and understand our spiritual condition. Help us to understand others' pain when we hurt them. Help me live a godly life that will please you. Forgive me of all my sins and if there is any sin that I need to repent, please help me repent."

(3) Wisdom to understand the Bible:
Prayer: "Holy Spirit, help me to have wisdom, knowledge, understanding, and revelation so I can understand the Word of God and live accordingly. Fill me with spiritual wisdom so that I can live a holy life."

(4) Pray to experience Holy Spirit:
Prayer: "Holy Spirit, I give all my worries and fear to your powerful hands. Fill my heart with your peace and joy. Help me to develop a relationship with Jesus and the Holy Spirit so I can understand that you are real."

(5) Pray to understand the Holy Spirit's voice:
Prayer: "Holy Spirit, speak to me clearly. Guide and direct me and help me to have a willing heart so I can follow you and obey you."

(6) Pray to understand God's plans for me:
Prayer: "God, help me to understand your plans, visions, and dreams for me so I can follow your plans instead of making my own plans and fall into sin."

(7) Pray for a new heart:
Prayer: "God, I ask for a new heart so I can follow you instead of following the worldly sinful desires. Please deliver me from all the cravings of sin and desires which will make me fall into temptation and sin. Wash me with the blood of Jesus and empower me to do what you want me to do."

(8) We can be a part of this revival:

I am asking people to join this prayer so God can help us change the history to a new movement of "The Flood of Revival" led by godly disciples of Jesus. We can show the world that God can transform us. Let's pray that God would help us change the history of our lives, history of our family, and history of our community, so instead of an increase in incarceration, we will see an increase in God's committed workers to bring revival.

Jesus said, "The harvest is plentiful but the workers are few." (Matthew 9:37) All Christians are called to be the harvesters. Talk is cheap. We have to live out our faith. James said, "As the body without the spirit is dead, so faith without deeds is dead." (James 2:26)

Prayer: "Lord Jesus, bless me with a passionate love for you and commitment to serve you."

A Prayer for Revival

God, in your mercy, come and save us.
We need you badly.
We need your presence.
We need the Holy Spirit.
We need revival in our hearts.
We need purification and repentance.
We need your forgiveness.

Pour down your Holy Spirit on us today, right now in this dry land, to our thirsty souls. Fill us with the Holy Spirit to touch our hearts, open our spiritual eyes and ears, so that we could see ourselves the way you see, and we could hear your voice, and have hearts to obey you.

Father, forgive us for underestimating your love and power in our lives. Forgive us for loving our flesh and the things in the world more than you.
Help us to repent of our sins. Break our hardened hearts and give us a new heart of love for you and others.

Forgive us for ignoring you so long, by not paying attention to your words,
by not praying, by ignoring the lost people who suffer from the bondage of sin and Satan, by disobeying the Word of God and the Holy Spirit.

Father God, save us. We need your mercy and compassion.
Don't turn your face away from us. We need your presence in our lives to survive.

Jesus, our hope and Savior and Prince of peace, save us.
You have done your part by shedding your blood on the cross and dying for our sins. Help us to understand your sacrificial love and help us to have love for you.

Holy Spirit, gentle and powerful divine God and Counselor, save us. We need your mighty saving, convicting power so we could be saved and filled with love for God and others, to have victory over sinful nature and Satan, to have courage to spread God's salvation message to others, so that we could die to save others as Jesus did.

God, bless pastors, evangelists, missionaries, teachers, and church leaders in the world. Fill them with the Holy Spirit so that they seek your face, and learn to love you and to live holy lives, so that they can be effective in ministry of serving God. Give them burning desires to help the lost people as you have.

Lord, Jesus, help me to be your disciple and follow you all the way to love you and serve you. Start a revival in my heart that I will have a burning desire to love you and serve you.

Note: To learn more about revival, read the book, *I Was The Mountain, In Search of Faith and Revival.*

Part Three

Chapter Twenty One

Why Do People Think About Committing Suicide?

When people's problems and stress are compounded and unbearable and they don't know how to cope with their pain, they can become self-destructive and suicidal. There are three kinds of pain: 1) Physical pain; 2) Emotional pain; 3) Spiritual pain. If you are suffering from physical pain, medical doctors can help you manage it. Counselors and psychiatrists can help you manage emotional pain. I believe spiritual pain can only be healed by applying God's principles and prescriptions revealed by the Bible and through a relationship with God. Those who have spiritual knowledge and understanding can teach others how to experience spiritual healing. Pastors, ministers or mature Christians can be guides healing through God's prescriptions which come from the Scriptures. The following are different types of pain and how they can affect people to have suicidal thoughts:

Three Kinds of Pain

1. Physical pain
When people are suffering from prolonged illness and pain and feel there is no hope of being cured, they might think ending their life is the only way to end the pain.

2. Emotional pain
(1) **Death and loss of loved ones:** Grief due to loss is a big common cause of emotional pain. Depending on the relationship the person had with the deceased, he/she may suffer from feelings of guilt, anger, resentment, loneliness, relief, shame, and many other emotions. People who do not know how to process grief and loss constructively can become suicidal.

(2) **Death of a relationship:** People who don't know how to deal with grief over a relationship break-up can become suicidal.

(3) **Feelings of unworthiness:** When a person suffers from helplessness, hopelessness, disappointment, boredom, guilt, shame, an unforgiving spirit, or self-hatred and despair for a long period, they can become suicidal.

(4) **Addictions:** Some people turn to alcohol and drugs when they are in pain. People are vulnerable to spiritual attacks when they are under the influence of drugs and alcohol. The spirits of despair, suicide and murder can take over and control their minds and tell them what to do to hurt themselves. If they follow the evil spirit's voice, even those who do not have any intention of killing themselves might end up committing suicide.

(5) **Financial problems:** When people are feeling desperate because of financial distress and think there is no way out, they might try to avoid the pain by ending their life.

(6) **Other's rejection:** People need to be understood, accepted, and affirmed. Sometimes, those who do not receive love from their significant others, especially from their family, might think ending their life is the solution. In some cultures, family affirmation and acceptance are more important than anything else. Once, an Asian man was incarcerated for a minor violation. When he heard on the phone that his family disowned him because his incarceration brought disgrace to the family, he committed suicide.

(7) **Lack of purpose in life:** When people do not have clear goals on how to live a fulfilled life, they may turn to destructive lifestyles to fill that void. When they lose possessions, relationships, or careers, they may be devastated. They may not feel there is a reason to live because they feel they have lost everything important to them.

(8) **Prolonged extreme stress and pain related to different situations:** When people suffer from intense pain and ongoing stress such as depression, war, incarceration, natural disaster, value conflict, mental illness and/or abusive situations, they are emotionally, mentally and spiritually exhausted. When they feel they don't have any way out, they may think that suicide is only way to get out of that situation.

(9) **Inability to process anger and forgiveness:** Some people don't know how to forgive or how to handle anger constructively, so they become self-destructive.

(10) **Desire to hurt their loved ones or others:** Some, however, may end up committing suicide to make other people feel badly when they don't get what they want.

(11) **Suicide in the family:** When people are overwhelmed with any kind of pain, they may think suicide is the way to stop, especially if a family member committed suicide. This is not always true, but they may think that since a family member chose this, it's okay for them to choose it.

3. Spiritual pain

Spiritual pain is caused by tormenting spirits. These spirits can hurt people in three ways:

(1) **Voices** — The spirit of despair plants the seeds of thoughts that the life we live is not worthwhile and human life is nothing but pain. This is twisted logic, and the voices of the devil people hear are real. Many people do not realize that it is the devil's voice they are listening and they accept it. Until they start to recognize these voices as the devil's, it's hard for anyone to win this spiritual battle.

(2) **Spirit of torment** — When people accept the voice of despair and start believing it, they are watering the poisonous plant of despair. It's like a disease spreading in the body; poisonous thoughts grow as pain increases. The cause of this pain is the spirit of torment. The spirit of torment will infiltrate the minds and hearts of people, attacking their spirits and oppressing them to the point that they feel immobilized with pain. The more people accept twisted logic, the more they are oppressed spiritually and feel intense pain.

(3) **Physical attack** — Not all physical sickness is demonic work. In some cases, virus, accidents, age, heredity, lack of nourishment or weak body parts play a role, and we get sick. However, demonic spirits can attack people and hurt with physical pain as well as spiritually. People can feel the pain in their body, but medically, nothing is wrong with them. When people rely on God and His Word, repent and start resisting the spirit of despair, the demon has to leave, and the physical and spiritual pain are healed.

Four Voices: There are four voices people hear in their minds: 1) Other people's voices; 2) Their own voice; 3) The devil's destructive voice; 4) The Holy

Spirit's voice. Other people's voices may be something that we remember from the past. Our own voice is our thinking and we make decisions on how we want to accept different voices.

We have freedom to make choices about which voices we will accept or resist. The devil's voice is deceptive and destructive in nature. If we accept and follow it, we will fall into sin and hurt ourselves and others. The devil will tell people many reasons why and how they should hurt and/or kill themselves. People are confused when they hear the devil's instruction to hurt and/or kill. They think they heard their own voice but that's because they have not learned to distinguish the devil's voice from their own voice.

We have a sinful nature, and our own sinful thoughts can do evil things. At the same time, we have consciences and God given characteristics to do good and to resist and avoid pain and misery. **Therefore, trying to kill oneself is not natural. It goes against the human natural instinct to survive.** We have a sinful nature but not to the point that we will turn against ourselves and end our lives.

The Holy Spirit will tell people to follow God and work toward the healing of souls to find peace, but the devil will hurt people by presenting how to hurt and/or kill. We should resist the evil voices telling us to hurt and kill. Many people who have suffered from suicidal thoughts have shared with me that they have heard the following destructive voices. There is a way to resist them, and God already has given us the answers in the Bible. Read the Bible whenever you can and you will learn to distinguish if the voice you hear is from God or the devil.

Destructive voices people may hear:
(1) **Voices telling you to end your life:** "The only way your pain will end is if you end your life." The devil uses this lie to get many people to commit self-murder. God can relieve your pain, and you can be freed from torment. Rebuke the spirit of suicide and murder in Jesus' name. (1 Peter 5:6-9) Ask God for help. He will heal you from your pain and suffering. "Ask and it will be given to you; seek and you will find; knock and the door will be opened to you. For everyone who asks receives; he who seeks finds; and to him who knocks, the door will be opened." (Matthew 7:7-8)

If you are depressed, sad, angry, and feeling hopeless and helpless to the point that you want to kill yourself to end your pain, call a suicide hotline immediately and ask for help. Talk to a counselor, social workers, mental health workers, pastors or chaplains until you can find someone who can help you process your pain.

(2) **Voices appealing to self-pity:** "Just end it now, those around you will be better off and no one will miss you. It will all be over after you kill yourself, because no one loves you. You are a burden to your family. They won't miss you when you are gone." If you end your life, you will be creating incredible pain and turmoil for your family. If you are trying to hurt your family by hurting yourself or committing suicide, think about some good memories that you have of them. You need to forgive the hurt they have caused you so God can forgive you. You don't really know what kind of pain others are going through.

You have to learn to care for your family and not just think about your needs. Get out of your selfish thinking that they have to take care of you. Take care of your family and let go of your expectations of them. Be a peacemaker. The devil uses self-pity to convince people to devalue life and to kill themselves. Get out of your self-pity, because it could kill you. There are other people who are worse off than you are, so learn from them how they have overcome their adversity. If you have children, think about how much they need you and will miss you and grieve for you for the rest of their lives. Learn how to process pain constructively by asking God for help.

(3) **Voices of doubt about God's love:** "God doesn't love you. He hates you. You are cursed." How can you think God hates you when He has given His best gift to you! God loves us and blesses us with many spiritual blessings. When we repent and accept Jesus as our Savior, we receive salvation, forgiveness and eternal life. Jesus said, "For God so loved the world that he gave his one and only Son, that whoever believes in him shall not perish but have eternal life." (John 3:16) God loves you. You are worthy of His love. That's why Jesus died on the cross for your sins.

(4) **Voices of doubt about God's forgiveness:** "God won't forgive you because you have done terrible things." The devil is good at making suggestions as to how to fall into sin. After you fall into sin, he will try to convince you that God will not forgive you. As soon as you ask for forgiveness and repent of your sins, God forgives you. If you keep hearing accusing voice that say you don't deserve forgiveness, remember that voice is coming from the devil to discourage you. God would not condemn us when we repent.

The devil tries to twist our mind into thinking that we don't deserve forgiveness. Then he tries to make us to fall into self-destructive behaviors and self-murder. No one can be saved by their righteous deeds but through having faith in Jesus. "For it is by grace you have been saved, through faith -- and this not from yourselves, it is the gift of God -- not by works, so that no one can boast."

(Ephesians 2:8-9) God already knows your sins, failures and weaknesses. We are all sinners: "for all have sinned and fall short of the glory of God" (Romans 3:23)

God blesses us if we only accept Jesus and repent of our sins. "If we confess our sins, he is faithful and just and will forgive us our sins and purify us from all unrighteousness." (1 John 1:9) Meditate on the Bible where it talks about God's love. Read Psalm 103 and read Chapter Four, "A Love Letter From Jesus," to understand how God forgives you.

(5) **Voices that tell you not to forgive yourself:** "How can you be so stupid as to make a mistake like that? You are a disappointment to everyone. You shouldn't forgive yourself. Just kill yourself. Then you don't have to make any more mistakes and you don't have to disappoint anyone else anymore." Feeling remorse is good if you can learn the lesson, repent, and not repeat the same mistake. But if you are guilt ridden and you hear a voice that tells you not to forgive yourself and to hurt yourself, this voice is not coming from the Lord, but from the devil. After people fall into sin, the devil will try to convince them that they don't deserve forgiveness, that they should not forgive themselves but go deeper into the sin of self-murder.

You need to forgive yourself and not focus on your failures instead focus on God's forgiveness and His grace. Jesus tried to help Judas repent before he betrayed him, but he refused to repent. After he found out he made a mistake, he still didn't seek God's forgiveness. He couldn't forgive himself, so he killed himself. I believe Judas would have been forgiven if he repented before or even after betrayal, but he didn't. Jesus gave Judas the last chance to repent and change his heart but he didn't.

There will be consequences for whatever we do. Hurting our loved ones for the rest of their lives is not something God wants us to do. You have to be gentle with yourself because Jesus died on the cross for your sins. If you don't forgive yourself, then you are saying that what Jesus did on the cross doesn't mean anything. David wrote, "The Lord is compassionate and gracious, slow to anger, abounding in love. He will not always accuse, nor will he harbor his anger forever; he does not treat us as our sins deserve or repay us according to our iniquities. For as high as the heavens are above the earth, so great is his love for those who fear him; as far as the east is from the west, so far has he removed our transgressions from us. As a father has compassion on his children, so the Lord has compassion on those who fear him." (Psalm 103:8-13)

We need to forgive ourselves as God forgives us and have compassion for ourselves as God has compassion for us.

(6) **Voices devaluing our core beings:** "You never should have been born. Your life is worthless." We are created in the image of God. We are God's masterpiece. "So God created man in his own image, in the image of God he created him; male and female he created them. God blessed them and said to them, "Be fruitful and increase in number; fill the earth and subdue it. Rule over the fish of the sea and the birds of the air and over every living creature that moves on the ground." (Genesis 1:27-28)

The devil wants to teach people to devalue what God has created. God rejoiced when you were born because you are His creation. He knew you before you were born. David recognized it. He wrote, "For you created my inmost being; you knit me together in my mother's womb. I praise you because I am fearfully and wonderfully made; your works are wonderful, I know that full well. My frame was not hidden from you when I was made in the secret place. When I was woven together in the depths of the earth, your eyes saw my unformed body. All the days ordained for me were written in your book before one of them came to be." (Psalm 139:13-16)

God creates human beings with love and to have a loving relationship with them, but the devil tries to deceive people so they will kill and go against God's plans.

(7) **Voices promoting self-hatred:** "You are incapable of being loved. You are a bad, stupid, ugly and unworthy person. You are a disgrace to everyone who knows you." What God created is good, but people have different ways of valuing beauty or worthiness. Many of us are too blind to see people as God sees them. When God created people, He liked what He created. "God saw all that he had made, and it was very good." (Genesis 1:31)

Everyone is beautiful in God's eyes. The devil tries to make people believe that they are not lovable, and that others do not value them. Self-hatred is one deception the devil uses to make people commit self-murder. The devil knows that if you hate yourself, you can hurt or kill yourself. Don't fall into this trap.

God created you as you are and loves you as you are more than you can imagine. Learn to love yourself as God loves you. What other people see may only be on the outside, but God sees your heart. God does not value one person more than another just because other people see them as more beautiful than the next. In fact, Samuel had to learn what God truly values. Samuel thought David's brothers were worthy to be anointed as king. "But the Lord said to Samuel, 'Do not consider his appearance or his height, for I have rejected him. The Lord does not look at the things man looks at. Man looks at the outward appearance, but the Lord looks at the heart.'" (1 Samuel 16:7)

(8) **Voices of false guilt and shame:** "Your parents committed suicide. You killed your parents." Many people who are affected by suicide, especially family members, suffer from false guilt and shame. The devil uses this guilt to make more people commit self-murder. Families of those who commit suicide do not have to feel guilt or shame for what their family member did. We do not have control over other's thoughts or actions.

People who kill themselves are responsible for their own actions, unless there is forced suicide, which is not suicide but homicide. The devil uses false guilt all the time. Don't be fooled by it. Other people made wrong choices by killing themselves. That doesn't mean you have to take responsibility for their mistake. However, if you continuously feel that you could have, should have, would have to prevent another's suicide, then ask God for forgiveness and forgive yourself. You need to forgive the person who committed suicide.

(9) **Voices of appealing to despair:** "You cannot do anything about problems with money, job, family and life. Life is not worthwhile. Just kill yourself, and you don't have to take care of it. They are not going to ask you to pay back what you owe if you are dead." Everyone faces difficulties and life challenges. The devil tries to make us focus on how we are trapped and cannot get out of misery and pain.

We may not be able to solve our problems with our own wisdom, but God can help us handle it. James tells us to ask God for wisdom. "Consider it pure joy, my brothers, whenever you face trials of many kinds, because you know that the testing of your faith develops perseverance. Perseverance must finish its work so that you may be mature and complete, not lacking anything. If any of you lacks wisdom, he should ask God, who gives generously to all without finding fault, and it will be given to him." (James 1:2-5)

God who made everything with words has infinite wisdom and power to help you. He can help us see the big picture and find purpose in life even in difficult times. Ask Him to help you.

(10) **Voices telling you how to kill:** "Your problem are too big. Just run into that other car and kill yourself, then you don't have to deal with them." Any voice that gives you directions on how to hurt or kill yourself is from the devil. When a person believes what the devil is saying, his/her goal in life becomes an obsession to end his/her life. This is against God's love and longing to have a loving relationship with His people. We are created to love God, ourselves and others. God created us to love, but the devil tells us to hate and destroy our own

bodies and our lives. Rebuke the spirit of suicide and murder. Make sure you turn to God for help by repenting of your sins.

Peter wrote, "Humble yourselves, therefore, under God's mighty hand, that he may lift you up in due time. Cast all your anxiety on him because he cares for you. Be self-controlled and alert. Your enemy the devil prowls around like a roaring lion looking for someone to devour. Resist him, standing firm in the faith, because you know that your brothers throughout the world are undergoing the same kind of sufferings. And the God of all grace, who called you to his eternal glory in Christ, after you have suffered a little while, will himself restore you and make you strong, firm and steadfast. To him be the power for ever and ever. Amen." (1 Peter 5:6-11)

"You know the commandments: 'Do not commit adultery, do not murder, do not steal, do not give false testimony, honor your father and mother.'" (Luke 18:20)

(11) **Voices that make you feel like a failure after you attempted suicide:** "You are a failure. You cannot even kill yourself right. Do it right the next time. Just do it and get it over with." Many people who have tried to kill themselves hear the voices that make them feel like a failure or worthless. That's one tactic the devil uses to make us feel that people God created are not good enough.

If you are determined to kill yourself, repent immediately and be humble before God. Ask Him for help because you are trying to destroy God's precious creation. You have become a partner with the devil if your goal is to destroy your life. You can be obedient to God's plan by choosing life, not death. God values your life, and you are to take care of our body and not destroy it.

Paul said, "Do you not know that your body is a temple of the Holy Spirit, who is in you, whom you have received from God? You are not your own; you were bought at a price. Therefore honor God with your body." (1 Corinthians 6:19-20) If you don't honor your body, you are dishonoring God, and that is a sin. Repent and start taking care of your body. The tormenting demon will run away if you start repenting and turn to God for help. Then you will be freed from pain with the power of the Holy Spirit.

"You, dear children, are from God and have overcome them, because the one who is in you (Holy Spirit) is greater than the one (the devil) who is in the world." (1 John 4:4)

Paul gives us insights on how to fight spiritual battle. He wrote, "Finally, be strong in the Lord and in his mighty power. Put on the full armor of God so that you can take your stand against the devil's schemes. For our struggle is not against flesh and blood, but against the rulers, against the authorities, against the powers of this dark world and against the spiritual forces of evil in the heavenly realms. Therefore put on the full armor of God, so that when the day of evil comes, you may be able to stand your ground, and after you have done everything, to stand. Stand firm then, with the belt of truth buckled around your waist, with the breastplate of righteousness in place, and with your feet fitted with the readiness that comes from the gospel of peace. In addition to all this, take up the shield of faith, with which you can extinguish all the flaming arrows of the evil one. Take the helmet of salvation and the sword of the Spirit, which is the word of God. And pray in the Spirit on all occasions with all kinds of prayers and requests. With this in mind, be alert and always keep on praying for all the saints." (Ephesians 6:10-18)

(12) **Voices telling you there is no reason to live and life has no meaning:** "Now, kill yourself. All the work you need to do is finished. No one needs you and you are in pain and it's time to rest." Many people, even that who believe in God, do not understand that God has plans for everyone to have a loving relationship with Him.

We are called to love and to spread this message of love. God didn't create us just to be miserable. He created us to love us and wants our love in return. We are to obey Him by teaching others to experience healing through Christ. The devil tries to make people forget why they have been created in the image of God. Resist any voices that say your life has no meaning.

Rebuke the spirit of despair to leave you in Jesus' name because we are to love God and love our neighbors. How can we love our neighbors if we are obsessed with killing ourselves?

The Scripture teaches us, "Love the Lord your God with all your heart and with all your soul and with all your mind and with all your strength. The second is this: 'Love your neighbor as yourself.' There is no commandment greater than these." (Mark 12:30-31)

Also, we are called to make disciples for Jesus. Jesus said, "But you will receive power when the Holy Spirit comes on you; and you will be my witnesses in Jerusalem, and in all Judea and Samaria, and to the ends of the earth." (Acts 1:8)

"Then Jesus came to them and said, 'All authority in heaven and on earth has been given to me. Therefore go and make disciples of all nations, baptizing them in the name of the Father and of the Son and of the Holy Spirit, and teaching them to obey everything I have commanded you. And surely I am with you always, to the very end of the age.'" (Matthew 28:18-20) Time is short. Many people are hurting and they need God's message of salvation and need to be freed from the devil's lies and torment. You don't need to hold on to the hand of the spirit of suicide and murder; the devil only brings pain, turmoil, despair, suffering and destruction. God has everything you are searching for: hope, peace, joy and fulfillment in life if you listen and obey.

Chapter Twenty Two

The Degrees of Pain

There are three degrees of pain:

1. **Green Light Zone — Normal stage:** A person is having some pain from life's challenges and stress. It's a normal thing to go through some stress, and you learn how to cope. In this stage people usually don't think about killing themselves. The emotional pain scale for this stage is 0-30 percent.

2. **Yellow Light Zone — Entering into a danger zone:** Many people who are under much stress caused by losses, death, abuse and trauma are in this stage. If a person doesn't learn how to cope with pain and stress caused by life's challenges, they might think that suicide is an option.

If they don't recognize how the devil works through twisted logic, they might accept whatever comes to their mind. The devil can encourage them to develop twisted logic in many different areas. At this stage, pain will increase, and the spirit of torment will attack and give suggestions of twisted logic to convince people that suicide is the best way to end their pain.

Many people don't realize that they are in a spiritual battle in their minds. They may believe the voices they hear are their own thoughts. The pain will increase as they accept more twisted logic. People might be pondering how to kill themselves at this stage.

When they accept suicide as a way to end pain, they may move on to the next stage. With God's help, some people learn to manage pain caused by grief and loss, so they learn to resist suicidal thoughts. They will be able to go back to the green light zone. The emotional pain scale is about 30-70 percent.

3. **Red Light Zone — Extreme danger zone:** A person feels intense pain and has accepted the twisted logic that suicide is the only way to end their pain. The urgency to commit suicide becomes so strong that they feel that there is some external force controlling their thoughts and behaviors. This is when a person's religious and cultural background plays a big role in making the decision to kill themselves or to change their minds to go back to the yellow or the green light zone. It depends on whether they have learned to process pain.

Many people feel helpless and hopeless because of the intense pain they have experienced. Many people do not realize that tormenting spirits are giving them suggestions on how to commit suicide. Their goal is to kill themselves. As the devil's voice becomes stronger, the pain goes deeper than ever. They try to end their lives, and some do take their lives. However, with God's help, they can learn to manage pain and go back to the yellow or the green light zone at any time. The emotional pain scale here is about 70-100 percent at this stage.

Chapter Twenty Three

Recovering from Suicidal Thoughts

If you are struggling with so much emotional pain that you want to hurt yourself or end your life, I urge you to call the National Suicide Helpline at 1-800-SUICIDE or 1-800-784-2433 or 1-800-273-8255(U.S) and ask for help. Take a moment to read the following and reflect on it: You don't have to end your life to overcome pain and despair! There are many other ways to deal with pain and life's problems. You are not alone in your anguish. God loves you. Others have walked the same path of pain and suffering and have learned to overcome it. They experienced healing to the point that today they are glad that they didn't take their lives. God can heal your pain. Learn to listen to God by reading the Bible, and not listening to the voices of destruction.

Here are some steps to help you change your way of thinking so you can experience healing:

The ultimate healing from pain comes from God who gives you peace, not pain. But, you have to take the initiative to get closer to God by reading the Bible and praying for healing. You also have to be determined to fight the voices of destruction moment by moment. Recognizing the battle you are in is the first step of healing, but you also have to go through the steps to resist the voices and to change your perception. You have the power to change your life by relying on God and making a decision to work through your problems in a constructive way.

To be healed from suicidal thoughts:

(1) **Decision** — You want to be healed from painful thoughts of suicide. Others cannot make the decision for you although they might have some influence on why you should decide to choose life, instead of death.

(2) **Change thoughts** — You need to recognize where you are and which area you need to work on so you can find direction in the area where you need healing. Recognize all the twisted logic that you have accepted. Start changing the way you think so you can change your behaviors.

(3) **Action** — Put plans for choosing life into action. In some cases, you may have to change your circumstances to get out of a painful abusive relationship

and to be healed from suicidal thoughts. You might have to change a job in some cases, or there may be other changes to make.

(4) **Persistence** — You need to continuously work on different areas until you are freed from pain and temptation to hurt and kill. You need to learn how to resist the voices telling you to kill yourself.

(5) **Healing** — You are released from torment and pain. You find peace, learn to love yourself, and are grateful for the gift of life. One caution here is that you need to remember healing is a process. There is a chance that you can go back to your old destructive self-murder mode anytime if you let your guard down. Keep working on loving God, loving yourself, and loving your family and significant people in your life. This will give you a strong foundation on which to be healed from self-murder. You can find peace and joy which comes from God. You will be surprised how much God can change your heart; healing from pain is possible with Him.

Following the right path will lead you to the healing of your spirit and soul. Suicide brings more pain and turmoil than you think, to all your loved ones. Work on changing your thought patterns, and in developing a close relationship with God. The following are areas that you can work on. Remember that your thought patterns have been developing for a long period of time, so don't expect that your thinking pattern will change in one day. You have to deal with many different areas of your life to be freed from suicidal thoughts. Rely on God, and He will help you find a way to find freedom from pain and turmoil.

1. Work on your relationship with God:
(1) **Read the Bible every day for 30 minutes**. Start by reading the gospels. (Matthew, Mark, Luke and John). There are two ways to do this: 1) Read any gospel for 30 minutes every day for the next 30 days. 2) Read one gospel every day for the next 30 days. Chart your progress each day. Get to know Jesus. He can help you in your healing process. He said, "Come to me, all you who are weary and burdened, and I will give you rest. Take my yoke upon you and learn from me, for I am gentle and humble in heart, and you will find rest for your souls. For my yoke is easy and my burden is light." (Matthew 11:28-30) "Peace I leave with you; my peace I give you. I do not give to you as the world gives. Do not let your hearts be troubled and do not be afraid." (John 14:27) Get to know Jesus and learn to worship him. Paul wrote, "He (Jesus) is the image of the invisible God, the firstborn over all creation. For by him all things were created:

things in heaven and on earth, visible and invisible, whether thrones or powers or rulers or authorities, all things were created by him and for him." (Colossians 1:15-19) Jesus has all the power to help you in your difficult time.

(2) **Memorize and meditate on the Scriptures.** Memorize and recite the following Scriptures day and night. Luke 4: 18-19, "The Spirit of the Lord is on me, because he has anointed me to preach good news to the poor. He has sent me to proclaim freedom for the prisoners and recovery of sight for the blind, to release the oppressed, to proclaim the year of the Lord's favor." This Scripture is for all God's children. Jesus gives freedom to spiritual prisoners. If you are in spiritual pain, you need spiritual freedom. Believers are called to help others find spiritual freedom in Christ by sharing the gospel. But unless you have that freedom in Christ, you cannot help others to find freedom. Work on your relationship with the Lord so you can be healed and find spiritual freedom.

(3) **Repent of all your sins, especially loving the world more than God.** Ask God to help you repent of all your sins to cleanse your soul if you have been ignoring God and living in sin. He will forgive you. "If we confess our sins, he is faithful and just and will forgive us our sins and purify us from all unrighteousness." (1 John 1:9) "'Come now, let us reason together,' says the Lord. 'Though your sins are like scarlet, they shall be as white as snow; though they are red as crimson, they shall be like wool. If you are willing and obedient, you will eat the best from the land.'" (Isaiah 1:18) When we don't love God above everything else, we start to lose the focus of who we are: we are made by God to give Him glory.

Prayer: "Lord Jesus, please forgive me for loving the world more than you. Help me to love you more than anyone or anything. Please forgive all my sins in the name of Jesus." (1 John 2:15-17)

(4) **Pray for healing of your mind and heart.** If you have lost someone or something, read Chapter Eight in this book: "Healing from Grief and Loss: A 30-Day Prayer Project" so you can experience healing. When you finally give your loved one to the Lord, it will help your healing process. What we have received is a temporary gift. Sometimes we must let go of someone or something in order for us to experience healing. With God's help, you will be able to let go of people, things, and situations that make you grieve. Find a professional grief counselor or grief support group and take care of your grieving heart. Writing a good-bye letter to a person you have lost will help you tremendously.

(5) **Practice listening to God's voice.** Many people suffer because they have been listening to the voice of the devil more than the voice of God. That's one of the reasons why they are in turmoil and hurting. The Holy Spirit's voice is gentle, kind, comforting and helps you find answers from God. Practice listening to God's voice in silence. The more you practice silence, the more you will be able to hear the voice of God, which will bring healing. Develop a habit of communicating your thoughts to God throughout the day and writing. Keep a journal of what you want to tell God and what He may be telling you. In this way, you can learn to listen.

Prayer: "Jesus, please speak to me. I am listening."

(6) **Recognize the devil's destructive voice and fight with the Word of God.** There are four voices we hear in our minds: 1) Our own voices; 2) The devil's voice; 3) The Holy Spirit's voice; and 4) other people's voices. The devil can speak to our minds, and lead us to make wrong choices. Resist the devil's suggestions and destructive voices. The devil tried to deceive Jesus into committing suicide by falling from a high place. Jesus fought back using Scripture. The devil is still working to destroy God's people with thoughts of suicide, murder and violent behavior. We need to resist the devil in the name of Jesus and with the Word of God. Any voice that tells you to do something to hurt yourself or others is not coming from the Lord but from the devil. You can learn to resist destructive, negative, critical voices; let go of them and read the Scriptures. Whenever you hear critical voices, read what Jesus has said: "For God so loved the world that he gave his one and only Son, that whoever believes in him shall not perish but have eternal life." (John 3:16) Learn to fight negative voices by replacing them life with transforming voices which come from the Bible. Lack of discernment can lead to the fatal mistake of self-murder.

(7) **Develop a habit of giving thanks and praise to God in all circumstances.** Spend time thanking God for the gift of life and His grace in your life. Praise God for what you have instead of grieving over what you don't have. Paul wrote, "Rejoice in the Lord always. I will say it again: Rejoice! Let your gentleness be evident to all. The Lord is near. Do not be anxious about anything, but in everything, by prayer and petition, with thanksgiving, present your requests to God. And the peace of God, which transcends all understanding, will guard your hearts and your minds in Christ Jesus." (Philippians 4:4-7)

(8) **Ask God for healing of painful losses and memories.** Some people suffer from constant emotional and spiritual pain due to grief and loss. Find

out from your doctor if you have any physical problems. If you don't have any physical problems, you might be suffering from trauma caused by grief and loss. You need to learn how to process grief and loss so you can experience healing. This pain may be caused by the spirit of torment. This tormenting spirit can lead some people committing suicide by telling them their pain will end if they kill themselves. You don't have to end your life to end the pain. This is a lie from the devil. Many traumatized people suffer from this spirit of torment and live in pain. The victims of these demons have a difficult time focusing. They are immersed in pain and grief. Ask God for healing of your mind. He can free you from the spirit of torment. God can heal your broken heart and free you from the spirit of pain and torment. God wants you to have an abundant life, and you can have it when you trust and rely on Him. You have to take the initiative to ask God to help you. Rebuke the spirit of pain and torment to leave you in Jesus' name.

(9) **Value what God values and avoid sin.** Suicide is the sin of self-murder and is a selfish act. Life is a gift from God and He values you so much that Jesus died on the cross for your sins. When you escape pain by ending your life, you break God's commandment, "You shall not kill." There is always a consequence of sin. You will hurt your family and friends with pain, anguish, guilt, shame, and regrets as long as they live. Resist the devil by saying: "In the name of Jesus, spirit of torment, hate and suicide, leave me!" Then, pray to God for help.

Prayer: "Lord, Jesus, I humbly ask you to help me to have the wisdom to recognize and to resist the devil's lies and temptation. I also pray for my family's and others' salvation. Come, Holy Spirit, and help me to love myself as God loves me."

(10) **Know that God has good plans for you.** "'For I know the plans I have for you,' declares the Lord, 'plans to prosper you and not to harm you, plans to give you hope and a future. Then you will call upon me and come and pray to me, and I will listen to you. You will seek me and find me when you seek me with all your heart. I will be found by you.'" (Jeremiah 29:11-14)

Prayer: "God, help me to understand your plans for my life. Holy Spirit, guide me with your wisdom, so I can love and serve you."

(11) **In place of addictive destructive thoughts, develop godly habits.** If you have the desire to know Jesus like Paul, and focus your thoughts on Jesus every day, you will be able to overcome destructive thoughts of suicide. You will be busy learning about Jesus, praying, and sharing Christ with others. Paul's secret to success in fruitful ministry came from his desire to know the Lord. He

wrote, "But whatever was to my profit I now consider loss for the sake of Christ. What is more, I consider everything a loss compared to the surpassing greatness of knowing Christ Jesus my Lord, for whose sake I have lost all things. I consider them rubbish, that I may gain Christ." (Philippians 3:7-8)

(12) **Develop a relationship with the Holy Spirit.** Pay attention to the small voice of the Holy Spirit. The Holy Spirit will tell you to follow the Word of God. Obeying the Holy Spirit is important in your healing process. Jesus taught us that the Holy Spirit will guide, direct, teach, comfort and lead us. "But the Counselor, the Holy Spirit, whom the Father will send in my name, will teach you all things and will remind you of everything I have said to you." (John 14:26) "But when he, the Spirit of truth, comes, he will guide you into all truth. He will not speak on his own; he will speak only what he hears, and he will tell you what is yet to come." (John 16:13) Spend time in prayer in silence and ask the Holy Spirit to speak to you.

(13) **Invite Jesus into your heart.** If you don't have a relationship with Jesus, this is your opportunity for you to invite Him into your heart.

Prayer: "Lord Jesus, I open my heart to invite you. Come into my heart and my life. I am a sinner. Please forgive me and baptize me with the Holy Spirit. Please fill my heart with your peace and heal my broken heart. Help me to see goodness in you and myself and others as well, so I can be delivered from the spirit of despair. I pray this in Jesus' name. Amen."

2. Work on transforming your mind according to the Scriptures and work on your character:

(1) **Forgive everyone, including yourself.** Write forgiveness letters to others. You don't have to mail them, but give all your grievances to God, and ask Him to forgive you. Ask God to forgive the people who have hurt you. "I, even I, am he who blots out your transgressions, for my own sake, and remembers your sins no more." (Isaiah 43:25)

(2) **Recognize the twisted logic of 1+1=5, and resist it.** Sometimes, after people have heard the destructive voices for so long, they might develop an illogical thinking pattern. It will take a while to recognize all the illogical thinking. Evaluate what you are thinking in each area and your life, and understand how you come to a conclusion. If your logic is, "You are in pain + kill yourself to end pain and find peace"; that is 1+1=5 logic. When you recognize your weaknesses and humbly open yourself to the Word of God, your heart will be healed. Listen to

other mature Christians. Your self-examination can help you at your darkest times if you rely on God's wisdom which comes from the Bible. Paul wrote, "Therefore, I urge you, brothers, in view of God's mercy, to offer your bodies as living sacrifices, holy and pleasing to God -- this is your spiritual act of worship. Do not conform any longer to the pattern of this world, but be transformed by the renewing of your mind. Then you will be able to test and approve what God's will is -- his good, pleasing and perfect will." (Romans 12:1-2) Note that God only wants the sacrifice of living our lives in a way holy and pleasing to Him.

(3) **Proclaim faith and victory in every area of your life that gives you concern.** Many times people undermine themselves by the words that they speak. Stop saying defeating words and speak the Word of life. Start proclaiming victory in Christ that you will come out all right in this very difficult process. Think of the areas in which you have been defeated. Those are areas in which you need to proclaim victory by faith.

Anything that you worry about, you need to speak about in faith. Proclaim victory in your situation and be persistent. Jesus said, "Because you have so little faith. I tell you the truth, if you have faith as small as a mustard seed, you can say to this mountain, 'Move from here to there' and it will move. Nothing will be impossible for you." (Matthew 17:20) I wrote a victory prayer for myself, my family and for my ministry. It's in Chapter Three. My first prayer is: "I claim victory that I made a decision to love Jesus. He is my first priority in my life." Write your own victory prayer.

(4) **Learn to love yourself as God loves you.** Meditate on the Word that talks about God's love. You were born to be loved by God, and He can give you peace, joy, and healing; but you have to seek it. Read the Scriptures that tell about God's love. "Dear friends, let us love one another, for love comes from God. Everyone who loves has been born of God and knows God. Whoever does not love does not know God, because God is love. This is how God showed his love among us: He sent his one and only Son into the world that we might live through him. This is love: not that we loved God, but that he loved us and sent his Son as an atoning sacrifice for our sins. Dear friends, since God so loved us, we also ought to love one another. No one has ever seen God; but if we love one another, God lives in us and his love is made complete in us." (1 John 4:7-12)

Prayer: "Lord Jesus, I thank you for the life you have given me. Help me to love myself as you love me. I let go of all my resentment, anger, hate, bitterness, guilt, and shame. Help me to stop all the destructive thoughts and behaviors that will hurt me, my family and others."

(5) **Invite positive thoughts.** Focus on God's grace and not on your own pain and misery. When Paul's prayer was not answered the way he wanted, he heard God saying, "But he said to me, 'My grace is sufficient for you, for my power is made perfect in weakness.' Therefore I will boast all the more gladly about my weaknesses, so that Christ's power may rest on me. That is why, for Christ's sake, I delight in weaknesses, in insults, in hardships, in persecutions, in difficulties. For when I am weak, then I am strong." (2 Corinthians 12:9-10)

When we learn to see God's grace in every situation, we experience healing from negative thoughts. You will become stronger when you have learned to see things that have happened to you in a positive light.

(6) **Develop a godly character with the help of the Holy Spirit.** From the following Scripture, find out which area you need to work on, and ask the Lord to help you change. "But the fruit of the spirit is love, joy, peace, patience, kindness, goodness, faithfulness, gentleness and self-control. Against such things there is no law. Those who belong to Christ Jesus have crucified the sinful nature with its passions and desires. Since we live by the Spirit, let us keep in step with the Spirit. Let us not become conceited, provoking and envying each other." (Galatians 5:22-26)

Prayer: "Holy Spirit, help me to develop a godly character that will please God and bring healing to everyone. Help me be a blessing to others."

(7) **Clean your heart through reflection and journaling.** Many people are overwhelmed because they don't know how to process many disturbing thoughts. Write journals and purge the thoughts so you can process your pain to find healing in your mind and heart.

(8) **Take care of distractions in your mind.** Anything or anyone that is consuming your thoughts and overwhelming you so you cannot focus on the Lord is a distraction. Take care of things that you need to take care of with God's help.

Jesus said, "So do not worry, saying, 'What shall we eat?' or 'What shall we drink?' or 'What shall we wear?' For the pagans run after all these things, and your heavenly Father knows that you need them. But seek first his kingdom and his righteousness, and all these things will be given to you as well. Therefore do not worry about tomorrow, for tomorrow will worry about itself. Each day has enough trouble of its own." (Matthew 6:31-34)

Prayer: "Lord, I give you all my worries, fears, and anything that is not holy. Create peace in my heart. Give me a new heart that is filled with love for you."

(9) **Avoid an addictions and ungodly practices.** Addiction has many different forms and manifestations: 1) alcohol, drugs, sex, TV, computer games, violent temper and many other ungodly behaviors; 2) Disturbing, immoral, hurtful thoughts; 3) Thoughts and urges to hurt oneself or others; 4) Addictions to people and things; 5) Constant fears, worries and immobilizing thoughts. Many people suffer from addiction, disturbing thoughts and behaviors, and live destructive lifestyles. Consequently, they cannot live the fulfilling, abundant, fruitful, joyful and peaceful life the Lord provides. Addicted people love the world or are obsessed with things and/or people more than the Lord. Ask the Holy Spirit to help you so He can direct your life away from your addiction. "Do not get drunk on wine, which leads to debauchery. Instead, be filled with the Spirit." (Ephesians 5:18)

3. Work on your relationship with your family:
(1) **Review your relationship:** Work on building your relationship with your family as much as you can. If you hurt your family with addictive, immoral, violent, destructive behaviors, do ask for forgiveness; however, don't expect your family to accept you or forgive you with just your words. Show them you have truly changed and that you are not going to hurt them anymore. If you are thinking about killing yourself, think about the people you love and who care about you, especially your family and children. Remember who will be receiving the news about your death if you commit suicide. How do you want to be remembered by your family and friends?

(2) **Bless your family:** Think about what your responsibility is. Make plans for ways you can bless your family and follow through. Go beyond your own needs and help your family and others who are grieving or hurting. Follow the Lord's lead by responding to the call to help your family.

4. Have positive people around you:
Surround yourself with positive people. Attend church worship services and Bible studies. These can help you find people who will help you and give you spiritual and emotional support. Find a mentor who can help you overcome spiritual and emotional pain. People who do not understand spiritual war in other people's minds may not understand you. You will need to find someone who can

give you spiritual direction and guide you on the right path. Talk to other people who can encourage you and help you, especially those who can understand your pain and guide you to experience healing.

5. Use your gifts to help others who are hurting:

Help others with your gifts. Your life is a gift to be shared. God gave you the gifts of life, talents and resources so you could use them to help others. Volunteer to help others in the community, church, or in missions. When you focus only on your own pain, the pain will grow, and you will be miserable. When you help others to relieve their pain, you will learn to deal with your pain constructively.

There are times we need to receive other's help, but if you are always focusing on what you want to receive from others, you will be miserable. There are many others who are less fortunate than you. God can fill our empty hearts with peace and joy when we have Him as our first love and first priority. As soon as we lose our focus on God, we lose peace and joy. We also lose joy when we only focus on our needs, but heal when we try to meet others' needs.

6. Find mentors or professionals who can help you:

(1) **Seek counseling from professional counselors, and/or medical doctors.** Find people who have special training and experience in helping people like you. Call the suicide intervention number if you have the urge to kill yourself. Find out if you suffer from depression. Medical doctors can prescribe medicine for you when you are dealing with physical and emotional pain.

(2) **Find a grief and loss support group and process your grief.** Many suicidal people have not processed their own grief and loss.

(3) **Develop life skills to cope in difficult and different situations.** Sign up for a life-skill class or other classes that will help you deal with stresses and life's challenges.

(4) **Ask for help.** Share your pain and how you struggle with suicidal thoughts with your family, friends, social workers, mental health workers so they can help you.

(5) **Seek counseling from ministers.** Talk to chaplains and pastors so they can pray with you and guide you to experience healing. Attend church and Bible studies and learn how to meditate and pray when you are overwhelmed with hurtful thoughts and pain. If you know someone who is suicidal, ask them to contact the suicide hotline to talk to professionals, and/or chaplains or pastors.

7. Change a situation or relationship, if necessary:

(1) **Let go of abusive relationships:** When you are in an abusive relationship and it is causing you so much stress that you are thinking about doing destructive things like suicide or murder, seek professional help. Find out the best way to handle the relationship so you can resolve it. You may have to remove yourself from the relationship in order to find healing and peace.

(2) **Change an abusive work situation:** You may have to change your job or your vocation, in some cases, to find hope instead of despair. You may need to make plans to pursue higher education, so you can find a job that you will enjoy and will give meaning to your life. Doing so may help you overcome destructive thoughts or behaviors.

8. Summary of reasons many people change their mind to choose life instead of death:

(1) **Changes within a person's heart and behaviors:**
- Self-forgiveness
- Forgiving others
- Learning to manage one's emotional pain
- Stopping alcohol and drug abuse
- Realizing life has purpose
- Learning to love oneself
- Learning to process grief and loss
- Recognizing twisted logic and changing it
- Getting rid of boredom by finding a new direction in life
- Healing from depressive thoughts

(2) **Family support plays a big part in changing hearts:**
- Not wanting to hurt the family
- Realizing how much the family loves them
- Having a supportive family
- Recognizing the value of their family

(3) **Help from professionals and others:**
- Professional counseling
- Pastoral counseling and spiritual guidance
- Supportive friends
- Medical doctors and prescriptions

(4) **Religious reasons that changed their hearts:**

- Finding hope in Christ
- Fearing eternal hell
- Not wanting to die in vain
- Finding comfort and encouragement in God
- Putting God first and loving God
- Reading the Bible, prayer and meditation
- Going to church
- Resisting the spirit of despair
- Having supportive believers
- Finding joy in serving God
- Freed from the spirit of torment
- Finding purpose according to God's plan
- Going on a mission trip to gain new insights
- Recognizing God's blessings in life

(5) **Change in situations and finding new meaning:**

- Getting out of abusive relationships
- Finding a new job and gaining confidence
- Deciding to go to school to prepare for the future
- Getting involved in helping others
- Meeting people who care about them
- Having children that they love
- Finding someone they love and being loved in return

Chapter Twenty Four

Spiritual Counseling After Suicide

I have counseled at the hospital in many critical situations. I have also counseled many inmates, individually and in group, in critical incidents such as delivering death notifications and counseling after a suicide. I will share one incident that might give you some insight on how to help others with spiritual guidance and share what I have learned from this experience.

A young man named Mike (not his real name) committed suicide while incarcerated. The housing unit he was assigned to was in turmoil. Many grown men were breaking down and crying. This happened right after I had received the news that my nephew committed suicide and just before I left for Korea.

First, I provided individual counseling for whomever needed to talk to a chaplain. Then, I went inside the housing unit where Mike died. I gathered all the inmates, about 27, and led group counseling for three days, about two hours each time.

We talked and processed many areas in those sessions. First, I asked them to write down any questions they might have concerning Mike. Then, I went over each question, answering them to help the inmates process grief and loss. Following are the questions I gathered from them and how I answered them.

Interestingly, the following questions are very common whenever I lead individual or group counseling, whether it's a hospital setting, jail or with individuals who have lost someone due to suicide.

1. Questions asked concerning suicide:

(1) **Eternal consequence of suicide:** "What happens to the soul when people commit suicide? Do they go to hell?" This is a controversial issue for many people. Different denominations have different beliefs because suicide is so troublesome and more unsettling than any other cause of death. Some people believe that when people commit suicide, they go to hell. There is no Bible verse saying that people who commit suicide will go to hell or heaven. Suicide is self-murder and it is sin, and salvation comes from believing in Jesus.

Some people believe that if the suicide was a believer, God will forgive them. There are others who believe that unless you repent of your sins before you die, you will go to hell, and people who commit suicide may not have repented. Both views believe that salvation comes from believing in Jesus, not by deeds. The difference between these two views are: the first group believes that once people are saved they are saved forever, no matter what kind of sin they commit. God can forgive even self-murder, suicide.

The second group believes that you can lose salvation if you don't follow the Lord all the way, and suicide is sin, following the devil's suggestion, a rejection of God's plan. The issue of salvation is complicated. We really don't know whether a person truly believed in God and had a relationship with Christ before they died.

We can't say whether the person went to heaven or hell. Salvation is between the individual and God. One thing is clear; the family members of the suicide victim become victims for the rest of their lives, live in hell with anger, regrets, shame, false guilt, grief and pain if they don't experience healing from God. In addition, many families agonize because they fear that their loved ones are in hell because they believe God does not forgive the sin of suicide.

I believe God's grace is greater than our sin and He covers our weaknesses and forgives us if we are children of God. I want to believe that my father is in heaven with God even though he committed suicide. However, I am not sure whether he truly believed in God. I don't know if my father is in heaven or hell. I rely on God's grace in that matter.

I am warning anyone who thinks God will forgive them even if they commit suicide. Don't commit a grave sin that will grieve your family and friends for the rest of their lives. God can heal your broken heart and can release you from pain if you will turn to Him for help.

Get help from people who can help you. Listen to the Word of God and reject the devil's deceptive lies. Paul said, "What shall we say, then? Shall we go on sinning so that grace may increase? By no means! We died to sin; how can we live in it any longer?...Therefore do not let sin reign in your mortal body so that you obey its evil desires. Do not offer the parts of your body to sin, as instruments of wickedness, but rather offer yourselves to God." (Romans 6:1-2, 12-13a)

(2) **Dealing with Blame:** "Who is responsible for the death?" Many times people either turn on the person who committed suicide and are angry with that person, or they blame someone else or themselves. I told the inmates that blame is a part of the grieving process when there is a suicide. People will try to understand why this has happened. People ask for explanations to the unanswerable questions, and in the process, they tend to blame someone. That is one aspect of grieving, but we should not stay stuck in it.

I assured them that it wasn't anybody's fault: if a person is determined to kill himself/herself, no one can stop them. They can be stopped one time, but will try again if their goal in life is killing themselves. Someone can only be released from suicidal and self-destructive behaviors when they wanting to change their mind to live instead of wanting to die.

One inmate shared that Mike was having relationship problems before he killed himself. A broken relationship is not to blame. Suicide happens when people cannot handle life's problems and don't know how to deal with them. A relationship problem may be just one more stressful event that happened to him, but I don't believe that is the only reason. There were many other losses Mike had experienced before the broken relationship has happened; he was not able to process them constructively.

(3) **Dealing with guilt and regrets:** "How do you forgive yourself for not being able to save that person from killing themselves?" I explained that there are two types of people who think about suicide. One is a determined person, whom we can stop repeatedly, but eventually they will kill themselves because they are determined to die.

Unless their way of thinking changes, no one can save them from killing themselves. I believe miracles can happen to those determined people, and they might change their minds. I have seen people change because they experienced healing through God. There is more of a chance that we can permanently stop someone who is momentarily suicidal because of a temporary distressful situation. The second type of suicidal person is who we can help. No one has the responsibility but the one who committed the crime of self-murder.

(4) **Dealing with anger:** Some express anger toward the person who committed suicide. Again, blame is a part of the grieving process when there is a suicide. I told the inmates that there are some people who cannot handle pain constructively and become destructive. So we need to have compassion for the persons who didn't learn how to process pain and end up killing themselves.

(5) **Dealing with sleepless nights:** Meditation on the Scripture and prayer will help. I asked the inmates to continuously pray for each other for healing, and especially to pray for the family.

(6) **Dealing with fear:** "Does the spirit of the dead hang around the pod?" Many inmates told me that they were afraid of even looking at Mike's room. I told them that I believe when a person dies, they either go to heaven or hell, so there

is no reason to fear their spirit. God can give us dreams and visions of a deceased person to give us comfort, but not to scare us.

God does not want us to seek communication with the dead through mediums. "Do not turn to mediums or seek out spiritists, for you will be defiled by them. I am the Lord your God." (Leviticus 19:31) Demons can disguise themselves to look like a dead person to deceive us. If that should happen and you are scared you, then rebuke that spirit, "Be gone in the name of Jesus." We don't need to be afraid of those spirits, because God is greater than they are.

(7) **Dealing with family:** "What about the family? How are they doing?" I told them that I was glad that Mike's mother wanted to talk to a chaplain, and I was able to communicate with her. She was in terrible pain and grief, so we need to pray for her and the rest of Mike's family.

2. Reflection on sessions:

After all the questions and answers, I led the inmates in prayer for healing of those who were affected by grief and loss, especially for the family. I handed out the brochure I wrote: "Healing from Grief and Loss: A 30-Day Prayer Project" to help those who suffer from grief and pain caused by death and loss. This prayer project is included in Chapter Eleven.

The second day I listened to the inmates talk about how they were doing. They talked about how they were feeling and ended with prayer.

The third day, it seemed everyone was much calmer than the first day because they had talked about their concerns and troubles. At this time, I said if anyone would like to write a letter to Mike's mom, now was a good time to do so. Some asked for more time, so I told them I would pick their letters up the next day. The following day, I gathered quite a few letters.

The discussions on how to process grief have helped the group. I saw lives being transformed from anxiousness to calmness. I answered many questions and helped the inmates process their grief and loss. Men who participated to talk in a group counseling had the time to talk and process different areas. The ones who broke down at first, seemed to be doing much better. Many shared that these group sessions helped them and brought healing.

Another man who also broke down the first day had trouble sleeping for a couple of days. Then, he had a dream that brought healing to him so he was able to process his grief. He shared that in one of his dreams, Mike appeared and asked him for forgiveness for lying and taking his life. This gave the man peace. He was able to sleep after that. I wrote a letter to Mike's mother and sent it to her along with the inmates' letters. Here is the letter I wrote to her:

Hi, I am Chaplain Yong Hui McDonald from Adams County Detention Facility. I have talked to you on the phone but wanted to write you this note because you have been in our thoughts and prayers.

I am very sorry about the loss of your son, Mike. Many of your son's friends in the same housing unit are grieving because of this horrible tragedy. Mike was a very good friend to many of them, and his loss hit them all very hard. To help them deal with this tragedy, I held meetings with them for three days straight. Many of them have been praying for you since this happened, and we prayed as a group for you, as well. We are all very, very sorry for your loss and the pain you are suffering.

All of Mike's friends felt the need to do something for you in this time of great sadness, so we are enclosing a card and individual letters they wrote to you expressing their feelings for Mike.

My father committed suicide years ago, and I am leaving for Korea tomorrow to comfort my older brother whose 32-year-old son recently committed suicide. I tell you this to let you know that in some small measure, I too have suffered, although I know I can never feel the depths of your pain as a mother losing a son. We will be praying for you and your family for comfort and God's healing presence. It is our hope that you might get some comfort through these letters and card. Here is the Scripture that comforts me, and I would like to share it with you.

"Do not let your hearts be troubled. Trust in God; trust also in me. In my Father's house are many rooms; if it were not so, I would have told you. I am going there to prepare a place for you. And if I go and prepare a place for you, I will come back and take you to be with me that you also may be where I am." (John 14:1-3)

God bless you and your family!

Sincerely,

Yong Hui V. McDonald

3. What did I learn from this tragedy?

After I told my supervisor how I handled this grief counseling, he told me I should write a book to help others learn how to counsel after suicide. A couple of months later, Mike's mother came to visit our facility and wanted to see me. She thanked me for the support and the letters, especially the inmates' letters. I still keep in touch with her. After this event, I made a brochure for those who are suicidal. I have written many other brochures to help people experience spiritual healing. I gave them to the facility medical unit, mental health and social workers, so they can have access to these brochures if they want to use them.

4. Is there any grief counseling needed for staff when a suicide happens?

At the hospital where I work, if there is a suicide, the hospital immediately provides professional counselors and chaplains for the staff. I have encountered deputies that go through the same stages of grief and loss when there is a suicide at the facility, especially when it happens in their module. For those who were open to it, I spent some time talking with them so they could process their grief and loss. The sooner they could handle different areas, the sooner they can go back to a normal stage. Grieving people cannot make sound judgments under stressful situations.

Conclusion

The goal of grief spiritual counseling is to help people recognize the areas they need to work on so they can work through different areas of grief and loss. Then, they will not get stuck in immobilizing pain. Healing depends on how they are able to process grief and loss. It's challenging to help others who are grieving, but there are also rewards after you help them to process their grief and come out emotionally, mentally and spiritually healthy.

Chapter Twenty Five

The Stages of Grief and Loss

The following are stages of grief that people experience. Some people may go back and forth between different stages, and not everyone goes through all the stages. Reaction to death depends on the relationship between the bereaved and deceased, where they were mentally and emotionally, what their faith background is and many other factors.

1. **Shock and denial** — They heard the news, saw the nursing staff trying to revive the person, or the body being taken out — Initial shock, traumatized, obsessed with incidents and death, numbness, confusion, emotionally immobilized, overcome with emotion, crying, screaming.

2. **Questioning** — Tension rising, anxiety, anger, blame, sleepless nights, nightmares, distress, and have many questions concerning death.

3. **Trigger feeling** — Guilt, regrets, depression, breakdown, shame, blame, deep sadness, unknown fear and theological questions. You will be breaking down whenever you are reminded of the deceased person.

4. **Processing grief and loss** — Finding answers for questions, acceptance, closure, clarity, understanding, compassion, knowledge, forgiveness, letting go, peace, healing and forgiveness.

5. **Acceptance of death and healing** — After you have gone through all the areas of grief and loss and let go of your loved ones, you will be able to go on with your life. You will find peace, live with good memories of your loved one, not grieve, and not suffer from triggers of sorrow or pain any more.

Note: To learn more about suicide and how to help others who are suicidal, read the book, *Twisted Logic, The Shadow of Suicide.*

Part Four

Chapter Twenty Six

Nine Areas of Spiritual Distraction

"My son, do not forget my teaching, but keep my commands in your heart, for they will prolong your life many years and bring you prosperity. Let love and faithfulness never leave you; bind them around your neck, write them on the tablet of your heart. Then you will win favor and a good name in the sight of God and man. Trust in the LORD with all your heart and lean not on your own understanding; in all your ways acknowledge him, and he will make your paths straight. Do not be wise in your own eyes; fear the LORD and shun evil. This will bring health to your body and nourishment to your bones." (Proverbs 3:1-8)

Prayer: "Lord, Jesus, teach me how to trust you in every way. Bless me with your wisdom so I can think, say, and do things according to your will. Help me avoid any distractions in life so I can follow you with no distractions but love for you and trust that you are with me no matter what. Teach me how to listen to your voice so I can obey you. Bless me with the gift of faith so I can always follow you and serve you. Teach me about your deep love, Jesus, and fill my heart with your love."

What is Spiritual Distraction?

Jesus teaches about the importance of loving God and serving God. "Hearing that Jesus had silenced the Sadducees, the Pharisees got together. One of them, an expert in the law, tested him with this question: 'Teacher, which is the greatest commandment in the Law?' Jesus replied: 'Love the Lord your God with all your heart and with all your soul and with all your mind. This is the first and greatest commandment. And the second is like it: Love your neighbor as yourself.'" (Matthew 22:34-38)

Moses teaches us about the importance of loving and serving God as well: Moses said, "And now, O Israel, what does the LORD your God ask of you but to fear the LORD your God, to walk in all his ways, to love him, to serve the LORD your God with all your heart and with all your soul." (Deuteronomy 10:12)

What is spiritual distraction? Spiritual distraction is anything that hinders us from fully loving and serving God. Every day we encounter many distractions in life. If we are not careful, we can be distracted and neglect to love the Lord our God with all our heart, mind, soul, and strength. We would be unable to fully serve the Lord our God. The world needs the message of God's love and the Gospel message of salvation that Jesus Christ has given us. If we are distracted from these messages, we will be unable to do what God wants us to do. Even when we have the passion, desire to love, and serve God.

Spiritual distraction will likely always be around us, big or small. This battle is not going to end until we are in our heavenly home. The purpose of this chapter is to give some insights into what exactly these spiritual distractions are: How to recognize them, how to avoid them. How to handle the distractions of life in a positive manner, so we can keep our focus on loving and serving the Lord with all our heart, mind, soul, and strength.

The causes of spiritual distractions

Every day we face many distractions with internal and external factors. There are many causes for spiritual distractions and here are some examples:

1. Our sinful nature:

Many of our distractions are caused by our sin. Sin opens the door to distractions and spiritual attacks. Our selfishness, unforgiving heart, lack of faith, spiritual immaturity, lack of spiritual discernment, impure and immoral thoughts, words, lifestyle, addictions, choosing the wrong friends, and love for the world bring spiritual distractions in our life.

When we love the world more than God, we fall into sin. John wrote, "Do not love the world or anything in the world. If anyone loves the world, the love of the Father is not in him. For everything in the world-- the cravings of sinful man, the lust of his eyes and the boasting of what he has and does-- comes not from the Father but from the world. The world and its desires pass away, but the man who does the will of God lives forever." (1 John 2:15-17)

Many distractions start in our hearts and minds, and we lose focus on God. Learning to live a godly life is done by obeying the Holy Spirit daily. Otherwise we end up living in sin and are challenged or overcome with distractions.

2. Others can become our distractions:

Our family, friends, spouse, and even both believers and non-believers can become our distractions. If their focus is not on loving and serving God, but loving and serving themselves, they will hinder our spiritual growth. Abusive situations can also open the door to spiritual distraction. When others become abusive and attack us, we begin to suffer from resentment, anger, hurt, pain, bitterness, and hate. When we don't forgive, and hold grudges, we live in sin. Sin opens the door for the devil to attack and torment. Handle distractions with wisdom from God's word, with the Holy Spirit's guidance.

We need to avoid people who will distract us from loving and serving God. We need to stay away from those who are self-centered, proud, abusive, violent, have bad character, and live immoral lifestyles having no fear of God.

Paul warns us: "Do not be misled: 'Bad company corrupts good character.' Come back to your senses as you ought, and stop sinning; for there are some who are ignorant of God-- I say this to your shame." (1 Corinthians 15:33-34)

Jesus also said that we can't follow him if we love our family more than him. "If anyone comes to me and does not hate his father and mother, his wife and children, his brothers and sisters-- yes, even his own life-- he cannot be my disciple. And anyone who does not carry his cross and follow me cannot be my disciple." (Luke 14:26-27) Hate doesn't mean we should mistreat, ignore or hurt our family. Hate in this context I believe is talking about our priorities. Whoever loves others and themselves more than Jesus can't follow him and do what God wants them to do.

3. Our weaknesses can become distractions:

There may be exceptions but most of the time our physical weaknesses can be beyond our control. Our sickness and pain can distract our walk with the Lord. The Lord understands us and He will help us if we rely on Him. We can pray and ask for God's help and sometimes the answer may be "no." That's what happened to Paul when he prayed in his weakness but he didn't give up loving and serving God.

Paul wrote, "To keep me from becoming conceited because of these surpassingly great revelations, there was given me a thorn in my flesh, a messenger of Satan, to torment me. Three times I pleaded with the Lord to take it away from me. But he said to me, 'My grace is sufficient for you, for my power is made perfect in weakness.' Therefore I will boast all the more gladly about my weaknesses, so that Christ's power may rest on me. That is why, for Christ's sake, I delight in weaknesses, in insults, in hardships, in persecutions, in difficulties. For when I am weak, then I am strong." (2 Corinthians 12:7-10)

4. Our hardships can become distractions:

When we try to serve God, there may be spiritual distractions especially where there is persecution of faith. Paul had escaped death many times because of persecution. He knew going to Jerusalem meant that he would be facing more persecution and possible death.

Other Christians prophesied that Paul would be imprisoned in Jerusalem and warned him not to go. Paul was not afraid of the hardships he would face. Paul said, "And now, compelled by the Spirit, I am going to Jerusalem, not knowing what will happen to me there. I only know that in every city the Holy Spirit warns me that prison and hardships are facing me. However, I consider my life worth nothing to me, if only I may finish the race and complete the task the Lord Jesus has given me-- the task of testifying to the gospel of God's grace." (Acts 20:22-24)

Paul knew how to handle distractions by listening to, understanding and obeying the Holy Spirit, not other people. Paul's determination to serve the Lord encourages us to follow the Holy Spirit in any circumstance. Also, his example teaches us to serve our loving God. Sometimes distraction is testing our faith. Paul shows us how we need to be faithful to the Father.

5. Ungodly culture and media can be distractions:

Spiritual distraction is much broader when social and cultural moral standards go against God's word. They can promote an immoral lifestyle. Fortunately, there is Christian media where God's values are presented. However, many of our media are controlled by people who don't love God and don't have biblical moral values. Therefore they promote immoral values. Unless we can filter or choose what we read, watch or hear, we will have distractions and hinder our spiritual growth. We have to guard our exposure to ungodly shows in media. Our minds will be affected and the door will be opened for the devil to attack us. It starts with impure thoughts that can be planted in our memories.

Our exposure to sexual perversion, pornography, and violence as acceptable behaviors in media promotes a lifestyle that is against the word of God. The Lord said, "Make every effort to live in peace with all men and to be holy; without holiness no one will see the Lord." (Hebrews 12:14) "But just as he who called you is holy, so be holy in all you do; for it is written: 'Be holy, because I am holy.'" (1 Peter 1:15-16)

We need to live a life that will reflect our holy God. If others tell us differently, we need to reject it. Otherwise they become our spiritual distractions.

6. Natural disasters can become distractions:

There are many things that we cannot control and this is one of them. How we handle this difficult distraction will determine whether the trauma can help us. We will either grow closer to God or it will stifle our spiritual growth, turning away from the Lord. If we interpret the disaster as God doing bad things to hurt us, our perception of our loving God will be distorted. Understand and accept that God is good no matter what happens. Natural disaster can happen to all.

Instead of blaming God, we should turn to Him for help. When we focus on God's goodness, we can be grateful for what He did to help us. We will be able to help others in times of distress. If we can find strength to see the God of mercy and compassion, our faith will grow.

Paul's journey as a prisoner to Rome wasn't a smooth one. The ship he was on, faced the storms. This was a natural course of weather. However, God helped all the ship crew through Paul. He received a message from an angel so Paul shared the message and encouraged others.

Paul stated, "After the men had gone a long time without food, Paul stood up before them and said: 'Men, you should have taken my advice not to sail from Crete; then you would have spared yourselves this damage and loss. But now I urge you to keep up your courage, because not one of you will be lost; only the ship will be destroyed. Last night an angel of the God whose I am and whom I serve stood beside me and said, 'Do not be afraid, Paul. You must stand trial before Caesar; and God has graciously given you the lives of all who sail with you.' So keep up your courage, men, for I have faith in God that it will happen just as he told me." (Acts 27:21-25)

7. Loving money can become distractions:

Whatever we receive are gifts from the Lord. We are the caretakers of what we have received. When we don't recognize this and place money before God and neglecting others, wealth becomes our distraction.

Paul wrote, "For the love of money is a root of all kinds of evil. Some people, eager for money, have wandered from the faith and pierced themselves with many griefs. But you, man of God, flee from all this, and pursue righteousness, godliness, faith, love, endurance and gentleness." (1 Timothy 6:10-11)

Jesus had a lesson for a rich young man about wealth. "Now a man came up to Jesus and asked, 'Teacher, what good thing must I do to get eternal life?' 'Why do you ask me about what is good?' Jesus replied. 'There is only One who is good. If you want to enter life, obey the commandments.' 'Which ones?' the man inquired. Jesus replied, 'Do not murder, do not commit adultery, do not steal, do not give false testimony, honor your father and mother,' and 'love your neighbor as yourself.' 'All these I have kept,' the young man said. 'What do I still lack?' Jesus answered, 'If you want to be perfect, go, sell your possessions and give to the poor, and you will have treasure in heaven. Then come, follow me.' When the young man heard this, he went away sad, because he had great wealth. Then Jesus said to his disciples, 'I tell you the truth, it is hard for a rich man to enter the kingdom of heaven.' Jesus said, 'Again I tell you, it is easier for a camel to go through the eye of a needle than for a rich man to enter the kingdom of God.'" (Matthew 19:16-24)

The rich young man chose not to obey and follow Jesus because he had a great wealth. The gifts we receive will be our spiritual distraction if we become selfish, serve only ourselves, and don't help other humans.

8. Traumatic losses can become distractions:

Loss of people, job, home, love, freedom or anything important to us, will start the grieving process. Difficulties caused by outside forces due to your loss or absence of loved ones can also become spiritual distractions. In times of grief and loss, not every believer understands just how important it is to continue our walk with God. He can bring healing and restore your broken heart. In this case, distraction can also become a blessing when you understand God's healing power and compassion.

To overcome distractions caused by losses, we need to see things from the Lord's perspective. Our lives here on earth are temporary. Our purpose is to love and serve God with a life that glorifies Him. When we get discouraged and lose focus on God because of things or people, we lose sight of why we are created. That's when we lose peace and joy in our hearts. We need to keep focused on God to gain strength, comfort, and healing.

"But our citizenship is in heaven. And we eagerly await a Savior from there, the Lord Jesus Christ, who, by the power that enables him to bring everything under his control, will transform our lowly bodies so that they will be like his glorious body." (Philippians 3:20-21)

9. Spiritual attack can become distractions:

The devil has ways to distract us in our loving walk with the Lord. Peter teaches us how we can defeat spiritual distractions. "Humble yourselves, therefore, under God's mighty hand, that he may lift you up in due time. Cast all your anxiety on him because he cares for you. Be self-controlled and alert. Your enemy the devil prowls around like a roaring lion looking for someone to devour. Resist him, standing firm in the faith, because you know that your brothers throughout the world are undergoing the same kind of sufferings. And the God of all grace, who called you to his eternal glory in Christ, after you have suffered a little while, will himself restore you and make you strong, firm and steadfast. To him be the power for ever and ever. Amen." (1 Peter 5:6-11)

God will guide us through times of distraction if we humble ourselves and ask Him to help us. We also need to recognize the devil's attack and resist it in Jesus' name. The devil tries to tempt us to fall into sin and sin becomes our distraction. We should be mindful of what we think, say, and do for the glory of

God, instead of our own. Whatever we choose, it will affect our relationship with the Lord. We need to avoid spiritual distractions so we can truly love God as we should. Serve Him by loving others as the Holy Spirit leads.

Summary of negative effects of spiritual distraction:

We may:
- Not be able to love God to the fullest.
- Become ineffective in spreading God's word.
- Fall into the sin of loving people and worldly possessions more than God.
- Fall away from God's grace and end up grieving the Lord.
- Not be able to use our spiritual gifts to serve the Lord to our potential.
- Be under spiritual attack: oppressed, tormented, and living in misery.
- Be distracted by someone who paired with a spirit of distraction.
- Become a distraction to ones who follow God, and others who want to grow in faith.
- End up ignoring the Holy Spirit and being disobedient.
- Lose our peace, in turn living in turmoil, confusion, and misery.
- Neglect our time of prayer and conversations with God.
- Live in sin and walk on the path of unrighteous.

Note: To learn more about how to recognize spiritual distraction, read the book, *Spiritual Distraction and Understanding*.

Chapter Twenty Seven

Characteristics of People Who Distract Others

People Who Distract Others

This chapter will focus on how our relationship with the wrong people can bring distractions. In Paul's teaching he taught people what kind of people they should stay away from.

Paul warns people in Rome:

"I urge you, brothers, to watch out for those who cause divisions and put obstacles in your way that are contrary to the teaching you have learned. **Keep away from them**. For such people are not serving our Lord Christ, but their own appetites. By smooth talk and flattery they deceive the minds of naive people." (Romans 16:17-18)

Paul warns Timothy about a man:

"Alexander the metalworker did me a great deal of harm. The Lord will repay him for what he has done. **You too should be on your guard against him**, because he strongly opposed our message. At my first defense, no one came to my support, but everyone deserted me. May it not be held against them. But the Lord stood at my side and gave me strength, so that through me the message might be fully proclaimed and all the Gentiles might hear it. And I was delivered from the lion's mouth. The Lord will rescue me from every evil attack and will bring me safely to his heavenly kingdom. To him be glory for ever and ever. Amen." (2 Timothy 4:14-18)

Paul had experienced people who distracted his spiritual journey and ministry. We need to be aware of others who can distract us from getting closer to God and being effective in ministry. There are people who are used by spirits of distraction. However, not all spiritual distractions are spiritual attacks. Also, we need to realize that the people who are used by the spirit of distraction are not any different from us. They could even be both believers and non-believers. Understand, anyone is vulnerable to be used by the devil to distract others and the person may not even be aware of it.

People who are used by the spirit of distraction can break the harmony in the body of Christ by justifying their sin and working with evil spirits. Paul talks about our sinful nature which distracts us from growing in faith and serving God.

He wrote, "The acts of the sinful nature are obvious: sexual immorality, impurity and debauchery; idolatry and witchcraft; hatred, discord, jealousy, fits of rage, selfish ambition, dissensions, factions and envy; drunkenness, orgies, and the like. I warn you, as I did before, that those who live like this will not inherit the kingdom of God." (Galatians 5:19-22)

Paul also wrote how the Holy Spirit can help us to bear good fruit to live a transformed life. "But the fruit of the Spirit is love, joy, peace, patience, kindness, goodness, faithfulness, gentleness and self-control. Against such things there is no law. Those who belong to Christ Jesus have crucified the sinful nature with its passions and desires." (Galatians 5:23-24)

We need to pursue godly life that will bear the fruit of the Spirit which can create peace and unity among people and honor and glorify God. There are people who can distract other's spiritual journey and here is the list of characteristics and behaviors associated with the spirit of distraction.

1. Characteristics of people who distract others

(1) Demand your time — They demand so much of your time in many ways by phone, email or in personal contact. They focus on themselves and have no consideration of others' time or wishes. We need to stand guard against anyone who demands so much of our time in our journey that we can't grow in faith.

(2) Passionate — They may seem to have passion for God, desire to grow spiritually and eager to serve God. However, their focus is to receive recognition and self-promotion. The problem is that they are not doing it for God's glory. Spiritual leaders are looking for people who are eager to serve, so it's easy for them to be happy with these people without determining or understanding their motivation.

(3) Critical — They have a critical mind and tongue. If they see something they don't agree with, or something that bothers them, they hurt others by attacking them with critical, negative, and brutal words. If these people are not accepted in other churches, or if you notice that many people are avoiding this person, that may be one of the reasons. People don't like to be hurt and these people don't see how much they are hurting others with their words.

(4) Can't take criticism — if others criticize them, they don't take time to see themselves. Instead, they immediately respond with offensive words and attack others with inappropriate behaviors.

(5) Some are leaders — They can be magnetic and charismatic leaders; however, it's not in a positive or productive way for the whole body of Christ. They are very good at convincing people through words and lies. The followers are vulnerable people who lack spiritual discernment. Many cults are born from these deceptive leaders.

(6) Gifted, but proud — some are very gifted in teaching or fundraising. This is a gift from God. Instead of giving God glory and credit, these people give themselves credit. Even though they give the glory to God, deep in their hearts they are only saying this while believing they did it.

(7) Attack leaders — They have no respect for spiritual authority and/or leaders who oversee them. Consequently, they attack leaders if they think the leader is not capable, or they may attack personal characteristics even without reason. They don't know how to solve problems peacefully. By bringing others down, they think they can elevate themselves.

(8) Blame others — Even though they are the cause of the problems, they cannot see that it is their fault because they are blind to it.

(9) Lack Emotional Intelligence — They don't realize how much pain they are causing in others. Their emotional intelligence is low as far as how much they understand pain, suffering, and turmoil in many people's lives.

(10) Don't forgive — They dwell on the past; past hurt, pain, and rejection by others. They are filled with anger and just don't want to forgive.

(11) Harass others — They contact people by phone, personal contact, email and any other means in order to abuse them. Even though they may have been told to stop contact, these people don't have any respect for others' wishes and keep attacking people emotionally, mentally, and spiritually. These people act like they have the right to go over the boundaries and intimidate people as much as they can. Some may stop this behavior when the other person puts a restraining order against them.

(12) Abusive — They abuse others mentally, emotionally and physically. These people have no fear of the law and they break the law. They act out their anger by attacking others who are weaker than they are. The only way to stop them is by restraining them through authorities and through prayer.

(13) Victim Mentality — They identify themselves as victims of rejection. They try to get others' compassion by bringing up how they were mistreated, but in reality, they cause hurt to others and create problems with them. Those with the "victim" mentality will tell others how they were mistreated to get sympathy. Those who lack spiritual discernment are the most vulnerable. Consequently, this can create a division among people and distract them from what they are supposed to do.

(14) Kicked out of organizations or churches — Their behavior is destructive which can, in turn, get them kicked out of the church or organizations where their destructive behaviors have been recognized.

(15) Lack Humility — They like to put themselves in the lime-light and give themselves glory more than giving God glory. This is what they do to get others attention and recognition more than focusing on serving God. Even though they may act humble, their humility is not their virtue. They have superior feelings that they are gifted more than others.

(16) Lack consistency — These people have two sides to their personality. To other spiritual leaders they are critical and brutal. To those who are not in a position of authority and perceive these people as leaders, they can be amazingly sweet and gentle.

(17) Seek position of power — Some seek a position of power, so they can control people and projects. They know how to work with systems so they work their way to a position of authority as soon as they become a part of the organization. Therefore, be aware of those who want to be in a position of power when they have been in the organization for a short period of time.

(18) Giving gifts to buy love — They shower people with gifts to get others attention and love. They may try to show others how generous they are. Even if people don't want gifts, they give them anyway because they think they need them.

(19) Aggressive — When they don't get what they want, they can become angry, critical, and abusive to others. They act immature and attack people. They have no regard for others wishes. Even if others told them not to contact them, they will contact them and have no concept of the consequences from their actions. They do not take into consideration how this affects others.

(20) Lack integrity — They will try to get what they want without consideration of whether it's right or wrong.

(21) Lack Logical thinking — They don't think about the consequences of their destructive actions. Their thoughts lack common sense.

(22) Control people — They try to control and manipulate people with funds and projects. If others are not open to their suggestions, they may take the funds and leave.

(23) Control funds — When they gather funds, they treat them as if it's their money instead of God's. They try to control funds on their own terms even though the funds were raised for a specific purpose.

(24) Create ungodly media — These people have such low moral values that they promote and create a sinful, lustful environment not only for themselves but others. They create lustful and immoral media in writing or movies. They also prey on others who lack high moral values and innocent victims. Unless you recognize their low moral values and resist by not participating with them, you can be affected negatively.

(25) They serve other gods besides God of the Bible — Spending time with people who are working with the devil can affect you. This is something that people who have a gift of discernment will recognize. Many times people who work with spirit of distraction are deceived, oppressed and tormented.

They may also hear the demon's voice telling them to take an action and carry it out and hurt themselves or others. People who do not know how to discern voices can also act compulsively without thinking about the consequences. If you spend time with them, the demons that work with these people can attack you and you may be tormented. It's best to avoid people who work with spirit of distraction if you can. Unless you have strong faith in God to help them and they are ready to open to God for healing, you can't help them.

Pray and ask the Lord's direction. If the Lord will tell you to avoid them, it's best to avoid them. If you cannot handle them spiritually, that means the demons working with them are much stronger than you, so avoid them.

(26) People may be suffering from addiction — Paul warns: "Do not be misled: 'Bad company corrupts good character.' Come back to your senses as you ought, and stop sinning; for there are some who are ignorant of God-- I say this to

your shame." (1 Corinthians 15:33-35) Many people fall into a trap of addiction because people around them were using them. There are times we may not be able to avoid addicted people who are not sober or abstaining, but if we can, we should avoid them.

Families and friends are distracted from their normal life and are in turmoil because of their loved one's addiction and addictive thoughts and actions. Some people you can help but unless that person who is addicted wants to change, they will become a distraction to you and you may have to have distance yourself from them if you can.

2. Spiritual distraction and spiritual bondage:

Have you come across people that have the above characteristics? If you find that your answer is "yes" on many of them, you may be affected by those who work with spirit of distraction. If you are overwhelmed because of people who distract you, there is a chance you are under spiritual attack. The more disturbing characteristics someone has, the more they are in spiritual bondage and work with spiritual distraction.

There are three kinds of people who become a distraction to others:
1) Those who don't recognize what they are doing and keep distracting others.
2) Those who feel they justify their destructive behavior and will not stop. They deliberately use distraction for self-satisfaction.
3) Those who recognize what they did was wrong. They repent and stop becoming a distraction.

One strong spirit of distraction uses people who seem to have many gifts and leadership skills. They continuously cause distraction for others. In fact, they not only distract others, they become abusive! If they succeed in attacking others, they can be negatively affected. It can be combined with spiritual attack and oppression so that they can't be productive in ministry. That's what the devil promotes among people who are not aware of spiritual attacks. This spirit of distraction uses people who do not have spiritual discernment. People used by the spirit of distraction often don't realize they are influenced by the devil.

How can we recognize these deceived people? Jesus teaches us how to discern this: "Thus, by their fruit you will recognize them. Not everyone who says to me, 'Lord, Lord,' will enter the kingdom of heaven, but only he who does the will of my Father who is in heaven." (Matthew 7:20-21)

People either work for God or promote the devil's destructive work. Unfortunately, there are people who are deceived, and they think they work for God but in reality they work for the devil. The devil will trick believers distracting other believers to fight against each other. This is a warning for all of us! We need to be aware of others who become distractions in our lives. Help with insight in the lives of leaders in the church. The devil will cause people to resist being humbled or prayer or accepting guidance from other godly people.

Be humble before God and ask if you have become a distraction to others in any way: First among our family and friends, then among other believers, non believers and spiritual leaders. If you feel the Lord is convicting you, pray, repent, and stop being disruptive or abusive toward others. If you don't fight the spirit of distraction's temptation, you may end up being a distraction to yourself and others.

3. Can spiritual "distraction" become "harassment" and "abuse"?

Yes, our spiritual distraction can become very serious. It will affect our daily life. There are three different degrees of relational spiritual distraction:

First stage - Mental and spiritual distraction. We can control and limit our contact with the other person.

Second stage - Distraction using words and actions and that person has crossed a boundary. There must be a limit on how much they can contact us. Phone, email, and any other unwanted or warranted means of invading our privacy is a spiritual distraction of harassment.

Third stage - Combines mental, spiritual, and physical abuse. This person has become abusive beyond your control. We have authorities intervene. Calling the police and placing a restraining order against person should stop their abusive behaviors. Be warned, this person is dangerous and may not stop. The only option is the police to save your life.

All distractions affect our walk with Christ. The negative distractions in the second and third stages are the most challenging and damaging. Distractions slowly but surely will get worse. Unwanted destructive words and actions of others affect our spiritual walk.

"Abuse" can be emotional, mental, spiritual and or can be combined with unwanted physical contact and violence. In America, harassment and physical abuse are against the law. God doesn't want us to be in any abusive relationship in any form. If you can stop harassment and abuse, do it. If you can't, get advice from others how to handle it. If it gets violent, you might have to call the police to make it stop. The sooner we can recognize and stop distraction, the sooner we can focus on God.

We become constructive living for His kingdom. Don't forget the most important aspect of life: loving God and serving Him in every way. You are worthy of God's love and protection and know the Lord has not left you in any situation.

Jesus is calling you to follow him to make disciples of nations. "Then Jesus came to them and said, 'All authority in heaven and on earth has been given to me. Therefore go and make disciples of all nations, baptizing them in the name of the Father and of the Son and of the Holy Spirit, and teaching them to obey everything I have commanded you. And surely I am with you always, to the very end of the age.'" (Matthew 28:18-20) "'Come, follow me,' Jesus said, 'and I will make you fishers of men.'" (Matthew 4:19)

Chapter Twenty Eight

Jesus' Spiritual Distraction

There were many spiritual distractions Jesus faced while he was on earth, before his ministry preparation and after he started ministry. Here is a story of when he was preparing for a ministry through fasting and prayer.

"Then Jesus was led by the Spirit into the desert to be tempted by the devil. After fasting forty days and forty nights, he was hungry. The tempter came to him and said, 'If you are the Son of God, tell these stones to become bread.' Jesus answered, 'It is written: Man does not live on bread alone, but on every word that comes from the mouth of God.' Then the devil took him to the holy city and had him stand on the highest point of the temple. 'If you are the Son of God,' he said, 'throw yourself down. For it is written: 'He will command his angels concerning you, and they will lift you up in their hands, so that you will not strike your foot against a stone.' Jesus answered him, 'It is also written: Do not put the Lord your God to the test.' Again, the devil took him to a very high mountain and showed him all the kingdoms of the world and their splendor. 'All this I will give you,' he said, 'if you will bow down and worship me.' Jesus said to him, 'Away from me, Satan! For it is written: Worship the Lord your God, and serve him only.' Then the devil left him, and angels came and attended him." (Matthew 4:1-11)

1. Appealing to physical needs more than spiritual needs:

This Scripture shows the devil tried to distract Jesus by reminding him of his physical needs. He asked him to turn stone to bread. Jesus answered, "It is written: Man does not live on bread alone, but on every word that comes from the mouth of God."

The devil tried to distract Jesus' fasting and prayer. When the devil tries to distract us, he appeals to our physical needs. We can forget about or neglect spiritual needs of knowing God's will and obeying the Holy Spirit. Jesus was trying to spend time with Father God to prepare his mission to save the world. The devil tried to distract Jesus' time with Father.

If we are only thinking about our own physical needs, we cannot focus on our spiritual needs. Jesus knew immediately how to resist the temptation by pointing out that not just physical, but spiritual needs can be met by the word of God. The word of God feeds our spirit. We should not neglect feeding our soul everyday by reading and meditating in the word.

2. Suggesting destructive behavior:

The devil also tried to distract Jesus by tempting him to hurt himself by suggesting a suicide attempt. The devil said God would send angels to protect him. Jesus came to the world with human flesh. He could get hurt if he jumped from a high place. The devil tried to distract Jesus by saying that God will save him. Jesus answered him, "It is also written: 'Do not put the Lord your God to the test.'"

Jesus has a full humanity and is also a divine nature God. That's why he was able to perform many miracles and was able to accomplish what Father God wanted on earth. However, throwing himself down to commit suicide was not God's plan. Jesus answered by saying we should not test God. God loves us and wants to take care of us. We should not listen to the devil's destructive suggestions and hurt ourselves in any way.

3. Appealing to desire for material possessions:

The devil's work is to make us worship something other than God, sometimes the devil himself. Jesus said to him, "Away from me, Satan! For it is written: Worship the Lord your God, and serve him only."

We need to rebuke the devil when he tries to tempt us to worship him. Only God is worthy of our love, worship and praise. Jesus showed us how we can fight spiritual distractions caused by the devil. We need to examine what we hear. The devil's attack starts by making wrong and destructive suggestions that appeal to us. If we are not aware and accept the devil's destructive idea, we fall into sin and turmoil. When this happens, we need to repent and ask for God's forgiveness and purification. "If we confess our sins, he is faithful and just and will forgive us our sins and purify us from all unrighteousness." (1 John 1:9)

Prayer: "Lord, Jesus, Help me to have wisdom to recognize spiritual distractions and avoid them. Help me to repent if I sinned in any way. Purify my heart. Forgive me for anything I did wrong. Purify my heart and teach me how to love you and serve you. Help me to live a holy life that will please you. Help me to live a godly life that will please you. I pray this is Jesus' name. Amen."

Note: To learn more about spiritual distraction, read the book, *Spiritual Distraction and Understanding.*

Part Five

Chapter Twenty Nine

The Holy Spirit and The Believers

1. How do you know you have received the Holy Spirit?

One way of knowing if you have received the Holy Spirit is to understand how the Spirit works with believers. There are some people who invite Jesus into their life, and they experience a supernatural experience right away. They know that the Holy Spirit is real. However, not everyone has this experience.

If you are one of those who have not experienced the Spirit in a supernatural way, how do you know that the Spirit is in you and working with you? If you believe in Jesus, you have received the Holy Spirit. The Spirit is with you and revealing things about God in different ways.

"Therefore I tell you that no one who is speaking by the Spirit of God says, 'Jesus be cursed,' and no one can say, 'Jesus is Lord,' except by the Holy Spirit." (1 Corinthians 12:3)

2. The Spirit helps you to know you are a sinner.

If you have felt and understood you are a sinner, this is the work of the Spirit. You cannot understand you are sinful unless the Holy Spirit reveals it to you.

"When he (Spirit) comes, he will convict the world of guilt in regard to sin and righteousness and judgment." (John 16:8)

Repentance: The Holy Spirit helps us see we are terrible sinners. We cannot help but ask for forgiveness from the Lord. Tears of repentance are the work of the Holy Spirit. This knowledge of God's holiness, knowing that He is not happy with our sinful desires, and actions comes from the Spirit. Understanding this will help us humble ourselves before God, knowing that we are not any better than others. We are all sinners in need of God's forgiveness. We should not judge others. If we are humble and want to change, the Holy Spirit will point out what is good and evil so we can live a life pleasing to God.

You feel bad when you do wrong: This is the Spirit teaching you, to learn what is right and wrong. Ask the Lord to forgive you and don't repeat the same mistake. The more you recognize your sin and repent, you will be cleansed and have a closer relationship with God. If you believe that God has forgiven you and you have peace, that is the work of the Spirit.

The Spirit asks you to forgive: If you have a nagging thought that is prodding you to forgive, the Spirit is speaking to you. The Spirit has started cleaning your heart. He is trying to help you let go of resentment, anger, bitterness, hatred, and a vengeful spirit so you don't fall into sin.

You will not have peace until you forgive. Take care of your soul by blessing, praying and loving others, even those who have hurt you. Then the Lord will reward you with peace, joy and healing from hurt and pain.

3. The Holy Spirit gives us spiritual understanding, knowledge, wisdom and revelation.

"There are different kinds of gifts, but the same Spirit. There are different kinds of service, but the same Lord. There are different kinds of working, but the same God works all of them in all men. Now to each one the manifestation of the Spirit is given for the common good. To one there is given through the Spirit the message of wisdom, to another the message of knowledge by means of the same Spirit." (1 Corinthians 12:4-8)

The Spirit opened your heart to understand the Bible: The Bible was a difficult book to read, but suddenly one day you opened it and you understood what the Word of God was saying. You understand the Bible is not the same as other books. The Spirit led people to write it and He will help you understand what the Word of God is saying.

You have come to believe what Jesus has done for you: You believe that Jesus died for your sins. You haven't seen it but you believe. There is no way you can understand and believe the Bible without the Holy Spirit revealing it to you.

"The man without the Spirit does not accept the things that come from the Spirit of God, for they are foolishness to him, and he cannot understand them, because they are spiritually discerned." (1 Corinthians 2:14)

The Spirit helps you understand God's love: You believe God loves you and He has forgiven you. How can a person believe that someone loves them without the help of the Holy Spirit? That's impossible but God can do it.

God gives you wisdom to understand your limitations: You realize that you cannot succeed in life or do anything that is significant without God's help. This humility and a humble heart does not come naturally. We want to do things our own way. We recognize that we cannot do anything right if we follow our own desires and plans, this is the revelation from the Holy Spirit.

The Spirit reveals other peoples' spiritual condition and calling: You somehow understand when someone is called by God or working for the Lord without knowing the person at all. This knowledge is not from you but the Spirit so you can help others. The Spirit revealed to Simeon who Christ was and this didn't come from anyone but the Spirit.

"Moved by the Spirit, he went into the temple courts. When the parents brought in the child Jesus to do for him what the custom of the Law required, Simeon took him in his arms and praised God, saying: 'Sovereign Lord, as you have promised, you now dismiss your servant in peace. For my eyes have seen your salvation, which you have prepared in the sight of all people, a light for revelation to the Gentiles and for glory to your people Israel.'" (Luke 2:27-32)

When God shares His heart and some information about others, ask the Lord what you should do with the information. If you don't hear anything from the Lord, you should wait until He gives you direction.

"However, as it is written: 'No eye has seen, no ear has heard, no mind has conceived what God has prepared for those who love him'--but God has revealed it to us by his Spirit. The Spirit searches all things, even the deep things of God." (1 Corinthians 2:9-10)

4. The Holy Spirit is our Guide, Counselor, and Director.

The Spirit is asking you to use your gift of writing, music or art: The Spirit gives us gifts and He will help us use our gifts. As you use the gift, you are filled with joy and fulfillment. You will know that obeying the Spirit is what you are supposed to do to glorify the Lord. There are many who write, but not everyone is led by the Holy Spirit. Those who are led by the Spirit will be enabled to write spiritual truths to reach out to others and make a difference in God's kingdom.

The Spirit guides you to share your resources and help others who are less privileged: God gives you the desire to donate money to churches, missions, or to people. The Spirit is leading you to be a part of God's larger mission to help the poor and to save more people.

The Spirit warns you to stay away from some people: You get a warning about people you need to avoid. This could come through uneasy and restless feelings, visions, dreams or through other people. The Spirit is warning you that you need to avoid these people and the temptations of falling into sinful life. Listen as the Holy Spirit leads; pray and ask for direction on how to avoid destructive people.

The Spirit can guide you to read the Bible and pray or fast: At times, you might have a thought come to you that you need to fast and pray for so many days for a certain issue or for some people. If you learn to recognize the Holy Spirit's voice, you will know if this is from the Holy Spirit. Sometimes you don't even know why you need to fast, but you know the Lord is asking you to. If you are not sure why you should, ask the Lord. Make sure that you have heard from the Lord and not just your own thoughts.

5. The Holy Spirit gives us godly desires.

The Spirit gives you the desire to read the Bible: You are desperate to read the Bible and pray. This desire is from the Holy Spirit, so you can grow. When you feel empty, that is coming from the Spirit. He is telling you that you need to turn to God to fill your heart with the Scriptures, prayer and praise for what the Lord has done in your life.

The Spirit gives you a desire to help others: You feel an urge to help others, but sometimes you resist and come up with excuses. The Spirit is trying to help you grow in faith. He is encouraging you to use your gifts to help others and build up God's kingdom. Your resistance shows that this is not your idea. The Spirit is trying to change your heart and lifestyle so you can be saved from being selfish.

The Spirit gives you the desire to share Christ with others: You want to tell others about Jesus. The Spirit gives you the desire to share what you have found in Christ. You are saved and you want others to be saved. This is coming from the Holy Spirit. Jesus said when the Spirit comes to us, we will be his witnesses. If we truly believe and the Spirit is working in us, we cannot help but share Jesus with others.

The Spirit gives you concern for the spiritual well-being of others: You have deep concern for the poor, homeless, prisoners, underprivileged and undervalued in society. The Spirit has given you a heart of compassion. You can only have this heart with the help of God. Your concern for other people's spiritual well-being grows as you are willing to help them. The Spirit has blessed you with the heart of Jesus and now you know what it is like to see people with Jesus' eyes.

6. The Holy Spirit gives spiritual gifts.

"To another faith by the same Spirit, to another gifts of healing by that one Spirit, to another miraculous powers, to another prophecy, to another distinguishing between spirits, to another speaking in different kinds of tongues, and to still another the interpretation of tongues. All these are the work of one and the same Spirit, and he gives them to each one, just as he determines." (1 Corinthians 12:9-11)

The Spirit gives the gift of faith: You have faith that there is a God. How can you believe someone you have not met or seen? You met God in your heart because the Spirit revealed it to you.

The Spirit gives you the gift of discernment: As your commitment to the Lord grows, the Spirit will reveal others spiritual condition to you, not to be judgmental or critical of others, but to help you to know how to help them.

The Spirit calls people to serve: Do you want to preach and serve God as a minister? That desire shows the Spirit has called you to the ministry. Don't try to find excuses, but ask the Spirit to open the doors to preach. Be prepared to go into the ministry in the area God is calling you. The Spirit will lead you step by step, guiding your path. You have to be open to His leading in order to be an effective minister for the Lord.

If you don't obey your calling, God will remind you. The Spirit will not let you rest until you make that final decision to follow.

If it is a good thing, you should do it. James says if it is a good thing and you don't do it, you sin. God has higher standards and moral values than humans, so you should obey.

The Spirit gives you love for others: Maybe you had a hard time loving some people, then one day you felt their pain and suffering. You have compassion instead of judgment. You realized that you are not any better than others and everyone is hurting. This is the work of the Spirit opening your heart to understand where other people are. We are all sinners and in need of God's grace and forgiveness.

7. The Holy Spirit gives spiritual gifts and visions and dreams.

The Spirit can give you dreams: You have a dream that may give you some understanding of a situation or tells you what's happening to others.

Nightmares are the work of the devil to torment people but sometimes they are a warning from the Holy Spirit to guide our path, preparing us to avoid problems in life. The Spirit can warn you about what is going to happen in the future.

The Spirit can give you visions: There are different visions. You may have mental visions which give you an understanding of a situation in your mind or visions that may appear like a short movie or a few scenes from a film clip. Visions can help you understand spiritual matters. This is the work of the Spirit and you should pay attention to your visions.

Remember the devil can also give us bad visions, which are impure, make us feel bad and bring us torment. Reject any visions that bring you turmoil and torment, in the name of the Lord.

The Spirit opened your spiritual senses to understand the Lord's presence: You feel the presence of the Lord in your individual prayer time and in worship services. You have no way of knowing or understanding the presence of the Lord without the help of the Spirit revealing it to your spirit. For those who have felt the Lord's presence in any form, they have been touched by the Spirit and He blessed them with supernatural experiences.

This is an outward experience but can also be felt inwardly—with our whole being, body and spirit. You can feel the overflowing of God's love, peace, and joy which are all the work of the Holy Spirit. You understand that spiritual senses can be felt and they are much deeper than physical senses.

The Spirit blessed you with spiritual discernment: You know when you are under spiritual attack by the devil. You will be able to recognize who works for God and who works for the devil. Paul was a good example of this.

"Then Saul, who was also called Paul, filled with the Holy Spirit, looked straight at Elymas and said, 'You are a child of the devil and an enemy of everything that is right! You are full of all kinds of deceit and trickery. Will you never stop perverting the right ways of the Lord? Now the hand of the Lord is against you. You are going to be blind, and for a time you will be unable to see the light of the sun.' Immediately mist and darkness came over him, and he groped about, seeking someone to lead him by the hand. When the proconsul saw what had happened, he believed, for he was amazed at the teaching about the Lord." (Acts 13:9-12)

8. The Holy Spirit communicates with us.

The Spirit uses Bible verses to speak to you: Sometimes a Bible verse pops into your mind and it is just what you need at the moment. Being reminded of the Scriptures that give us guidance, comfort and direction are from the Spirit. Our Lord Jesus said the Spirit will teach, direct, counsel, and comfort us. That's what the Spirit is doing, reminding you of the Scriptures to build you up and encourage you.

The Spirit can speak to you: You may hear His voice clearly in your mind or through your dreams and visions, giving you comfort and direction. Sometimes the Spirit can speak to you with words or without words or understanding.

You know what the Spirit is saying to you. Pay attention to Him and if you have any questions, ask the Lord. Since you started recognizing the voice of God, you will hear His answers to your questions.

There are four voices people hear in their minds: 1) Their own voice; 2) The voices of other people; 3) A bad voice (The devil's destructive voice; 4) A good voice (God's voice).

Other people's voices may be something that we remember from the past and it could be good or bad. Our own voice is in our own thoughts, which can be good or bad. We have the freedom to make choices about which voices we will accept and this will determine how we think and how we live. If we accept bad voices, we will be in turmoil and could fall into sin by following them. If we accept the good voices, which is God's voice, we will find comfort and healing.

Remember, the devil can speak to your mind also. Sometimes with an audible voice to confuse you and bring turmoil. If it does not help you grow in faith, gives you doubt about God's love, does not glorify the Lord, or suggest you hurt yourself or others; it is not from the Lord. Resist such thoughts in the name of the Lord Jesus Christ.

The Spirit speaks to you through others: The Spirit is telling others to help you and many who understand how the Spirit leads, understand why they are helping you. They were told by the Spirit to help you in times of need.

The Spirit guides your ministry path: The Holy Spirit gives us gifts and calls us to the ministry.

"In the church at Antioch there were prophets and teachers: Barnabas, Simeon called Niger, Lucius of Cyrene, Manaen (who had been brought up with Herod the tetrarch) and Saul. While they were worshiping the Lord and fasting, the Holy Spirit said, 'Set apart for me Barnabas and Saul for the work to which I have called them.' So after they had fasted and prayed, they placed their hands on them and sent them off." (Acts 13:1-3)

Paul and Barnabas were chosen to be missionaries. Other people who are walking with the Lord may recognize your calling. That's what happened to these people, who were praying and listening to the Holy Spirit, they recognized the calling on Paul and Barnabas.

9. The Holy Spirit gives joy.

The Spirit gives you joy: When the Spirit is not pleased with your thoughts and activities because you are on the wrong path, you are not going to have joy. He is telling you that you need to change.

The Spirit gives you joy when you serve the Lord: Whenever the Spirit leads you to serve and you help others, you will have joy from the Holy Spirit. That's how the Spirit communicates that you are on the right path. If you don't obey the Holy Spirit's leading, you will have feelings of restlessness. Until you obey you may feel miserable. So, obey the Spirit to find joy and peace.

10. The Holy Spirit heals us.

Healing from a broken heart: You have lost your loved one and are grieving. Deep in your heart you feel God is asking you to give your loved one to Him. The Spirit wants to bring healing to your broken heart. Until you give your loved one to the Lord, you will not find peace and healing. Having peace and joy is a sign, showing you have experienced healing from the loss of your loved one.

The Spirit heals you from an anxious mind: When you were in turmoil, and you prayed, you may have been flooded with peace, this is the work of the Spirit. God has freed you from anxiety and brought healing to your mind. Healing from tormenting spirits: Many people, including myself, have been healed from terrifying nightmares, and seeing evil spirits. The Holy Spirit can deliver you if you humble yourself and ask for help.

Physical healing: God can bring healing. However, no one lives forever. Remember, whatever God gives you is a gift, and life is a gift to glorify and serve the Lord.

11. The Holy Spirit comforts us.

"In the same way, the Spirit helps us in our weakness. We do not know what we ought to pray for, but the Spirit himself intercedes for us with groans that words cannot express. And he who searches our hearts knows the mind of the Spirit, because the Spirit intercedes for the saints in accordance with God's will." (Romans 8:26-27)

He grieves with you: When people hurt you or hurt God, you grieve for their sin. You have cried the deepest you can cry. You may feel deeply hurt or grief to the point that you are wailing. The Spirit is grieving inside of you, crying, and understanding your hurts as well.

The Spirit can bring healing through tears: There are tears of sorrow, hurt and pain. Not all tears are the work of the Holy Spirit. But when we feel the presence of the Lord, many times tears can come. Also, when the Spirit starts cleansing our heart, tears come. Some people are flooded with tears for a long period of time and their hearts are changing for the better.

Note: To learn more about the Holy Spirit, read the book, *Invisible Counselor, Amazing Stories of the Holy Spirit.*

Part Six

Chapter Thirty

Stories of Spiritual Healing

1. "God Delivered Me" by Stephanie

I felt the Holy Spirit one time in my life back in 2003 in a cell at Denver Women's Correctional Facility. At that time I believed Jesus died for my sins and was the true son of God. After killing my numbers in 2005 from the hold I managed to stay out of prison for ten years…My girlfriend cheated on me with different people in revenge for my violence. During this time of abuse we lost the house. In addition, I lost my car, my job, and my kids' custody rights. I did everything I could in my power to mend the relationship….I became bitter, angry, and mad at God.

One day, I was so desperate to make my relationship work, I lit a candle and called on the spirit of the dead and prayed to her. This was the beginning of my deep trouble and painful walk. Ironically, the place I lit the candle was where I committed a violent crime and that's why I am in jail today.

I've been here for eight months. This is the third time I've come to ACDF. I had a vision that a woman came to me and said, "Come to me." I thought this must be the Virgin Mary so I trusted her, thinking she was going to give me comfort. I leaned my head against her shoulder. I felt her hands on my cheek at first then her hands turned into sharp nails. Her nails turned into skeletons, and then I heard this screaming from far away. I was filled with terror. She turned into a demon and held me by my throat and then started choking me. I struggled to get away but I wasn't strong enough to push her away. Then I saw another bigger demon that looked like a dragon with wings and horns standing next to me, hovering over me.

I saw long horns grow out of my back, feathers started to grow out and around to cover them. Then the wings flopped down, the feathers stretching out, touching each other, making shrieking metal sounds. Two short horns grew on my forehead, and my hands were wounded as if someone stabbed my palms and I saw a black spot that looked like oil in the middle of my hands. I was hurting very badly. Black smoke came spewing out of my mouth and I couldn't move because the women skeleton was holding my neck in place. I was screaming for help but I was alone in the room and no one came.

The whole time I was rebuking the demons in Jesus' name, but I wasn't able to free myself. Nothing seemed to work. This must have lasted for 30 minutes. I was so exhausted. Finally, when I was freed, I couldn't stand straight because of the heavy weight of the wings on my back. My hands were hurting badly as if someone stabbed them and the black holes were still there. I thought I was the devil. I kept rebuking the demons in Jesus' name and praying but couldn't free myself from this heaviness.

Then the third day, Chaplain McDonald came to our housing unit to pray for people. I asked, "Please pray for my soul. I am afraid I will go to hell."

While everyone was praying for me, something came to me from behind and cut off my wings, and then the horns on my forehead just disappeared, like they evaporated in the air. The wounds in my hands started healing and became scabs except no one was able to see what was happening to me. I saw in a vision of what happened. I experienced God's power and He answered my prayers. I was overjoyed and said, "They are gone. My horns, they are gone!"

Others couldn't understand what I was saying. They couldn't see it but I saw it. God healed me that day! Since then I asked the Lord to forgive me for lighting the candle and seeking other demonic spirits and the many other things I have done wrong to hurt others. I've written down the names of all the people I need to forgive and people I need forgiveness from. I gave it all to God. After this, I feel the Lord has forgiven me but I am still working on forgiving myself.

You see, I am gay and I believe that is a hindrance and distraction in my journey with Jesus. I feel the Lord is saying to me that I need to change my lifestyle so I can follow Him. I decided to follow Jesus and I started growing my hair to make changes. Now, I have peace in my heart. I have forgiven others. The Lord is helping me hold my temper and I am thankful for it. God has listened to my prayers. He delivered me from the bondage of sin. The devil tries to make me feel bad at times and remind me what I did wrong, but I am aware that this is a spiritual battle and I am going to keep praying to Jesus to help me win this battle.

I read devotions everyday along with the Scriptures. Many books helped me in my walk with Jesus. The Maximum Saints Forgive book helped me with powerful stories of other inmates. It also has prayers that gave me spiritual insights. Tornadoes of Spiritual Warfare helped me understand what I was going through and how to deal with my situations. Journey With Jesus helped me understand the pitfalls we can fall into. When we need to hold on to our faith, rely on God and not to give up; Jesus will show us the way. I am on a journey with Jesus and he does see us as children. Jesus gave me peace and love in my empty life.

I am thankful to the Lord for everything: my life, my deliverance and my daily blessings that I am continually blessed with. Now, I have peace in my heart. I have a violent temper but I am asking God to help me with that now. I want you to know that Jesus died out of love for you. All Jesus wants is your love in return. Everything that hurts you is healed with his love. My favorite Scripture is Romans 8:31-39.

Note: This story is from the book, *Repentance, Spiritual Battle of Bill's Story, Satanic Cult & Torment.* This book is not for everyone because you can have spiritual attacks while reading it. You have to pray a lot and understand spiritual warfare so you can handle spiritual attacks. Before you read this book, read *Tornadoes of Spiritual Warfare, and How to Recognize & Defend Yourself From Negative Forces* to understand what spiritual warfare is about. Then, read *Repentance, Spiritual Battle of Bill's Story, Satanic Cult & Torment.*

2. "The Miracle of Life" by Christopher

I'd be the first one to admit that I'm not like most of the people here at ACDF. I'm not from a broken home. I've never done drugs. I'm here because I messed up. I was raised as a Christian, but never had things explained to me in a way that I understood. All of my friends were Christian, I always envied that they got it and I didn't. So, I faked it. I talked the talk, but I never knew how to walk the walk.

I joined the military right out of high school. With that I also fell away from Christianity. I figured since I didn't get it after eighteen years, that I should look elsewhere. I looked everywhere; Buddhism, Islam, Hinduism. These were off the top of a very long list. Eventually I found tarot cards.

After I left the military, I went to college. First to become an aircraft mechanic, then when that didn't pan out I went to get my degree in Criminal Justice to become a cop. (Oh the irony!) This is the first time I've been incarcerated. I don't intend to make a habit of it. I tried to help a friend, but she tried to manipulate me into buying drugs for her. I said no. We ended up fighting and she died. Instead of calling the cops, I tried to hide what I'd done.

That was the worst mistake of my life. I felt terrible and eventually decided to commit suicide. I wrote out my note, explaining what I'd done and apologizing. Just as I was trying to think of how to finish my note, God gave me an understanding that I should turn myself in. I turned myself in the next day.

It wasn't until a month after I was incarcerated that I found God. At first I was very angry and depressed. Most people would have said that I was the dark spot in the room. They had prayer circle every evening in F 2200. One day I went in with them to pray. I felt the Holy Spirit call to me. On July 26, 2014, after lights out I knelt down by my bunk and started to pray. I prayed and cried while kneeling down by that bunk for three hours confessing my sins and just pouring my heart out to God. When I stood up, I had to literally bite my tongue to keep from yelling and waking everyone up to tell them about the love I felt. In an instant I said, "God, I'm yours now."

I suddenly understood all of the Scriptures I'd learned as a kid. Everything clicked in a way that it never had before. Even though my body is imprisoned, I tell everyone that I am freer in ACDF than I ever was before, and I thank God for that freedom every day.

Note: This story is from the book, *Repentance Volume 2, The Way to Spiritual Freedom.*

3. "Spiritual Attack and Victory" by Yong Hui McDonald

In my early years, the evil spirits attacked me so often that I became physically and emotionally exhausted. I could sometimes see demonic faces and bad spirits that worked in people. As these demonic spirits attacked me, I felt it physically. I was scared and my mind wasn't clear. My weapons were my faith in God, reading the Bible, praying, and rebuking the demon to leave in Jesus' name. These things freed me from spiritual attacks.

When I speak with people who are attacked by tormenting spirits, I usually feel badly physically. It feels like someone is poking me with sharp needles or I feel pressure in my head. At first, I didn't know what was happening; then I finally recognized that it was demonic attacks. When I rebuked the demons in Jesus' name, this poking and pressure in my head left.

When I lead worship services, if there is someone who is attending worship who is tormented by demons, I sometimes feel the demons attack me as well. When that happens, I lead prayer. Sometimes, I ask people to put their hands on their heads while I pray for them. I ask the Lord Jesus to anoint them with the Holy Spirit and bring healing to them. If the Holy Spirit asks me to, I pray for others. I recite Luke 4:18-19 during the prayer to remind people that Jesus can free them from spiritual oppression. Usually, by the time I finish the prayer, there is no attack and I feel peace in the atmosphere. The evil spirits have left.

Many people are tormented. When I met Mr. Perez, the Lord asked me to write a book on spiritual warfare to help others who suffered from spiritual attacks. I specifically asked Mr. Perez to contribute his testimony on spiritual warfare. He said he would be glad to do it.

I watched him as he began to write. Suddenly, he started rubbing his right arm saying, "Boy, that hurts! That hurts more than any other time they have ever attacked me. I know the demons are upset that I am writing about them and what they do."

I assured him, "The demons don't want you to expose their methods and strategies on torturing others. Your story will help others to win spiritual battles."

Another time, I watched Mr. Perez writing his testimony. He said, "What you told me to do is working. I have been praising God for even my hard times and the demons are attacking less."

As soon as he said that, he started rubbing his right arm and shook his head. "That hurts. The demons don't want me to talk about how God is helping me. It's like a long needle being inserted into my arm."

A few minutes after he said this, I felt a long needle poking in my right arm in several places. I had never experienced that kind of pain in my arm. I was rubbing my arm and I just couldn't understand why I had that pain. Then, I realized that the tormenting spirits that attacked Mr. Perez were also attacking me. This actually helped me to understand what kind of spirits were after him. I am glad that I learned how to rely on the Lord for this battle. I can't win this battle by myself but having the Word of God and also having faith in Jesus, I am winning this spiritual war.

4. "Strange Lights and Poking Demon" by Ernie

I came to Adams County Detention Facility on 11-22-2011 and I began asking God to take the evil out of me because I had done many bad things. About two months later, I was lying in my bed when I felt something that seemed to be the shape of a jelly fish, round in shape, with red, green, and blue colors. I have never seen anything like this before.

At first, I thought it was a good spirit or guardian angel, but then I realized they were not nice. The green ones were the mean ones and they felt like a bunch of little needles that shocked like a spark plug. I started to play with them because at first they weren't too mean. I asked them questions like, "Are you the Holy Spirit? Are you my guardian angel?"

I could make them change colors with my thoughts, but only green, red, and blue. They would come to me in the form of bubbles. I thought they had given a 'yes' answer, so I started taking them and breathing them in, but the more I played with them, the meaner they got.

One day after I had just finished praying, I started to chase them around the room, first with my hand breaking up the round spinners, then I would chase them with a towel spinning it like a fan. I noticed there were a few that I couldn't reach. There were about four of the blue ones that went real high in the air. They just stayed there on top of the fire sprinkler in my cell…I began thinking that this is the evil I've been asking God to take out of me and it just doesn't have anywhere to go…

I signed up for church with Chaplain McDonald and as I was sitting in worship, I was thinking to myself, "Is she talking about spirits?" And sure enough she was talking about a wall that might be preventing me from having a strong relationship with God.

I was almost going to raise my hand during her sermon, but decided to wait until the end. As I was sitting there in church, I happened to look up and saw what the spirits were doing. They were really close to the ceiling in the form of a light red and purple fog. At the end of church services, I talked to Chaplain McDonald and told her what was going on, and we sat there and prayed. She gave me some Scriptures to memorize and asked me if she could come and see me occasionally to check on how I'm doing. I said, "That's fine."

Actually, I was happy she asked that because I didn't know if she thought I was crazy or delusional, but I tell you, it's real!…One instance that comes to mind is when I was praying the "Armor of God" prayer. When I looked around to see what the spirit was doing, I noticed something that appeared like a bubble around me. It was about 4 inches thick all the way around my body. The spirit then had a black cloud appearing around the green entity.

Also, when I am sleeping these spirits drain me. When I wake up I feel drained like I've never slept. My eyes are heavy and sometimes I almost don't want to wake up. I know in my heart that they want me to be asleep because when I'm sleeping I can't rebuke them. I noticed the spirits are after my heart or my face.

I make myself get up and the first thing I do is grab my Bible and start to read. Since I took the advice of Chaplain McDonald and started thanking God for everything He has given me and taken away, it seems to have lightened up!

As I said, when I write about them, they shock me and it feels like one needle that pokes me then leaves. One night, I went to bed after reading my Bible and the next morning I woke up and was taking a shower. I noticed a scratch about 4 inches in length going down my left arm.

A few nights later, I woke up and the back of my neck had a scratch that was the same size as the scratch on my arm. I couldn't have scratched myself because I don't have finger nails that are sharp. When I'm nervous I bite them off.

After I saw the first two green entities, I started rebuking them in Jesus' name and since then they have lightened up a whole lot. I know from this whole ordeal that the spiritual world is more powerful than you could ever imagine…One day, a couple of guys and I were in my cell trying to pray about these spirits I was seeing. We said the Armor of God prayer. Towards the end of the prayer, I became very nauseated to the point that I would start to gag. The feeling caused dizziness and was a distraction towards our prayer.

The guys saw what I was experiencing and couldn't believe their eyes. We continued to pray other Scriptures, but it was only the Scriptures that were about spirits and the devil that got this reaction.

That brings me to the present day. I'm still fighting with the help of my Bible and Scriptures. They haven't let up, but I know they will eventually get tired of tormenting me and leave. I know that all the praying I've been doing has helped me in a way that is unbelievable. I never thought that prayer could be as strong as it is. So, if you are just getting to know God, just keep on praying because He is real. Right now as I'm writing this, I just got a strong shock on my right arm. This happens every time I talk about or write about these spirits.

Note: These stories are from the book, *Tornadoes of Spiritual Warfare, How to Recognize & Defend Yourself from Negative Forces.*

5. "Founding Joy" by David

When I first found God at ACDF in 2005, I was so filled with joy and started reading the Bible every day. I knew God was real and I was sharing Christ with others for about a year. Those were the happiest times in my life.

In 2006, I lost my grandmother, then I lost my children to social services. I felt God had forsaken me because of all the hardships I was going through. I lost all my faith in God and became angry with Him. In reality, it was me who had forsaken the Lord and turned away from Him. At the time I felt so distant from the Lord and I lost all joy in my life. When I went to prison, someone introduced me to another religion and I started worshipping other gods. I tried to find happiness from these gods but I couldn't find it. I knew I was missing something but I didn't know what. For the last ten years, I've been worshiping other gods and I didn't know how to find joy. I wanted to find the joy that I had had before. However, I couldn't find it. I finally decided to go back to God.

I prayed, "Lord, I ask for forgiveness for worshipping other gods when I should have been worshipping you. I ask for your forgiveness. Please shut all the doors that I have opened. I also prayed for the ones who are lost and are in need of you."

I started reading the Bible and praying to Jesus again. All of the sudden, I was filled with joy. I am truly happy again. I never thought that I would ever have this joy again. All of my burdens are lifted and I am free. I thank God for all the things He has given me in this life. Last night I started a Bible study in the pod and a brother accepted Jesus Christ as his personal Savior. He is saved. That was a happy moment for both of us. It's the most awesome feeling to help someone find God. Now I am walking around happy even in jail. I found the Lord again.

I am thankful for God's gift of life. There were many times in my life that I should have been killed or just died. I had grown up around gangs, drugs, and guns. Thankfully, God has seen to it that I survived because He has a bigger story for my life. So you see, finding joy has been very hard for me, but as I sit here in my cell in 2016, I have asked God to forgive me for worshipping other gods. I have also asked for help on closing any and all doors that I opened.

So you see something has happened, not only have I started to read the Bible, I have also seen many things start to happen in my life again. It's God's grace. I asked God for forgiveness and I repented. I know He has been at work in my life. I have found joy again and have received many blessings.

I have a wonderful lady waiting for my return home. I could not ask for someone as special as she is. I am staying faithful to the word of God, walking and talking with the Lord. I'm so thankful that God sent His only begotten Son to die on the cross for all of us and to forgive our sins.

Note: This is a story from the book, *Repentance Volume 2, The Way to Spiritual Freedom.*

6. "Closing Doors" by Amanda

I am 29 years old. I would like to share my stories and prayers so that it may help many others to get through spiritual warfare. I believe my first door opened to spiritual attack when I was 11 or 12 years old. I used to play around with a Ouija board. I didn't realize I was putting myself in danger nor did I realize the lack of faith I had in the Lord. About a year ago, I had opened another door, actually many doors this time. I started reading tarot cards not knowing that was opening many doors. I started having demonic attacks. First I started hearing strange voices of women, men, and children. They would sometimes tell me things that upset me.

Then one day, I was lying in bed and something that I couldn't see was touching me. It was scary and weird so I started to get curious about these spirits.

I started talking to them thinking I could help them not knowing they were all demonic. Then I started getting these physical attacks, and when it would happen, they would hold me down and choke me, shake me, and wouldn't let me get up. I didn't understand why this was happening. I would be so scared that I would grab the Bible and start praying, asking God to please help me. I thought that I should help free these spirits but I was wrong. Instead of being curious, I should have ignored the bad spirits and kept my faith with the Lord. If I would have done that from the beginning I wouldn't have so many doors to close now.

I also opened the doors when I started using drugs. I have been addicted to almost everything from the age of 11 years old. First alcohol then cocaine, crack for six years with the mix of crystal meth, then turned into heroin.

Now I am in jail fighting addiction and demons. I have had three attacks since I've been here at ACDF. I have seen two girls get attacked in their sleep and they didn't even know it. Every day I have been praying and focusing some of the prayers from the Scripture. Luke 4:18-19 and the Jericho Walking Prayer. I am thanking Jesus all throughout the days and nights. Also, I have been spreading God's word and love around the pod with all the other women.

My faith has become stronger and I have more understanding of spiritual wisdom. But I still have a long road to face and I will not give up and every day I come closer to our Father. Before, I was selfish and I thank Chaplain for her prayers and her teaching. I also thank all of the other inmates at ACDF for their incredible stories. I hope I can help other's spiritual warfare. It's up to us to keep our faith in God. I will keep spreading His word and His love every day until we are all with Him in heaven.

I am getting released soon and I am not going to use drugs again. If I do, I am opening more doors to spiritual attack. I have my Lord Jesus in my heart. I will be focusing on the Lord and that's what I will replace my addiction with.

Prayer: "Lord, please forgive me for not having faith in you. I am ready and willing to give you my heart and life. I love you my Father. Please give me your shield of faith and your knowledge to teach others. I will trust in you and only you. Heavenly Father, show me the light. I want to be closer to you. I will not let go of my Father. I am coming to you asking you to please close these doors for me. Lord, I never should have opened them. Please forgive me and close them forever. I forgive myself and also others. I only want you. You are my forever light and you give me hope. Lord, please close these evil doors for me."

When I was writing this testimony, the devil was pulling my hand and trying to stop me from writing, but I prayed and didn't let these evil spirits stop me. The chaplain had to say a prayer for me to help me to keep writing.

I pray that everyone who reads my testimony will follow Jesus and know that our Father is strong. We should not fear anything or anyone, only fear God. Trust in our Father for He is our almighty.

I am still fighting and struggling but soon I will have more peace and strength to succeed because my faith is becoming so incredibly strong every day. I will continue and fight with the devil by having faith in Jesus. I will not let evil win. So to everyone going through spiritual warfare, just know that it's not easy but do not give up. You will be attacked more by Satan if you do. Just keep fighting with prayers and the more you do, the more faith you will have, and the more protection God will grant you. You have to keep faith to win this spiritual battle.

To anyone who is going through hard times, keep your faith and pray to God. These days I haven't experienced strange voices and spiritual attacks at all. Praise God!

Note: This is a story from the book, *Repentance Volume 3, Lost and Found.*

Part Seven

Chapter Thirty One

Do's and Don'ts for Prison Chaplains, Volunteers, and Inmate Leaders

1. Don't underestimate the inmates' knowledge of the Bible, but teach them the methods of how to grow.

I heard from an inmate that they didn't like some preachers to come and preach to them because they already know all the stuff. They want to know how to grow and get to know God better, not just the Bible knowledge. This is something I try to balance between new believers and the ones who already believe and read the Bible 40 times. Inmates have more time and less distraction.

Inmates need basic Bible knowledge but they also need to know how to grow in faith so they can serve God. That's why I try to teach them how to listen to God's voice, recognize the Holy Spirit's leading and how to serve God daily. They want more than just Bible knowledge but methods how to win spiritual battle and find peace. So, "how to" repent and "how to" forgive and "how to" prayer projects are what they told me that helped them.

Everyone's needs are different, but I learned to ask four basic questions concerning their walk with God. I ask the following questions in worship services and individual or group counseling to understand where they are:

1) **Are you saved?** That means if they believe in Jesus and his sacrificial death on the cross for their sins.

2) **Have you experienced the Holy Spirit?** If so, explain how? Many people in jail experienced the Holy Spirit's leading in their lives, but some have experienced it but don't know how. I would say that those who believe in Jesus and are saved have received the Holy Spirit.

3) **Do you recognize God's voice?** The question that I was asked the most is "How can I listen to God's voice?" Listening to God's voice is a skill we can learn. People can learn to wait and be silent so they can hear God. "How to Listen to God's Voice" is created for people who want to learn how to listen. It's a relationship people have to develop with the Lord and many don't know that they have to learn to quiet their minds and listen in silence.

4) **What is your calling?** There are some who understand their calling but not too many people know since they have not developed the heart to listen to God. So, by teaching them how to listen to God's voice and suggesting they ask the Lord how to serve Him daily, in this process they can learn to hear God's voice and also their calling will become clear.

These four questions give me understanding of where they are in their spiritual walk with the Lord and give me ideas how to help them to go forward and grow.

2. Don't bring your own personal political agenda to worship or Bible studies.

When people bring their own personal agenda to worship services or Bible studies, it can create controversy. Inmates come to worship to experience God and be comforted by God, not to go into controversial issues that are not beneficial to their spiritual walk with God.

Once I had an intern who said in his preaching that undocumented people should go back to their own country. I knew he made a big mistake. About 40 percent of inmates who attended that worship were Hispanic. Right after that, one Hispanic inmate raised his hands and said angrily, "Since you said that, I can't listen to what you are saying. If my family is starving, I will do anything to feed my family."

I immediately asked my intern to sit down and I said, "There are two comments I would like to make here. This is a worship service. We are here to worship God and this is not a political debate group gathering. So, we should stop this political conversation. Also, until we know where other people have walked, we cannot justly make comments about other people's lives." The second comment was for the intern who made a grave mistake.

I led the worship service until it was over. Then I went to the same housing to gather the second group for worship. An inmate told me, "Chaplain, you saved that man." After the second worship was over, I spent one and a half hours explaining to my intern why he made an inappropriate comment in the worship service. I told him how God was upset when the Israelites mistreated foreigners. Not all the Hispanic people attended were undocumented. Many were U.S. citizens.

After the intern had left, I called out leaders from each pod who came to the worship services. I told them that the intern made a mistake and I apologized for his mistake. Then I asked, "What should we do?" Then one of the inmate leaders said, "He comes here to help us. He is our brother in Christ so we should forgive him." Everyone agreed with him and we all ended with prayer. This was a good thing. This intern was able to minister to the inmates after that.

3. Don't tell inmates not to come to worship or Bible study anymore unless there is danger to others.

In 15 years of my chaplaincy at ACDF, there was only one time in my worship that I had to ask a deputy to remove a person who tried to attack others and fight physically. Still, I never told the inmate, "Don't ever come to worship." I knew once I said that he might completely withdraw from all the worship services and Bible studies.

Even if someone may be disrupting the worship, unless the inmate is hurting others physically, don't try to tell them directly not to come to the class. When that happens, gently say, "Let's focus on worship" or "Let's pray about it" or "Can I visit you alone so we will have more time to talk?" Or, "Let's give others time to talk" or "Let's focus on the Bible." In that way you don't discourage one individual but help them to be more considerate of others and God.

Once I was counseling after Bob committed suicide. I didn't know who Bob was but he was a young man who suffered from depression. Many inmates I counseled angrily told me that a volunteer told Bob not to ever come back to the Bible study because he was argumentative. Bob took this hard and he never went to any worship services or Bible studies. Other inmates tried hard to convince him to attend another worship, but he never came out of depression and committed suicide.

When our facility had an annual volunteer training, I shared Bob's story with them. Volunteers may think it will be easier to make some inmates stop coming to their own class but an inmate can take it as if God didn't want him at all. So, my suggestion was that when they have someone like that, gently change the subject or refer them to the Chaplain so I can visit. Many times inmates are hurting and they need to learn how to process pain. Many carry lots of baggage and it comes out in worship or Bible studies but you can give them hope by redirecting them to focus on healing.

4. Don't ask inmates what their charges are unless they want to share with you.

If the inmates want to share, they can share. I don't ask people what their charges are. I never look at their records. My job is not to remind them of what they are accused of, but to share that God's grace is bigger than our sin when they repent.

I usually attend worship services with interns a few times to see how they lead worship. In one of the worship services, one of my interns asked the inmates what their charges were. Immediately, I knew he made a mistake. The inmates' faces froze and the atmosphere changed but the intern didn't seem to notice this at all. When the worship was over, one inmate told him that she came to find comfort in God in worship but she found more turmoil and hurt.

This intern didn't understand why she said that. I told him, "I know why." I explained to him that he shouldn't have asked the inmates what their criminal charges were in front of everyone. In fact, I don't ever ask what their charges are, but listen if they want to share it. When the charges are heavy, I advise inmates not to talk about their charges with other inmates because some inmates can use it to be judgmental and turn against them.

It's our responsibility to bring God's love and forgiveness to those who are in need of comfort but what this intern did was remind them of all the rest of the daily issues in jail.

I told the intern that where they live and what they see reminds of them of their miserable condition. They can't escape thinking that they made grave mistakes and now society seems to perceive them and calls them convicts and criminals. Some are innocent and are housed in the facility until their charges are cleared. This intern couldn't quite understand what I was saying.

After that, I visited an inmate who made some negative remarks to the intern before she left. She was very upset. The next time when she and I were with the intern she told him that it really hurt her when he asked what her charges were. She explained that she was innocent but because of her charges, others in the pod were treating her like a criminal and she didn't want other people to know what her charges were.

Then he finally admitted that he was sorry. In the worship I remind inmates how loving God is, how Jesus' love can free us from all our guilt and sin, and the Holy Spirit bring healing to broken hearts. If we fail to bring this message, we have failed to proclaim the message of salvation and forgiveness.

Volunteers including chaplains need to have respect for inmates' personal privacy when it comes to their charges. If they want to share, that's fine but it's not our place to judge and be critical of them or even ask them. The judge and the Lord will do that. Our place is to tell them how much God loves them and forgives sinners. You have to create a safe place for people to bring their heart to God who is compassionate. We have to focus on the message of God, not focus on pointing out others mistakes or problems.

5. Don't bring an attitude that you are better than inmates.

Some volunteers have the idea that they are better and more righteous than inmates. You don't have to tell them but inmates can read your mind from your mannerisms. Once I was in shock when a man who volunteered to come and lead worship start pointing out to them how they were messed up. This man was an older man and it seemed the inmates who came took it gently like a grandfather. I never invited this man ever again. With that kind of attitude, he will make more casualties from a condemning critical attitude toward inmates.

Some people think that we have to confront the sin of others and make them feel bad. This is always done by judges but as Christians, we should let the Word of God and the Holy Spirit do the work. When they finally come to understand that they need to change because of the Holy Spirit's conviction of sin, that's when transformation happens.

If just reminding them of what they have done can change a person, the court system can do the work of God. But it doesn't work that way. The way to help them is to help them to learn how to repent through the Scriptures. I suggest Daniel's prayer and this changed many people's lives from repenting, hearing God's voice, being finally able to pray, and experiencing God's presence. The reason for that is Daniel's prayer helps them to repent.

If we don't throw away this attitude of superiority over inmates, it will discourage the inmates who are trying to find hope and encouraging words from God. Just being in jail or prison itself is condemning and mentally choking. Without God's love and forgiving heart preached, there is no hope in prison. Inmates are desperate to hear God's message of love, hope and forgiveness.

Many inmates are under spiritual attack because they already know they are messed up, feel so bad, and all the evidence of just being jail is hard for them to accept. Then there is spiritual war going on in many inmates' minds because the devil condemns them about how worthless they are. So, if anyone thinks they are going to show them they are better than them, I say, "You are in the wrong place."

If you learn to be humble and know that you are not any better than inmates, you can reach the people who need God. We are all sinners and yes, some didn't get caught even though they have done lots of things they need to be punished for. We should all be grateful for the Lord to protect us so we can keep open minds.

6. Don't forget that you are in a spiritual war zone when you start prison ministry.

After my first visit to prison, I had a dream that I will never forget. I was chased by a big demon who tried to kill me. I was so scared, but when I finally got into a room, my mother was holding the door for me to keep the demon away from me. The demon was so strong that my mother was having a difficult time holding the door. The message was that I stepped in the territory of the devil when I started prison ministry. The devil was going to scare me to stay away from prison ministry. But my mother's prayer was keeping me safe. Prayer is what we need to do and keep relying on the Holy Spirit and the angels' protection when we minister to inmates.

I have met some people who started prison ministry and had so many spiritual attacks that they thought they should rest from prison ministry. This is not the answer. The answer is to keep praying and go forward with spiritual warfare by ministering to people. My first night terror after prison ministry made me realize that there is no turning back. I can always be afraid of the devil's attack and be defeated or learn how to fight the battle.

Also, I had no idea why I was so exhausted whenever I went to Denver Women's Correction Facility(DWCF) to minister. Finally I realized that I had been spiritually attacked and beaten by the evil spirit so that I felt weak when I left the prison. So, I started praying more and that helped me. As time passed, I have many who pray for me. This gives me strength.

Even in my individual and group counseling or in worship services, at times, I feel the devil's attack. When that happens, I realize that there are some inmates who are tormented. I then stop the worship by asking inmates to put their hands on their heads and close their eyes and pray for them.

I recite the Bible verse for them and to let the devil know that Jesus has the power over everything, including spiritual war. Luke 4:18-19 "The Spirit of the Lord is on me, because he has anointed me to preach good news to the poor. He has sent me to proclaim freedom for the prisoners and recovery of sight for the blind, to release the oppressed, to proclaim the year of the Lord's favor."

After that, I pray for their healing and the tormenting spiritual leaves. This is the Scripture I give to others who are under spiritual attack. I ask them to memorize Luke 4:18-19, meditate and pray and believe that Jesus can free them from the spiritual torment and attacks. I have seen many who were delivered from demonic attacks by having faith in Jesus and relying on the powerful Scriptures.

Another Scripture I ask people to meditate on is Ephesians 6:10-19. "Finally, be strong in the Lord and in his mighty power. Put on the full armor of God so that you can take your stand against the devil's schemes. For our struggle is not against flesh and blood, but against the rulers, against the authorities, against the powers of this dark world and against the spiritual forces of evil in the heavenly realms. Therefore put on the full armor of God, so that when the day of evil comes, you may be able to stand your ground, and after you have done everything, to stand. Stand firm then, with the belt of truth buckled around your waist, with the breastplate of righteousness in place, and with your feet fitted with the readiness that comes from the gospel of peace. In addition to all this, take up the shield of faith, with which you can extinguish all the flaming arrows of the evil one. Take the helmet of salvation and the sword of the Spirit, which is the word of God. And pray in the Spirit on all occasions with all kinds of prayers and requests. With this in mind, be alert and always keep on praying for all the saints."

When you start prison ministry, you might have problems that you never had before. You might be under attack. Keep praying. With your faith in Jesus and prayer and Scriptural knowledge, you can win this battle. Don't give up just because you feel spiritual attack. That's the time to pray more and be strong and help others who are under spiritual attack.

7. Don't make fun of another religion even if you don't agree with it.

I ask chaplains and volunteers to be open to what God has for all of us through Jesus, not to focus so much on which denomination people are coming from as long as they believe in God and Jesus and his work on the cross for our sins.

I heard that some volunteers are pointing out that Catholics are wrong and that created lots of tension among inmates. Instead of finding unity through knowing and believing in Jesus, this volunteer made some Christians feel that they have the salvation message and Catholics didn't. This is wrong. We need to realize that our salvation is not based on some doctrine but our relationship with Jesus. When people try to divide people by focusing on just denomination, this is destructive. It's best to create a respectful attitude toward each other instead of division among inmates. They have to live with each other for 24 hours each day and only unity and openness to each other can help them to grow in faith.

I learned that just carrying the right Bible does not promise salvation but their relationship with the Lord and how they are walking with Jesus. I lead worship for everyone who wants to come to worship and some are not accepted by traditional religion, but they believe in Jesus and I believe they are saved.

Some volunteers criticize other religions or the books inmates carry. This happened with one inmate I will call him "John" (not his real name). He was a Jehovah's Witness who faithfully attended the worship service I lead. He believed in Jesus and he believed that Jesus died on the cross for his sin. He tried to help others to know Jesus. He grew up with the Jehovah's Witness Bible and that's what he preferred.

Then I asked a pastor volunteer to come and fill in for me because I was out of town. After this pastor came and led worship once, somehow John didn't come to worship anymore. One day John wanted to see me. He told me three things that this pastor who filled in for me had done. 1) Pastor told him that he was carrying the wrong Bible and made fun of him which made John upset. 2) the pastor brought some political issues that has nothing to do with the Bible. John challenged him by saying "Can we study the Bible? That's why I came." 3) The pastor perceived that John was argumentative and told the deputies that John should not ever come to worship again. This was a grave mistake this volunteer made.

When John wanted to see me, I found out what had happened. John was in tears. He wanted to come to worship but the deputies didn't let him because of what that pastor had said. I let John come to worship after that and I told him that I was sorry about what happened. I confronted the volunteer and told him about one incident where an inmate committed suicide when he was told not to come to worship anymore by a volunteer. I told him not to do that to anyone. I never invited him to lead my worship services after that.

Many attend church but they don't know who Jesus is and they don't realize they are sinners. Therefore, they don't even know why Jesus died on the cross for their sins. But there is hope. At any moment, the Holy Spirit can reveal to them that they are sinners and Jesus died for their sins.

So, I encouraged them to keep learning about Jesus. I don't point out that they have a wrong Bible or right Bible according to human standards. In the worship I lead, we talk about Father God, Jesus, and the Holy Spirit. I am grateful that they attend worship to worship God with others who may not believe the same way they do.

8. Don't share inmates' crime history with volunteers or others.

When I was working as an intern chaplain at DWCF, my supervisor chaplain had a visit from his denomination. They had met some inmates in worship and after inmates left, this chaplain said that out of 9 people they saw, three of them committed murder. This immediately changed the atmosphere. I would have told the chaplain how bad that was but I didn't. His practice was to look up everyone who came to worship and find out what they had committed. This I think creates the wrong attitude and a judgmental attitude toward inmates.

I am aware that you can find out from inmate finder website to find out each inmate's background. But that's not what chaplains and volunteers should focus on. What we should focus on is the message of God's love and forgiveness.

People who committed murders also are human beings who made mistakes. They already are paying the price with regret and remorse. If they don't, then that's between themselves and God. We have no right to point out others mistakes unless if you are involved in after care and how you can help.

People who committed murder can be changed. Moses, a great leader, and someone we look up to, committed murder and God forgave him and used him. God can use anyone who repents and many of the inmate leaders I have met committed murder but that's in the past. God has forgiven them and I have no right to dwell on it.

Many people are not mature enough to have a loving attitude toward everyone, including chaplains and volunteers but we need to strive to focus on what we are here for: That is sharing God's message not our own prejudice against people who made mistakes.

I think it would have been better if that chaplain didn't share that kind of information with others. As soon as he shared it, everyone was quiet and seemed to have a different attitude, like condemning attitude toward inmates who came to worship service.

I learned my lesson from that. I said to myself, "There is no way I will be looking at inmates' background check. I am a human and can easily point fingers at others and I don't want to do that. That's not why God sent me to minister to inmates. The message I heard was clear, "Go and tell them that Jesus died for their sins and Father God has forgiven them." This is the message I try to share, nothing else.

Also, the Lord told me to treat them like my brother, which is to not have a condemning heart but with gentleness. I try to see them as my older brother who was incarcerated three times in his teen years. If I can do that, there is no judgmental attitude toward any prisoner but love and acceptance. They are also forgiven sinners just like me. Jesus said, "For I have not come to call the righteous, but sinners." (Matthew 9:13) Actually, inmates' records are public and they can check out what they have done. But unless you are trying to screen out whom you want to help with aftercare or help them after they are released, I think most people will be affected negatively. If you want to minister, minister the word and don't bring your own prejudice which hurts people.

9. Don't be discouraged when others don't have a passion for prison ministry.

I used to grieve for other people and churches' lack of concern for prison ministry. I don't do that anymore. I just let the Lord bring people to work with me. Even in the book projects, I just let the Holy Spirit find people to help me.

The Lord has done that I have found some dedicated people who worked with me for more than ten years with book projects.

Not all the people who call a chaplain and say that they are interested in prison ministry end up helping inmates. But they have to find out. Just having a zeal for prison ministry sounds good but in reality, many don't have the passion or true calling. When people call me and tell me that they want to be a volunteer at ACDF, I asked them to go through the background check, attend worship to observe, and listen to God if that's what He wants them to do. I learned that many just have passion and zeal, but not calling so they ended up stopping coming. There are some passionate people who come to volunteer for many years. Unless you have love for prisoners, you really can't minister to them.

Actually, that love comes from the Lord and I believe the Lord has given me that love. If any volunteers don't have love and respect for inmates, I should say, they shouldn't be ministering to them because eventually their true face will manifest and they end up causing hurt.

Once I had a chaplain who didn't have much love and understanding of inmates. I didn't know that at first. The facility hired him because we needed a chaplain and not many people applied for it at the time. His first worship service was a disaster. He talked to inmates so disrespectfully that one inmate asked, "Are you a cop?" A week later, when this chaplain went to gather people for worship, no one came to worship. I understood why. This chaplain was displaying his prejudiced attitude toward inmates and the inmates saw it. Eventually, this chaplain quit since prison ministry was not his calling. He only applied for financial needs when he couldn't find a church. He confessed to me before he quit that it took a year for him to finally realize that God also loves prisoners. I was in shock.

Prison ministry is not for everyone. If someone is looking to fill in for money, I would say you should find work somewhere else so you don't damage people with your wrong attitude. Unfortunately, this chaplain didn't realize how much he was hurting prisoners. We work independently from the other chaplain so I had no idea what was in his mind at the beginning. I would say, don't do it for money. Let others who have passion to serve, serve.

10. Don't be discouraged if you don't see any progress of inmates.

I met a chaplain who was so disgusted with some inmates who came back to jail again. There are many reasons why people keep coming back to jail and prison. Some are homeless and some still struggle with addictions. Jail and prison is a place of healing of their soul when they could be dead on the street or die from overdose. There are many other reasons but lack of the support of family and community is a big part and being poor and unable to pay for fines so serving time instead is another.

An inmate you worked with before who returns to jail or prison is not your fault. Thus you should not blame yourself. Likewise, it is not God's fault when a former inmate returns to jail. Everyone makes their choices and God wants best for them. Sometimes being jail is a lifesaving place for some people who could have been dead with overdose or on the street with fights. We just have to keep patiently helping each inmate to grow until they can get support and they can stay away from prison.

Once an inmate came out to worship covering his face and I told him it's good to see him in worship. If they don't come to worship, there is a more deep issue so I told him I am glad that he came. I have seen so many transformations and the Holy Spirit's healing power at ACDF that I am very thankful that the Lord called me to the prison ministry.

When people start being discouraged, they are not seeing the big picture. I am also aware that as a chaplain I see more transformation of people than many others. I saw when they came in and I see that they are changing. Many volunteers who may not come in to the facility do not see this progress and can be discouraged. But I try to see it from God's point of view. We have failed God in many ways and He waited for us patiently. God has patience and we need to be patient.

One inmate just came back and she was so discouraged. I told her that God must have some more lessons to teach her and to not be discouraged. I told her to keep growing in faith.

11. Don't be discouraged when you have to deliver other religious books.

After chaplains are told to deliver books of other religions, I sometimes ended up delivering other chaplains religious books. Chaplains are considered as chaplains to everyone. In that I don't believe I will compromise my belief in Jesus but just show respect to others as if they are in our care. I had a difficult time with this at first. I wish I don't have to do it since I only believe that the Bible is what people need to find God, salvation, and eternal life.

One time the Lord sent me to minister to a Satanist. The Lord asked me to write a book about him and this man agreed. He wasn't ready to change his religion but the Lord sent me to him so I can share the gospel with him. He only repented 50% but he didn't completely turn to the Lord. He still is a Satanist. I did my best to plant the seed and I will be surprised if I see him in heaven. But who knows? God's compassion and mercy might save him at the end. So, I encourage you to reach out to others with respect.

This is a key. We want others to respect our religion. I believe all the people who have not found God are searchers. They are still looking and in the process, they can find God. That's what I pray and then I am their friend. I have seen many who turned to God even after they received the wrong book. I pray for them that they will find God and some did find God. Praise God!

12. Don't break the rules of the facility if you want to minister to inmates.

Without the help of the staff and deputies, we can't minister to inmates. So, it's very important that we follow rules and respect the deputies who are trying to help. Yes, there are many reasons why the facility has rules and they are to protect people. Unfortunately, not all the inmates will take advantage of chaplains or volunteers or staff. But there are some who have been trying to take an advantage of the kindness of volunteers or chaplains. There are reasons for these rules.

One of the chaplains who got fired was giving inmates phone calls and made phone calls to inmates' families. This chaplain had a kind heart, just trying to help but the facility saw that he was going over the boundaries so the facility had new rules not to call out. He did anyway but the problem was the inmate's wife had a restraining order against him. He shouldn't have asked the chaplain to contact the inmate's wife. The wife of the inmate immediately called the facility, reported it, and the chaplain got fired from his job.

Each facility has rules. Chaplains can only give phone calls to inmates from chaplains when family of the inmates call for a death or serious sickness notification and has been verified from the facility.

Another area is boundaries. Chaplains and volunteers in our facility can't correspond with inmates. One of my interns got fired from the facility after he started corresponding with one of the inmates in our facility. This is not allowed in most facilities.

Chaplains and volunteers are not permitted to have individual contact after inmates leave the facility and also while they are incarcerated. I had to make a decision if I should do prison ministry outside or inside. My calling is inside so I tell inmates they can't write to me or contact me after they leave.

This one intern lost his privilege of coming to the facility because he broke this rule. He sent me an email saying he made a mistake and he was paying the price. There was another intern that was drunk when he came to lead worship and staff smelled alcohol on his breath. He had a warning before from me but he told me he wasn't drinking when he came to the facility.

This time, the deputies went to the contact room and tested his breath and his alcohol was so high that he wasn't allowed to drive. He called someone to come and pick him up. He lost the privilege of ministering to the inmates.

13. Always show respect to the deputies who are trying to help you to be safe.

I never had any problems with inmates so far and I am very thankful for that. I am also glad that in most part, I have no problems with deputies. The deputies have so much going on all day long, tending to the inmates, feeding them three times a day, keeping watch for nurses, sending people out to medical, classes, worship services, GED classes, and many other classes all day long. They also give out books, mail and all personal items every day. They have to take inmates to the hospital if they get sick and during the lockdown time they are supposed to walk around every 30 minutes to make sure that everyone is safe, etc.

Safety and security are deputies' concerns and sometimes I can't have worship services when the whole facility is on lockdown or if there is a lack of deputies. If something is missing in the kitchen, there is another lockdown to search for the missing item. The deputies have to stop fights between inmates and sometimes the deputies get hurt in the process. All these things that the deputies must do all day for the safety of the community is not recognized by other people.

Chaplains and volunteers need to appreciate what the deputies do and show them respect. When we are trying to lead worship or see an inmate, try to be patient and be considerate that the deputies are also trying to perform all their duties. I am more and more appreciative of the deputies who are actually putting their lives at risk on the streets and even at the jail where violent fights can erupt. They try to protect inmates and the staff.

The Scripture says that we should respect authority. Everyone should show more respect and appreciation for the deputies who try to protect people inside and outside of jail. This is hard among some inmates if they are mistreated by some deputies. Still chaplains and volunteers need to teach them to forgive.

I have seen a man who even forgave the deputy who broke his nose. I was touched by this inmate by his forgiving attitude. He was smiling and I am so thankful that God's love is working through many inmates. Another inmate told me that he did say some harsh things to a deputy and the Lord told him that he made a mistake so he asked the deputy to forgive him. So, peace is possible if we learn to listen and forgive each other.

I tell the deputies that I can't do my chaplain's job without their help and thank them when I can and they appreciate it. Many police officers are underappreciated. We need to show them more appreciation and I sincerely respect them because without them, there will be no peace but turmoil. Their sacrifice is not recognized in many people's hearts and I try to install it in inmates' hearts as well. After all, that is learning how to obey God's word.

14. Don't think that you can meet all the needs of the inmates.

In our facility we have more than 1,000 inmates. How can I have peace when there is so much need? This is an impossible task so I pick and choose. What is my first priority? That's worship and to help individuals who are open to God and are in need of guidance. I don't spend too much time with one inmate but use "Torment Room" to assess their spiritual needs and help them guide their experiences according to their own needs. You can ask them, "What area you are troubled the most?"

They will tell you what bothers them the most and that's where you can start. Some inmates ask me if I can visit them once a week. I flatly tell them, I can't do that when we have more than 1,000 inmates but write a kite (request form) to see me than I will try to answer when I can. But there are inmate leaders I mentor so they can help many others and I pay more attention to the inmate leaders. There are some inmates who just want a chaplain's attention; they don't get it in our facility because I am very brief about what I can do and what I will do. I help them with books a lot. Also, I listen to the Holy Spirit about whom I should help individually.

15. Do treat all the inmates with respect.

If inmates know and understand that you respect them and you are there for them, they will respect you. They read your thoughts through your tone of voice and if you treat them with respect, they will treat you with respect. There are some who are mentally ill and angry at the world and everything. These people may not respond to you with respect but still it is your place to treat them with respect. If you have problems with some inmates, you need to bring it to your supervisor to help solve the problems. But always listen more than just responding and giving them answers. They will know where you come from when you do that.

16. Don't lose professionalism and keep your boundaries.

In our facility, any volunteers, chaplains, or staff are not allowed to contact inmates after they leave the facility. As volunteers and chaplains gets to know inmates, they might loosely give information about their personal life. Some inmates looks for that and think that they can visit them after they get out of the facility even though they know that the facility rule is not to contact any volunteers, chaplains or staff.

In that matter, our facility tells the volunteers not to give out their personal information. There are some staff that look kind and gentle while they deal with inmates. An inmate showed up at this staff's doorstep and she called the police. There are some volunteers and chaplains who don't have any respect for inmates and there are some who fall into a trap of forgetting the rules because they forget their boundaries. There were some staff who lost their job because they kept their relationship by corresponding with an inmate after the inmate's release. You can either lose your work or ministry opportunity to many people if you try to have one relationship that violates the rules. That's prison and jail work and you have to keep a professional distance.

17. Don't be afraid of the prison setting but be aware what's going on.

Many people asked me if I am afraid of working with inmates. I said no. People also asked me if I feel safe in prison setting. To me, jail and prison are safer than walking on the street where you don't know anyone. In fact, the only people who can have weapon is deputies, unless inmates make their own weapons. Inmates can't have guns, but almost anyone can have guns outside.

There have been times that the staff was attacked in another jail and some got injured or even killed. Most of the time the deputies are right there when I counsel. Even though I am alone with inmates and lead worship, I feel safe with people who come to worship. However, not everyone feels that way. Once a person visited worship to observe to find out if she wanted to come and minister to inmates. As soon as the metal door shut behind her, she was scared. She never came back. So, everyone is different.

I had to go through 6 metal doors when I was visiting the maximum unit in one prison as an intern chaplain. I never got scared. I felt at home in prison and jail. This is a place of human beings and many are hurting and they need God. In my position as a chaplain is helping inmates so I haven't had any safety problems so far and I am thankful for it. Inmates are the most appreciative people I have found. They are so happy to just receive a Bible. I am glad that the Lord called me to prison to minister to people who are hungry for God.

18. Don't be afraid of helping people with spiritual attack. They can be freed from attacks with God's help.

Not all the Christians are equipped to fight this spiritual battle even when they say that they are ministers or serving God or even those who believe that they have strong faith in God. My greatest learning about spiritual warfare, attack and torment came when God asked me to write a story of a Satanist.

This book is not for everyone. If you don't have faith in Jesus and are not a praying person the devil can attack you while you are reading it. Even if you are a Christian, the devil can attack you so you will be distracted and may not be able to finish the book. I believe the devil doesn't want people to read this book. This book exposes the devil's lies, tricks and traps that people fall into by ignorance, curiosity, and lack of faith in God and Jesus' power to deliver them.

If you feel you need more information about spiritual warfare, and want to help people how to be freed from the demonic attack, I suggest you to read this book, prayerfully, so you don't have to have fear. Also, don't fall into a sin of pride that you can read this book without any spiritual attack. The devil knows where you are and we always have to guard ourselves from falling into sin of pride.

Not everyone is attacked by demons while they read this book, but many people who have spiritual senses of what the spiritual world is like did. The demons know whom they can attack and they try to attack anyone. Even if we are attacked, we have the weapon which is our faith and all we have to do is rebuke the demon to leave in Jesus' name. If spiritual attack won't stop, you need to ask the Lord to give you wisdom on how to win this battle as you read the Bible and pray to listen. Or you may not be ready for this book. In that case, I say, wait.

Spiritual weapons are our faith in Jesus and we have the Word of God that strengthens us and the devil knows when we get stronger spiritually as we keep reading and obeying the word of God. Spiritual attack can happen in four different ways: When you look into "Torment Room" there are the first four categories on the left: (1) Physical attack, (2) scary, unholy and terrifying visions or even friendly visions which are demonic and deceptive (3) demonic voices in mind and also audible (4) attack through dreams and having nightmares and physical attack can be combined in this one.

There are many reasons for spiritual attacks. I would like to share four different categories of people who can be vulnerable for spiritual attacks.

1) **Active devil worshipper or curious people** – There are non-Christians who are involved with Satanism, witchcraft, or are curious about the demonic world and open the door by reading witchcraft books or books that are written by people who are working with demons. Many who are tormented have opened the wrong door. I can only help people who

believe in Jesus and are willing to repent of their sin of serving the devil. I saw demons attacking people right in front of me and yes, I prayed for that person to get help but it was only when I was there he had relief. After I left, since he still worshipped Satan, he was tormented again. This is the Satanist the Lord asked me to write about. His story is in the book, "*Repentance, Spiritual Battle of Bill's Story, Satanic Cult and Torment*" and if you want to be a spiritual leader and want to help others spiritually, this is a must read book to learn to understand how others are tormented and deceived. I also had a spiritual attack while preparing this book but the Lord gave me strength to finish it with many people's help. I learned what kind of demons were torturing this man. God helped me to make "Torment Room" after this book came out. There was a lesson I had to learn through that experience so I can help others.

2) **Environment** – Those who do not actively seek the spiritual experiences of the devil but have relatives or friends or have contact with them, or even being in jail with someone who works with the devil in the same pod. Innocent children can be in this category. When I try to lead prayer meeting, counsel people, and even in worship, the devil attacks if there are some who are attacked by demons. Actually, this helps me to know how to help people so I pray for them and give them instruction on how to be freed from torment. One inmate was attacked by demons physically after she was housed in jail and I asked her to read Luke 4:18-19 over and over again and meditate and believe that Jesus can free her from demonic attacks, and rebuke the demons to leave in Jesus' name. In two days, she was completely freed from the demonic attacks. She found out the real power of Jesus and the word of God through this experience. She said, "God is alive."

3) **Those who are traumatized by abuse or experienced grief and loss** – this is a vulnerable time, the devil takes advantage, and attacks people. When my sister died in a car accident, I started having spiritual attacks: seeing demons in people's faces, beaten by the demons on the street, hearing voices of despair, and suffering from nightmares. I saw my sister in my dreams and at the end, I was choked by unseen demons. My mother told me that if what I saw in my dream is not comforting to me, it's not from God but the devil. She even said my sister I saw in my dream was not my sister but the demonic attack since I was choked by demons. She told me to rebuke the demon in the name of Jesus. She was right. The demons can manifest like my sister and can torture me. So I rebuked the demons and eventually all the spiritual attacks stopped. Many inmates are

suffering from grief and loss of their loved ones. Many are traumatized by tragic death of their loved ones.

4) **Those who are Christians but curious about other spirituality** – Some Christians don't know the danger of opening wrong doors and they end up being attacked. I saw some inmates who were so peaceful and then suddenly attacked by demons and they were in turmoil. I asked one person how she opened the door. She was reading tarot cards and another said she was reading a witchcraft book with curiosity. I asked them to ask the Lord to forgive them and they did. Then they only read the Bible and put the other spirituality book down. They didn't have any more attacks.

God is more powerful than the devil. The devil is a creature and God is the Creator. Remember, without having faith in Jesus, you have no power over the devil. So, when I help others, I have a list of things that I ask them.

(1) **Do you have faith in Jesus and that he died on the cross for your sin?**

(2) **Is there anything that you did to open the door?** Ask the Holy Spirit to help you repent. Work on repentance with Daniel's prayer for the next 30 days for purification

(3) **Is there anyone you need to forgive?** I lead four prayers from "The Torment" Room: 1) Repent and ask God for forgiveness and Him to take away your anger if you can't forgive someone or yourself. 2) Ask the Lord to forgive all those who have hurt you and your family and help them to repent. 3) Tell God you forgive everyone including yourself. 4) Ask the Lord to close the door of torment for you and also ask Him to help you close the doors you need to close. There are things only God can do and there are things you have to do to close the doors.

19. Don't be afraid of helping grieving people. You can help them with resources.

Many people I have encountered in jail have not learned how to grieve when they lost their loved one. Many are holding anger. In the "Torment Room" the door of "Grief and Loss" is a big open door for many who are suffering greatly. Many spiritual leaders don't know how to help them because they think there isn't much they can do other than allow time. That's not true. I have learned to let go of my husband after he died in a car accident in 2008. Within three months, I was completely healed from grief and loss, and triggers which made me breakdown everyday whenever something reminded me of my husband and his death.

The Lord helped me in my grieving process step by step and helped me to let go of my husband. If you are suffering from grief and loss, you can't really help others fully. I was in that stage and I couldn't even get to work until God gave me a vision of my husband dancing in the sky. Then I still wasn't willing to let my husband go. Eventually, I had to because God asked me to and I couldn't live in pain anymore.

The Lord completely healed me from grief and loss that I don't even miss my husband but my heart is full of love for Jesus. I don't even have lonely feelings because Jesus filled my heart with contentment, joy and peace. This is not just for me. It's possible for others to experience it.

The Lord helped me to write "*Dancing in the Sky, A Story of Hope for Grieving Hearts.*" You can order all the books that I wrote from Amazon.com. All the proceeds goes to Transformation Project Prison Ministry(TPPM), a nonprofit which publishes and distributes books free of charge to prisoners and homeless.

The Lord asked me to add "A 30-day Prayer Project: How to Grieve & Experience Healing from the Death of Loss of Your Loved One." Many who are grieving are also suffering from spiritual attacks because they have not processed many different areas such as anger and blame. In the "Torment Room" the "Anger" door opens many other doors such as spiritual attacks, flashbacks, confusion, depression, and more. I ask you to look into a prayer project for "Healing from Grief and Loss" and follow different areas to process grief and healing. Then I ask them to write a goodbye letter to their loved ones to let them go.

Holding people you have already lost is like holding a fire in your heart. It will burn and immobilize you. Also, the dead person can become like an idol worship to the point that you forget about God. This doesn't please God. So when I ask people to write a letter, such as expressing your thoughts like, "I love you, I miss you. I am sorry, please forgive me or I forgive you." You can also write at the end, "You are a gift from God, but I have to give you back to God and say Goodbye."

This letter writing helped many people to experience healing from pain caused by grief and loss. I praise God for their healing! I also remind them of Job's prayer. "The LORD gave and the LORD has taken away; may the name of the LORD be praised." (Job 1:21b)

Everything we have is not ours but the Lord, including our lives. Our spirits live here in our body but our eternal home is in heaven. This is a hard concept. People seem to think they will live here forever but life is short.

"A voice says, 'Cry out.' And I said, 'What shall I cry?' 'All men are like grass, and all their glory is like the flowers of the field. The grass withers and the flowers fall, because the breath of the LORD blows on them. Surely the people are grass. The grass withers and the flowers fall, but the word of our God stands forever.'" (Isaiah 40:6-8)

Most everyone experiences grief and loss sometime in their life. If we can learn to focus on why we are here, it will help focus on what's important. "Jesus replied: 'Love the Lord your God with all your heart and with all your soul and with all your mind.' This is the first and greatest commandment. And the second is like it: 'Love your neighbor as yourself.'" (Matthew 22:37-39)

Remember loving God has to be the first priority and loving our neighbors are second. So, focus and love God first and then love others. I was going to grieve for my husband until I died but the Lord didn't let me. He wanted me to focus on loving Jesus and following him. I made a decision to follow Jesus and let go of my desire to hold on to my husband. That brought complete healing in me. I don't grieve and I don't even miss my husband anymore.

I have met some inmates who didn't want to let their loved ones go at first. Then eventually they realized how painful it is to grieve every day and they decided to let them go. After that they experienced healing from grief. God has power to bring healing in broken hearts and people need to learn how to process grief and healing. Chaplains have the privilege to help grieving people and I am grateful for the Lord teaching me to help others through my own grief and healing process.

20. Don't hesitate to mentor leaders for worship services and listen to the Holy Spirit in that area.

There are some amazing inmate preachers and teachers. I lead 8 worship services every week and I often find great inmate preachers and teachers.

But what about those who want to teach and lead but need some training and help? What I have been doing in some modules is that I found two people to lead and I provide the Scriptures to read and they can explain. At some other times I have lessons ready and have them read and they can make comments.

This worked out well with two people. I try to give them the teaching materials early so they can go through and pray about it. I have seen remarkable results with training inmate leaders to teach. There were many times I can tell how other inmates can agree with their inmate leaders teaching because they are on the same page and they understand what others are going through.

There were times that if they talk about anything that is not related to the Scripture or lessons, I remind them to go back to the original text. But most of the time inmate leaders have more time than me and they prepare for the text thoroughly. I am so thankful that the Lord asked me to train the leaders from the beginning of my ministry. That is the reason I always try to locate the potential leaders who can grow. I have seen both men and women inmates transformed after they started preaching and teaching. They finally discovered their gifts and some decided to go into the ministry because of their experience of preaching and teaching.

In fact, some of the inmates know so much about the Bible and they are ready to teach. I am encouraging any chaplain or even volunteer to train leaders and give the inmate leaders the opportunity to not only share their testimony but also give them time to preach and teach. The Lord is the one who leads me to do this when I have some volunteers.

The Lord often tells me which inmate is called to the ministry and they need to preach. This makes my job easier but the Lord doesn't always reveal that to me unless there is a specific reason, for example, that I should mentor someone. People who are called to the ministry recognize it and they have the desire to preach and teach so I try to give the opportunity to inmates who desire to do that unless the Lord stops me or I see character fault in them.

The Holy Spirit has been leading worship services and many times if the Lord doesn't give me any words to preach, that means there is another in the worship service who should preach. Yes, there is always someone the Lord prepared to preach when He doesn't give me the words. This not only true with me but also with one of my interns. God leads the worship services.

One intern, who was an excellent preacher, stood to preach. The Holy Spirit told me to ask him to sit down and ask inmates to preach. I hesitated at first but I finally said to my intern, "I am not sure how you will take this but the Holy Spirit is asking me to ask you to not to preach but let some inmates preach." At this the intern said, "I am so glad that you are asking me to sit because the Lord is not giving me anything share." I was glad that this intern was sensitive to the Holy Spirit's leading. That day, there was an inmate who had to share his amazing transforming story of how God was helping him. Everyone was so blessed by the Lord's presence that day. The Lord knows who needs to speak and made it known to me and to the intern.

Another time, a young man with very gifted musical talent contacted me on the phone and wanted to visit ACDF and minister to the inmates in chaplain's worship which I usually lead. Just before I met him for the first time face to face at the front desk of ACDF, the Lord asked me to tell him not to minister to inmates but be ministered by the inmates. He was a humble man to accept my words and in the worship service, he only shared his story briefly and he gave inmates time to share. That day, the Holy Spirit blessed the service through many inmates who shared their faith story. This man who came to minister was so filled with the

Holy Spirit's joy that he told me and others that that was the most powerful worship service he has ever attended. He told me he talked about this for a week.

Many people think that when they go to prison, they minister. I don't think that way. The Holy Spirit is ministering to hurting inmates and I am just there and enjoying the feast. Yes, I contribute to teaching and make room for worship but that is also God's grace that I can do that.

I encourage everyone to mentor inmate leaders and teach them how to help others with the gospel message. Also, listen to the Holy Spirit and see how the Holy Spirit wants you to mentor and whom to mentor. The Lord will bless you so much in the process of mentoring inmates. There are many pastors and missionaries who are inmates. If we can help them, they can help many others.

21. Don't make worship primarily a time of discussion, but give people time to listen to God's voice.

When I lead worship services, this is the order:

1) Praise song and many inmates know what they want to sing.

2) Prayer of listening after I say, "Thank you Father God for being here. Thank you Lord Jesus for being here. Thank you Holy Spirit for being here. We are here to worship you and listen. Please open our hearts so we can listen to you." Then I ask inmates to put their prayer requests aside but ask the Lord to speak to them and try to listen in silence. I usually pick out some background music. I listen to the Holy Spirit and ask which song I should play for this.

3) I ask people to share what they are thankful for so God knows that we are grateful for what He is doing in our lives.

4) I ask inmate leaders to preach with the materials I already gave them. Also, most of the time, these leaders have written sermons or Scripture meditation.

5) After inmate leaders' preach, I ask rest of the people to share their comments from the lesson.

6) I usually lead prayer of either repenting or four prayers of healing from "Torment Room" with background music.

7) I lead Holy Communion in every worship service.

8) We end the service.

While I was attending Iliff School of Theology, I organized prison ministry. I learned this very important lesson of teaching inmates how to listen to God's voice when I was ministering to inmates in 8 different jail and prison facilities. When I was asking people to start conversations with Jesus during prayer and meditation, inmates were touched. Some had heard God's voice and felt the presence of the Lord. I learned that what we say is not that important and many worship services are what we say and end there. Chaplains and volunteers can intentionally have a quiet time to give inmates time to listen to God's voice. I believe that will make a remarkable difference in many inmates' spiritual growth.

One reason why we don't grow is because we never learn to listen but have head knowledge of the Bible. When God starts to speak to people, they are transformed. They start understanding God's love and His heart. I think many people think what they say to inmates are important but from my own experience teaching inmates how to converse everyday with the Lord is more important than just listening to my sermons. Many inmates have learned to listen to that small, still voice speaking to their hearts and they are never the same person again.

To teach inmates how to listen to God's voice, you can refer them to the prayer project, "How to Listen to God's Voice." In worship and Bible teaching time, ask people to converse with the Lord. When they start asking God questions, He may not answer right away. But if they can learn to wait, eventually the Lord will speak to them and they will get the message. This is a beginning of a deeper relationship with the Lord. It's critical we teach inmates how to listen if we want to see them change their lives. Transformation doesn't just start automatically: it's the work of the Holy Spirit. When inmates learn to listen, they can understand God's heart and there will be healing in many areas.

22. Don't give yourself glory, but do praise God for all the good things that happen in ministry.

Chaplains and volunteers are human beings. We need affirmation and encouragement. I would say if you are truly serving God not yourself, you will get that affirmation from the Lord. Other people's affirmation is a bonus and not many people get that bonus.

Don't look back on your ministry and pat your own back. It's all God's grace that you are in ministry. You saw some fruit of that ministry because of the Holy Spirit's work. Yes, your part is obedience and the Lord did the work. If you give yourself credit, the Lord won't be pleased with it. Your ministry shouldn't be the first priority, but pleasing and loving the Lord. That is giving God all the glory for what He has done.

The Lord cannot use you effectively if you focus on the success of your ministry more than loving God and pleasing Him. I was reminded of it when I fell in love with prison ministry. He asked me, "Choose what you love the most, ministry or loving God?" I had to choose God of course because that's the most important thing in my life.

When I first started prison ministry the Lord said, "I am looking for people that I can trust with my power to transform other people's lives." Trust is the word. If God can trust you, He will use you. You will learn what trust means: be obedient and put God first in every situation as He wants. You have to pay the price of gaining God's trust. At times He will test your obedience. Read the book, "*I Was The Mountain*" and "*Loving God*" to understand this part more.

Don't focus on the result of ministry and don't be discouraged. It's your heart for obedience that He will be looking for, not the result. The result is something that the Lord will help you achieve. You can rely on Him that all things will work out in the end, for His glory.

"What, after all, is Apollos? And what is Paul? Only servants, through whom you came to believe-- as the Lord has assigned to each his task. I planted the seed, Apollos watered it, but God made it grow. So neither he who plants nor he who waters is anything, but only God, who makes things grow. The man who plants and the man who waters have one purpose, and each will be rewarded according to his own labor. For we are God's fellow workers; you are God's field, God's building." (1 Corinthians 3:5-9)

"If anyone speaks, he should do it as one speaking the very words of God. If anyone serves, he should do it with the strength God provides, so that in all things God may be praised through Jesus Christ. To him be the glory and the power for ever and ever. Amen." (1 Peter 4:11)

"So whether you eat or drink or whatever you do, do it all for the glory of God. Do not cause anyone to stumble, whether Jews, Greeks or the church of God--even as I try to please everybody in every way. For I am not seeking my own good but the good of many, so that they may be saved." (1 Corinthians 10:31-33)

"'Come, follow me,' Jesus said, 'and I will make you fishers of men.'" (Matthew 4:19)

Appendices

An Invitation to Accept Jesus

Do you have an empty heart that doesn't seem to be filled by anyone or anything? God can fill your empty heart with His love and forgiveness. Do you feel your life has no meaning, no direction, no purpose, and you don't know where to turn to find the answers? It's time to turn to God. That's the only way you will understand the meaning and the purpose of your life. You will find direction that will lead you to fulfillment and joy. Is your heart broken and hurting, and you don't know how to experience healing? Until we meet Christ in our hearts, we cannot find the peace and healing that God can provide. Jesus can help heal your broken heart. If you don't have a relationship with Christ, this is an opportunity for you to accept Jesus into your heart so you can be saved and find peace and healing from God. Here is a prayer if you are ready to accept Jesus:

Prayer: "Dear Jesus, I surrender my life and everything to you. I give you all my pain, fear, regret, resentment, anger, worry, and concerns that overwhelm me. I am a sinner. I need your forgiveness. Please come into my heart and my life and forgive all my sins. I believe that you died for my sins and that you have plans for my life. Please heal my broken heart and bless me with your peace and joy. Help me to cleanse my life, so I can live a godly life. Help me to understand your plans for my life and help me to obey you. Fill me with the Holy Spirit, and guide me so I can follow your way. I pray this in Jesus' name. Amen."

An Invitation to Transformation Project Prison Ministry (TPPM)

The Transformation Project Prison Ministry, a 501(c)(3) non-profit organization, produces and publishes books and DVDs and distributes them to prisons, jails, and homeless shelters free of charge nationwide. TPPM produces Maximum Saints books and DVDs containing transformation stories of inmates at Adams County Detention Facility, in Brighton, Colorado. Your donation is 100% tax deductible. If you would like to be a partner in this very important mission of reaching out to prisoners and the homeless or want to know more about this project, please visit our website: tppmonline.org. You can donate on line or you can write a check address it to:

Transformation Project Prison Ministry
P.O. Box 220
Brighton, CO 80601

Website: tppmonline.org
Facebook: http://www.facebook.com/tppmonline
Email: tppm.ministry@gmail.com

Transformation Project Prison Ministry is started in Korea. Contact: Rev. Lee Born, Director of TPPM

변화 프로젝트 교도소 문서 선교 지부장: 이본목사
Website: http//blog.daum.net/hanulmoon24

한국연락처: South Korean Contact Person:

이본 목사, 밝은빛교회,
Rev. Lee Born, Bright Light Church
인천시 남동구 구월동 1299-21, 청솔빌라 다동 301
Inchon-city, Namdong-gu, Guwal-dong, 1299-21, Chungsolbila, Da-dong 301
Cell: 010-2210-2504, 교회전화: 070-8278-2504

About The Author

Yong Hui V. McDonald, also known as Vescinda McDonald, is a United Methodist minister, chaplain at Adams County Detention Facility (ACDF) in Brighton, Colorado. She is a certified American Correctional Chaplain, spiritual director and served as an on-call hospital chaplain for 14 years. She is the founder of Transformation Project Prison Ministry (TPPM).

Education:
- Suwon Bible College, Christian Education (1976~1979)
- Multnomah University, B.A.B.E. (1980~1984)
- Iliff School of Theology, Master of Divinity (1999~2002)
- Asbury Theological Seminary, Doctor of Ministry (2013~2016)

Books by Yong Hui:
- *Journey With Jesus, Visions, Dreams, Meditations & Reflections*
- *Dancing In The Sky, A Story of Hope for Grieving Hearts*
- *Twisted Logic, The Shadow of Suicide*
- *Twisted Logic, The Window of Depression*
- *Dreams & Interpretations, Healing from Nightmares*
- *I Was The Mountain, In Search of Faith & Revival*
- *The Ultimate Parenting Guide, How to Enjoy Peaceful Parenting and Joyful Children*
- *Prisoners Victory Parade, Extraordinary Stories of Maximum Saints & Former Prisoners*
- *Four Voices, How They Affect Our Mind: How to Overcome Self-Destructive Voices and Hear the Nurturing Voice of God*
- *Tornadoes, Grief, Loss, Trauma, and PTSD: Tornadoes, Lessons and Teachings —The TLT Model for Healing*
- *Prayer and Meditations, 12 Prayer Projects for Spiritual Growth and Healing*
- *Invisible Counselor, Amazing Stories of the Holy Spirit*
- *Tornadoes of Accidents, Finding Peace in Tragic Accidents*
- *Tornadoes of Spiritual Warfare, How to Recognize & Defend Yourself From Negative Forces*
- *Lost but not Forgotten, Life Behind Prison Walls*
- *Loving God, 100 Daily Meditations and Prayers*
- *Journey With Jesus Two, Silent Prayer and Meditation*
- *Women Who Lead, Stories about Women Who Are Making A Difference*

- *Loving God Volume 2, 100 Daily Meditations and Prayers*
- *Journey With Jesus Three, How to Avoid the Pitfalls of Spiritual Leadership*
- *Loving God Volume 3, 100 Daily Meditations and Prayers*
- *Journey With Jesus Four, The Power of The Gospel*
- *Tornadoes of War, Inspirational Stories of Veterans and Veteran's Families*
- *Maximum Saints Never Hide in the Dark*
- *Maximum Saints Make No Little Plans*
- *Maximum Saints Dream*
- *Maximum Saints Forgive*
- *Maximum Saints All Things are Possible*
- *Bitter Wind, A Memoir of War in Korea (Yong Hui's Mother Hui Chae Lee's Story)*
- *Restorative Justice, Grace, Forgiveness, Restoration, and Transformation*
- *Restorative Justice, Reasons for TPPM's Grow of the Project and Motivation of the Volunteers*
- *Spiritual Distraction and Understanding*
- *Callings, Finding and Following Our Callings*
- *Repentance, Spiritual Battle of Bill's Story, Satanic Cult & Torment*
- *Repentance Volume 2, The Way to Spiritual Freedom*
- *Repentance Volume 3, Lost and Found*
- *Repentance Volume 4, Finding Peace*
- *A Guide to Inner Healing: 16 Prayer Projects and Meditation Guides as Resources for Chaplains, Ministers, and Counselors*

DVDs:
- Dancing In The Sky, Mismatched Shoes
- Tears of The Dragonfly, Suicide and Suicide Prevention (Audio CD is also available)

Books translated into Spanish books:
- *Twisted Logic, The Shadow of Suicide*
- *Journey With Jesus 1~4, Visions, Dreams, Meditations and Reflections*
- *Maximum Saints Forgive*

Books translated into Korean books (한국어로 번역된 책들):
- 『예수님과 걷는 길, 비전, 꿈, 묵상과 회상』
  (Journey With Jesus, Visions, Dreams, Meditations & Reflections)
- 『치유, 사랑하는 이들을 잃은 사람들을 위하여』
  (Dancing In The Sky, A Story of Hope for Grieving Hearts)

- 『꿈과 해석, 악몽으로부터 치유를 위하여』
  (Dreams & Interpretations, Healing from Nightmares)
- 『나는 산이었다, 믿음과 영적 부흥을 찾아서』
  (I Was The Mountain, In Search of Faith & Revival)
- 『하나님의 치유를 구하라, 자살의 돌풍에서 치유를 위하여』
  (Twisted Logic, The Shadow of Suicide)
- 『승리의 행진, 미국 교도소와 문서 선교 회상록』
  (Prisoners Victory Parade, Extraordinary Stories of Maximum Saints & Former Prisoners)
- 『네가지 음성, 악한 음성을 저지하고 하나님의 음성을 듣는 영적 훈련』 *(Four Voices, How They Affect Our Mind)*
- 『하나님 사랑합니다, 100일 묵상과 기도』
  (Loving God, 100 Daily Meditations and Prayers)
- 『영적 전쟁에서의 승리의 길』
  (Tornadoes of Spiritual Warfare, How to Recognize & Defend Yourself From Negative Forces)
- 『예수님과 걷는 길 2편, 침묵기도와 묵상』
  (Journey With Jesus Two, Silent Prayer and Meditation)
- 『우울증과 영적 치유의 길』
  (Twisted Logic, The Window of Depression)
- 『하나님 사랑합니다 2편, 100일 묵상과 기도』
  (Loving God Volume 2, 100 Daily Meditations and Prayers)
- 『예수님과 걷는 길 3편, 영적인 여정에서 위험한 함정들』
  (Journey With Jesus Three, How to Avoid the Pitfalls of Spiritual Leadership)
- 『자녀들의 영적 성장을 위한 지침서』
  (The Ultimate Parenting Guide)
- 『멀고도 험한 길의 회상집, 미 육군 유격대 리키의 이야기』
  (The Long Hard Road, U.S. Army Ranger Ricky's Story with Reflections)
  리키 라마와 이영희 지음(Ricky Lamar and Yong Hui V. McDonald)
- 『매서운 바람, 한국전쟁을 기억하며』
  (A Memoir of War in Korea)(Yong Hui's Mother, Hui chae Lee's story)
- 『전쟁의 폭풍속에서, 퇴역 군인들과 그 가족들의 회상록』
  (Tornadoes of War, Inspirational Stories of Veterans and Veteran's Families)
- 『용서의 기쁨』
  (Maximum Saints Forgive)
- 『예수님과 걷는 길 4편, 복음의 능력』
  (Journey With Jesus Four, The Power of The Gospel)

- 『용서가 낳은 치유의 은혜』
  (Tornadoes, Grief, Loss, Trauma, and PTSD: Tornadoes, Lessons and Teachings, – The TLT Model for Healing)
- 『하나님 사랑합니다 3편, 100일 묵상과 기도』
  (Loving God Volume 3, 100 Daily Meditations and Prayers)
- 『평화를 찾은 사람들』
  (Tornadoes of Accidents, Finding Peace in Tragic Accidents)
- 『세상을 이끄는 여성 리더십』
  (Women Who Lead, Stories about Women Who Are Making A Difference)
- 『선교의 꽃 9편, 회개, 사탄숭배자의 영적인 번민과 고통』
  (Blossoms Volume 9, Repentance, Spiritual Battle of Bill's Story, Satanic Cult & Torment)
- 『승리의 행진 2편, 교도소의 영적 부흥과 문서 선교 회상록』
  (Prisoners Victory Parade Volume 2, Inspirational Stories of Prisoners & Volunteers)
- 『숨겨진 보배, 성령님』
  (Invisible Counselor, Amazing Stories of The Holy Spirit)

Books translated into Vietnamese books:
- *Journey With Jesus 1~4, Visions, Dreams, Meditations & Reflections*

Books translated into Farsi books:
- *Twisted Logic, The Window of Depression*
- *Journey With Jesus 1~4, Visions, Dreams, Meditations & Reflections*
- *Loving God, 100 Daily Meditations and Prayers*
- *Four Voices, How They Affect Our Mind*
- *Twisted Logic, The Shadow of Suicide*

Books translated into Hindi books:
- *Journey With Jesus, Visions, Dreams, Meditations & Reflections*
- *I Was The Mountain, In Search of Faith & Revival*
- *Prisoners Victory Parade, Extraordinary Stories of Maximum Saints & Former Prisoners*

Made in the USA
Columbia, SC
20 June 2018